School Counseling
Classroom Guidance

SAGE was founded in 1965 by Sara Miller McCune to support the dissemination of usable knowledge by publishing innovative and high-quality research and teaching content. Today, we publish more than 850 journals, including those of more than 300 learned societies, more than 800 new books per year, and a growing range of library products including archives, data, case studies, reports, and video. SAGE remains majority-owned by our founder, and after Sara's lifetime will become owned by a charitable trust that secures our continued independence.

Los Angeles | London | New Delhi | Singapore | Washington DC

School Counseling Classroom Guidance

PREVENTION, ACCOUNTABILITY, AND OUTCOMES

Edited by

Jolie Ziomek-Daigle
University of Georgia

Los Angeles | London | New Delhi
Singapore | Washington DC

Los Angeles | London | New Delhi
Singapore | Washington DC

FOR INFORMATION:

SAGE Publications, Inc.
2455 Teller Road
Thousand Oaks, California 91320
E-mail: order@sagepub.com

SAGE Publications Ltd.
1 Oliver's Yard
55 City Road
London EC1Y 1SP
United Kingdom

SAGE Publications India Pvt. Ltd.
B 1/I 1 Mohan Cooperative Industrial Area
Mathura Road, New Delhi 110 044
India

SAGE Publications Asia-Pacific Pte. Ltd.
3 Church Street
#10-04 Samsung Hub
Singapore 049483

Copyright © 2016 by SAGE Publications, Inc.

Printed in the United States of America

Cataloging-in-publication data is available from the Library of Congress.

ISBN 978-1-4833-1648-2

This book is printed on acid-free paper.

MIX
Paper from
responsible sources
FSC® C014174

Acquisitions Editor: Kassie Graves
Editorial Assistant: Carrie Montoya
Production Editor: Olivia Weber-Stenis
Copy Editor: Erin Livingston
Typesetter: C&M Digitals (P) Ltd.
Proofreader: Jennifer Grubba
Indexer: William Ragsdale
Cover Designer: Candice Harman
Marketing Manager: Shari Countryman

15 16 17 18 19 10 9 8 7 6 5 4 3 2 1

BRIEF CONTENTS

DETAILED CONTENTS

SERIES EDITORS' FOREWORD: INTRODUCTION TO THE SERIES

COUNSELING AND PROFESSIONAL IDENTITY IN THE 21ST CENTURY

While school students in the 21st century are living in an exciting era, they also face more challenges than ever before. These challenges are faced not only by them but also school teachers and school educational leader teams. As pointed out by the American School Counselor Association (ASCA) on its website, to respond to the challenges faced by today's increasing diverse school student population school counselors have played a pivotal role on the educational leadership team by providing valuable assistance to these students at elementary, middle, and high schools and beyond. In order to deal with these challenges and provide quality services school counselors must equip themselves with adequate counseling knowledge and skills and become competent to meet the students' needs. The primary purpose of *School Counseling Classroom Guidance* is to assist school counseling students to gain evidence-based fundamental knowledge and skills that school counselors need to conduct classroom guidance programming for comprehensive school counseling programs.

School Counseling Classroom Guidance is a blueprint of the valuable role that school counselors play in responding to almost all challenges that the students face at school. Through reading this book school counseling students will be able to gain a comprehensive understanding of classroom guidance as a delivery service and student development pertinent to classroom guidance programming in academic, career, social, and emotional areas. The book further targets the growth of school counseling students in helping them develop a holistic comprehension of their role as school counselor through designing, delivering, assessing classroom guidance programming as well as managing student behaviors and classroom dynamics.

Besides integration of outcome studies and identification of future directions for classroom guidance programming *School Counseling Classroom Guidance* is the book which assists school counseling students to develop their professional identity while they are in training. The text defines the nature of professional identity, its value to the Profession and the Professional and ways to further develop one's professional identity while in training.

While we are proud of the depth and breadth of the topics covered within this text we are more than aware that one text, one learning experience, will not be sufficient for the development of a counselor's professional competency. The formation of both your Professional Identity and Practice will be a lifelong process. It is a process that we hope to facilitate through the presentation of this text and the creation of our series: *Counseling and Professional Identity in the 21st Century.*

Counseling and Professional Identity in the 21st Century is a new, fresh, pedagogically sound series of texts targeting counselors in training. This series is NOT simply a compilation of isolated books matching that which is already in the market. Rather each book, with its targeted knowledge and skills, will be presented as but a part of a larger whole. The focus and content of each text serves as a single lens through which a counselor can view his/her clients, engage in his/her practice, and articulate his/her own professional identity.

Counseling and Professional Identity in the 21st Century is unique not just in the fact that it "packaged" a series of traditional texts, but that it provides an *integrated* curriculum targeting the formation of the readers' professional identity and efficient, ethical practice. Each book, within the series, is structured to facilitate the ongoing professional formation of the reader. The materials found within each text are organized in order to move the reader to higher levels of cognitive, affective, and psychomotor functioning, resulting in his/her assimilation of the materials presented into both his/her professional identity and approach to professional practice. While each text targets a specific set of core competencies (cognates and skills), competencies identified by the Council for Accreditation of Counseling & Related Educational Programs (CACREP) as essential to the practice of counseling, each book in the series will emphasize each of the following:

a. the assimilation of concepts and constructs provided across the text found within the series thus fostering the reader's ongoing development as a competent professional;

b. the blending of contemporary theory with current research and empirical support;

c. a focus on the development of procedural knowledge with each text employing case illustrations and guided practice exercises to facilitate the reader's ability to translate the theory and research discussed into professional decision making and application;

d. the emphasis on the need for and means of demonstrating accountability; and

e. the fostering of the reader's Professional Identity and with it the assimilation of the ethics and standards of practice guiding the Counseling Profession.

We are proud to have served as co-editors of this series feeling sure that all of the books included, just like *School Counseling Classroom Guidance,* will serve as a significant resource to you and your development as a professional counselor.

Richard Parsons, PhD

Naijian Zhang, PhD

PREFACE

It is recommended that at least 80% of the school counselor's time be spent providing direct and indirect services to students.[1] Classroom guidance programming is one of the delivery systems in which counselors design structured lessons as a part of the larger school's academic curriculum to help students gain competencies, skills, and knowledge. Classroom guidance programming is an integral component to a comprehensive school counseling program where lessons are built in collaboration with teachers and administrators. School counselors are fortunate to have access to children for seven hours each day, and classroom guidance programming offers the best chance for counselors to work with all kids and provide universal interventions.

Counselor education programs have been remiss over the years and do not provide nor capture opportunities for students to learn, practice, and refine the skills necessary to deliver classroom guidance programming. You will not find classroom guidance programming as a stand-alone class. It may be a section covered in a foundations and seminar course or later, during internship. There is certainly an expectation that students will deliver classroom guidance programming during practicum and internship, and evaluations of fieldwork will always include items on classroom guidance programming. A disconnect remains between what is expected of our students during field placement and as practitioners and the content we include in the curriculum. In other courses, students learn skills related to group work, interpersonal relationships, and advocacy, and this learning is applied during field placement. Students need to learn the skills specific to classroom guidance programming to help ensure that this delivery and their overall comprehensive school counseling program is effective.

---

[1]American School Counselor Association (ASCA). (2009). *The ASCA national model: A framework for school counseling programs*. Alexandria, VA: Author.

The book is targeted as a text to teach fundamentals, strategies, and research outcomes of classroom guidance programming for comprehensive school counseling programs. Prevention and preventative care is increasingly being recognized by federal and state agencies as a way to improve and promote wellness. Classroom guidance programming is unique in that programming can also be rooted in promotion and prevention. Programming can also be universal and expose 100% of the student population to the same content, skill sets, and competencies.

The book is divided into four major parts. In Part I, the history of school counseling, classroom guidance as a delivery service, and the American School Counselor Association's (ASCA) three broad domains of student development (academic, career, and social/emotional) relating to classroom guidance programming will be presented. Part II discusses the contextual and developmental considerations of classroom guidance programming and the unique challenges the different grade levels offer. In Part III, the nuts and bolts of how to design, deliver, and assess classroom guidance programming will be described along with ways to manage student behavior and classroom dynamics. Finally, in Part IV, sections on school counselor as active collaborator, outcome studies, and future directions of classroom guidance programming are included.

Further, multiple-choice questions and responses and short essay questions are provided with each chapter to help guide instructors with assessment for this learning. It is my hope that this book fills a gap in school counseling training programs and provides professional development to those already in practice. Trainees and practitioners need to be comfortable and skilled in delivering classroom guidance programming. As I have always said, "School counselors are the luckiest people on earth to have access to kids seven hours every day." Let's make that time count, let's reach more kids, and let's make the school safer and better for everyone.

ACKNOWLEDGMENTS

I would like to recognize a number of individuals who have provided valuable support, encouragement, and feedback as I wrote this book. I carefully selected all of the chapter authors and all have added immensely to the overall success of this book. They are a group of talented practitioners and researchers and I am so grateful for their trust in me. Kassie Graves and Carrie Montoya have been instrumental in shaping this text and this first-time book author could not have picked a better home than with these women and SAGE. Also, I would like to thank the reviewers, who provided excellent suggestions and generated new ideas for me to consider.

I would also like to acknowledge my colleagues and students at the University of Georgia and my mentors. Throughout my career, I have been especially fortunate to have opportunities to learn from the very best, including my professors, site supervisors, counselor colleagues, peers and friends from my graduate training, colleagues at UGA and other institutions, counselors in Clarke County School District and throughout Georgia, inspiring doctoral students, excited master's students, and supportive staff. Finally, I would be remiss if I did not acknowledge my family for giving me opportunities to do the work I love and for providing the very best of case examples I use in class.

SAGE wishes to acknowledge the contributions of the following reviewers: Tiffany L. W. Bates, Louisiana Tech University; Kathy Fuller, UCLA Extension; Chris Hennington, Lubbock Christian University; Rochelle L. Hiatt, Northwest Missouri State University; Ken Jackson, University of Georgia; and Jeannine R. Studer, University of Tennessee, Knoxville.

About the Editor

Jolie Ziomek-Daigle, PhD, LPC, graduated with a master's degree in guidance and counseling from Loyola University New Orleans in 1997. While completing her graduate coursework, she was employed as a psychiatric technician at DePaul/Tulane Behavioral Health Center and worked with acute and inpatient children and adolescents. In 1998, Dr. Ziomek-Daigle became employed with New Orleans Public Schools and worked as a school counselor at a secondary career academy. In her final year of employment with New Orleans Public Schools (2004–2005), she worked as an elementary school counselor. In 2002, Dr. Ziomek-Daigle began doctoral studies at the University of New Orleans. She graduated in 2005 with a doctoral degree in counselor education and supervision with a minor in school counseling and emphasis in play therapy. Additionally, in 2005, she accepted a position as an assistant professor in the school counseling program at the University of Georgia. In 2011, she was promoted to associate professor with tenure and assumed coordination of the master's in education program in school counseling. She has published extensively on remediation and retention issues in counselor education, the clinical preparation of school counselors, school-based counseling interventions, and school-based play therapy services in the following journals: *Journal of Counseling and Development, Professional School Counseling, Guidance and Counselling, Middle School Journal,* and *The Family Journal,* among others. Dr. Ziomek-Daigle teaches clinical core courses such as interpersonal skills, counseling children and adolescents, psychodiagnosis, play therapy, service learning, and internship. Currently, she serves in the role of Professor-in-Residence for Northeast Georgia Regional Sharing Agency (NE GA RESA) and Rutland Academy, which is the area's educational therapeutic school site. In this position, Dr. Ziomek-Daigle coordinates a two-semester service-learning program, provides supervision to master's and doctoral students who are practicing on-site, and expands the therapeutic model through grants and contracts. She is the 2014 recipient of the 2014 Association for Counselor Education and Supervision (ACES) Counseling Vision and Innovation award and is currently a service-learning fellow at the University of Georgia.

About the Contributors

Kristin Avina works for the District of Columbia Public Schools as a professional school counselor and team leader at Truesdell Education Campus. She received her bachelor's degree in psychology from the University of California, San Diego, and her master's in education and human development from George Washington University. Kristin has a passion for group work and instilling a growth mindset in her students.

Stephanie Eberts is an assistant professor in the professional counseling program at Texas State University. Dr. Eberts received her bachelor's degree in foreign language education from the University of Georgia and her master's in professional counseling from Loyola University in New Orleans. Dr. Eberts worked as a school counselor (at both the elementary and middle school levels) in New Orleans for six years prior to returning to school. During her doctoral training she worked with Safe and Drug-Free Schools of Gwinnett County in Georgia. After completing her PhD program at Georgia State University in 2010, she moved to Austin to work at Texas State University. In fall of 2015 she will begin working as a school counselor educator at Louisiana State University.

Melinda M. Gibbons is an associate professor in counselor education in the Department of Educational Psychology and Counseling at The University of Tennessee. Her research interests include career development for underserved populations and counselor identity development. Her work has been published in scholarly journals including *Professional School Counseling, Career Development Quarterly,* and *Journal of College Counseling.* She is currently the associate editor for *Professional School Counseling*, a peer-refereed journal. She earned her PhD from University of North Carolina at Greensboro.

Natoya Hill Haskins is an assistant professor at the University of Georgia. She holds a doctorate from the College of William and Mary, a master's of education from Virginia Commonwealth University, and a master's of divinity from Virginia Union University. She has worked with urban and suburban adolescent populations as a secondary school counselor. Her lines of inquiry include professional and educational supports and challenges for faculty of color and students of color, school counselor advocacy, and supervision with counselors in training.

Amber N. Hughes is an assistant professor in the School of Professional Counseling at Lindsey Wilson College. Her research interests include career counseling with underserved populations, online teaching in counselor education, and technology in counseling. Her work has been published in *Career Development Quarterly, Adultspan,* and *Wisconsin Counseling Journal.* She earned her PhD from The University of Tennessee at Knoxville.

Christopher Janson is an associate professor and interim Chair of the Department of Leadership, School Counseling, and Sport Management at the University of North Florida. Prior to his work in academia, Janson was a public school teacher and counselor. His scholarly interests include school practitioner development; educational leadership; career, academic, and motivational development of urban school students; and community-based development and learning. Janson was a national leadership team member of the Community Learning Exchange (CLE), a W. K. Kellogg Foundation initiative seeking to build collective leadership capacity within and among historically marginalized communities. The transformational practices for community development through the CLE process are described in a forthcoming book Dr. Janson has co-authored, titled *Reframing Community Partnerships in Education: Uniting the Power of Place and Wisdom of People.* Janson has published in journals such as *Professional School Counseling, Journal of School Leadership, Journal of Research in Leadership Education, Education and Urban Society,* and the *Journal of Special Education Leadership.* He received his bachelor's and master's degrees from Central Michigan University, his teaching certification from Michigan State University, and his PhD from Kent State University.

Dana Jenkins works for Chicago Public Schools as a professional school counselor. He is the multi-tiered systems of support (MTSS) and social emotional learning (SEL) specialist for PK–8th-grade students. He received his bachelor's in sociology and Spanish from Knox college and his master's in education and human development from George Washington University.

Andrew J. Knoblich is a professional school counselor at the secondary level in Alexandria, Virginia, with Fairfax County Public Schools. His research interests include student engagement, adolescent career development, and dropout prevention. He earned his master's of education from the University of Georgia.

Christy W. Land is an assistant professor at the University of West Georgia in the clinical and professional studies department. Dr. Land has twelve years' experience as a professional school counselor at the elementary and middle school levels. Dr. Land also maintains a small private practice, where her work focuses on clients through counseling, consultation, and supervision. Her areas of expertise include bullying prevention, stress and anxiety management with children and adolescents, group counseling, and supervision. Dr. Land prides herself in working as a change agent for the field of counseling, particularly in the school setting, to best support and advocate for/with all clients.

E. C. M. Mason is an associate professor in the counseling program at DePaul University in Chicago. Erin is active in professional school counseling organizations and legislative work at both state and national levels. She has published in scholarly journals with a focus on the professional identity of school counselors. She is the co-author of the 2013 book *101 Solutions for School Counselors and Leaders in Challenging Times*. Erin is a regular presenter in her field on a variety of topics and served as the 2012–2013 president of the Illinois School Counseling Association. In recent years, Erin's work has turned to the use of technology in school counseling. Erin developed SCOPE, School Counselors' Online Professional Exchange (www.scope4scs.org), as a site for highlighting practical tech tools for school counselors with concrete examples of how they are being used in the field.

Sophie Maxis is an assistant professor of school counseling in the Department of Leadership, School Counseling and Sport Management at the University of North Florida. Dr. Maxis's current work as a counselor educator is embedded in local schools and emphasizes the culturally responsive ways in which professional school counselors engage school communities for the best interests of students and their families. Many of her research interests are informed by her background as a secondary school educator and her affiliation with university–urban school partnerships, college access outreach, and retention initiatives on behalf of historically minoritized populations in higher education. She integrates culture-centered pedagogies and community-centered approaches in her research frameworks and teaching practices. Dr. Maxis primarily uses Q methodologies and survey methods for research inquiries.

Clare Merlin is an assistant professor in the department of counseling at the University of North Carolina at Charlotte. Her research focuses on multicultural education and school counseling, with an emphasis on prejudice reduction in K–12 schools. She also studies social justice practices in counselor education programs. She received her PhD in counselor education and supervision from the College of William and Mary.

Joy Rose is a professional school counselor at Columbia Heights Education Campus in Washington, DC, where she directs a middle school counseling program. She received her bachelor's in psychology from the University of North Carolina at Chapel Hill and her master's in education and human development from George Washington University. Joy has published and presented on school counseling and achievement issues and is currently doing research on group work with middle school ELL students.

Sam Steen has extensive experience in research and practice in public schools. He served as a K–12 professional school counselor for ten years at both elementary and secondary schools. One goal of his research is to close the achievement gap for students of color and those from low-income backgrounds through evidence-based group counseling interventions. One of Dr. Steen's publications, "The Preparation of Professional School Counselors for Group Work," was awarded the Best Research Article of the Year by the *Journal for Specialists in Group Work*, Dr. Steen has published over 25 articles and book chapters. Most recently, Dr. Steen won two research grants that culminated in a complete training and preparation video funded by the Association for Specialists in Group Work (ASGW), an American Counseling Association (ACA) division that focuses on infusing multicultural considerations in group counseling for children.

Amy W. Upton is an assistant professor and the school counseling coordinator at University of South Alabama. Prior to moving into higher education in 2013, Dr. Upton spent 16 years working as a middle and high school counselor and supervisor. Her research and teaching interests are in school counselor development and professional identity, school counselor program development and implementation, school counselor leadership, and student resiliency.

Lauren Stern Wynne is an assistant professor of counselor education at Longwood University in Farmville, Virginia. Prior to moving to Virginia, she was an elementary and high school counselor for 9 years in Gwinnett County, Georgia, served as a clinical assistant professor in the school counseling program at Georgia

State University, and worked with children and families in private practice at the Anxiety and Stress Management Institute in Atlanta. She has trained school- and community-based mental health practitioners in school-based mental health and play therapy locally, regionally, and nationally with the goal of encouraging collaborative and developmentally/multiculturally appropriate approaches to help all students achieve. Her research and training interests include school-based group work, play therapy, and consultation/collaboration as well as best practices in school counselor education and supervision. She earned her master's and EdS degrees in mental health counseling from the University of Florida and her K–12 school counseling endorsement and PhD in counseling from Georgia State University.

*This book is dedicated to my husband, Chris; my children, Brennan,
Chance, and Vivienne; and my family. Every day, you continue to inspire me, fuel
my passion, challenge me to be my very best.*

"I have looked at you in millions of ways and I have loved you in each."

Part I

The Specialty of School Counseling and Classroom Guidance as a Delivery Service

Chapter 1

HISTORY OF COUNSELING, EMERGENCE OF SCHOOL COUNSELING, AND CLASSROOM GUIDANCE

JOLIE ZIOMEK-DAIGLE
University of Georgia

> *The Bureau does not attempt to decide for any boy what occupation he should choose, but aims to help him investigate the subject and come to a conclusion on his own account, that is much more likely to be valid and useful than if no effort were made to apply scientific methods to the problem. Our mottoes are Light, Information, Inspiration, Cooperation.*
>
> (Parsons, 1909, p. 92)

The quote that opened the chapter points to our profession's commitment to facilitating development and the empowerment of clients, even in the very early days of counseling.

This chapter will present a brief history of the counseling profession, the school counseling specialty, and the trends in the profession over the last century. Accountability measures and shifting from day-to-day crisis work to prevention programs will be further discussed. A review of accreditations standards, professional standards, and ethical codes and the inclusion of developmental classroom guidance programming in these standards will follow.

After reading this chapter, the reader will be able to

- understand the emergence of counseling, school counseling, and classroom guidance programming over the course of the last century,

- describe the changes in school counselor certification and the tightening of the field as a result of accountability measures,
- explain prevention models and how these models can be applied to classroom guidance programming, and
- understand the Council for Accreditation of Counseling & Related Educational Programs (CACREP) 2009 standards and the American School Counselors Association (ASCA) Mindsets & Behaviors for Student Success as they relate to classroom guidance programming.

A RICH HISTORY

Vocational Guidance

As we know it today, school counseling began as vocational guidance at the turn of the 20th century. The roots of school counseling began through the work of Frank Parsons and others due to concerns over the vocational needs of youth of the day. Impending social issues at that time included child labor, immigration, and urbanization, thus the vocational guidance movement was created to assist in transitions from school or home to the workforce (Herr & Erford, 2011).

Guidance as Integrated in School Systems

Primarily due to the work of Frank Parsons, vocational counselors were introduced into schools in Boston, Massachusetts, and the Vocational Bureau was created so that students could gain valuable skills for the workforce. Many advocates of vocational guidance of the time (i.e., George E. Myers and Anna Reed) believed that career exploration should be integrated into an academic curriculum, just as traditional subjects such as math and science were. During this period, it was also stated that the guidance process needed to be more thorough than just meeting the vocational needs of students (Sink, 2005). Subsequently, a decade later, educational guidance was delivered through classroom programming and incorporated broader topics that dealt with everyday experiences such as living at home, becoming a good citizen, taking care of oneself, and getting along with others.

Exercise 1.1 invites you to explore our counselor roots in career and college counseling.

EXERCISE 1.1

EXPLORING OUR ROOTS IN CAREER AND COLLEGE COUNSELING

In some ways, we are seeing a renewed focus on further refining the career and postsecondary needs of students. For example, the Georgia BRIDGE Act (2010) and First Lady Michelle Obama's Reach Higher initiative provides opportunities for school counselors to deliver career activities and assessments to all students enrolled in Grades K–12. Talk with a partner about our roots as school counselors and how this relates to our roles now. What are the similarities? What are the differences?

The Launch of Sputnik

The next few decades brought further definition of the school counseling specialty as well as special recognition and support of the profession from the federal government. This change occurred post-World War II. The launching of Sputnik in 1957 led the government to conclude that the country was behind in math and science advances. The concerns resulted in the passing of the National Defense Education Act of 1958 with an end goal of identifying high-achieving students and encouraging them to attend college. The concern over the country's lagging math and science achievements was identified by the federal government as a concern and influenced the shape of the field by asking guidance counselors to have training in assessment and testing administration. Federal funds were then allocated and spent on the preparation and employment of school counselors who, in turn, would identify talented students for college majors in engineering, mathematics, and science. Herr and Erford (2011) concluded that this was the era when legislation and professionalization defined the field of school counseling. The professionalization of the school counseling specialty included the emergence of several national organizations such as ASCA (formerly American Personnel and Guidance Association) that created distinct standards and educational requirements for the professional field. At the same time, state certification requirements were emerging and universities were responding with distinct training programs in guidance and counseling.

Exercise 1.2 asks you to explore how external influences impact the school counseling field.

EXERCISE 1.2

EXPLORE HOW EXTERNAL INFLUENCES IMPACT THE SCHOOL COUNSELING FIELD

Currently, some would say our space program in the United States is nonexistent or on hold. How might another global advancement—whether in sea, space, or cyberspace—by a competing country spur new government training programs? In what ways do events like these situate school counselors for leadership positions?

Guidance and Counseling in the Schools

Several acts were passed during the next few decades that increased responsibilities for school counselors. The Carl D. Perkins Act of 1984 and the Elementary School Counseling Demonstration Act of 1995, along with local and state mandates for school counselors to become involved in student issues of child abuse, drug abuse, and career education, were influential events during this time. Due to school counselors assuming more responsibilities across developmental domains (i.e., academic, career, and social/emotional), comprehensive program models began to emerge to ensure accountability and cohesion of program components (Gysbers & Henderson, 2006). Also, toward the end of this era, we saw the birth of the Transforming School Counseling Initiative (Education Trust, 1997) and the passage of No Child Left Behind (NCLB) Act of 2001. The following section will describe how the school counseling profession increased accountability measures in training and practice and began to merge the practice of providing guidance *and* counseling in the areas of academic, career, and social/emotional development for K–12 students.

Changes in State Certification

As the school counseling profession began to better define itself, a shift was also occurring, allowing individuals to receive school counseling certification without a teaching degree. This movement was monumental in opening the doors for those with graduate degrees in counseling to become professionals in the school. The educational and work experiences of school counselors were becoming more diverse and varied and the profession was expanding beyond the lens of those who were former teachers. By eliminating the prior teaching requirement for state certification, most states opened the doors to all counselors who have an interest in working in the schools. Presently, very few states still maintain the requirement for state certification as a school counselor.

Exercise 1.3 requires you to examine the school counselor certification requirements in your state or in the state you would like to work.

EXERCISE 1.3

EXAMINING SCHOOL COUNSELOR CERTIFICATION REQUIREMENTS

Do you know what states you may work in? Is prior teaching experience a requirement? Check out ASCA's website (http://www.schoolcounselor.org/school-counselors-members/careers-roles/state-certification-requirements) for specific information.

There continues to be a lack of evidence indicating that teaching experience equates to more effective school counseling. However, practice in the classroom, understanding the dynamics of effective management in the classroom, and using the classroom to serve larger groups of students are needed skills of the school counselor. Many of the evidence-based practices that will be discussed throughout the book are delivered through classroom guidance programs such as the Student Success Skills and Why Try?

Evidence-based practices + serving larger numbers
of students = school counselor accountability and impact

COUNSELING TODAY

Accountability and the Transformed School Counselor

The mid-1990s brought standards-based reform, accountability measures, and advanced technologies in software and communication (House & Martin, 1998). Leaders in the field wanted school counselors engaged in critical conversations regarding student achievement and prepared to show evidence-based results, particularly in student outcomes. Discussions as to whether school counselors should address issues of equity and access as well as assume roles as advocates and educational leaders were occurring (Paisley & Hayes, 2003). This transformative shift in school counseling would leave behind a more clinical, mental-health model focused on the individual needs of students and create a greater focus on comprehensive program development in the areas of academic, career, and college aspirations of all students. As a result of this discourse and as a response to the educational climate, many training programs made a commitment to value all the contributions school counselors could offer and to meet both the academic and mental health needs of youth. To date, several programs have adopted a training model that develops counselors who become skilled practitioners and educational leaders in the schools through innovative coursework and purposeful field placements (Paisley & McMahon, 2001; Ziomek-Daigle, McMahon, & Paisley, 2008).

Educational reform efforts during this time also stimulated organizations such as ASCA to develop national standards for programs. Additionally, ASCA's standards development concentrated on student competence/outcomes in three broad domains: academic, career, and social/emotional. Soon after, ASCA published the *ASCA National Model: A Framework for School Counseling Programs* (ASCA, 2012b) to assist counselors in developing standards-based programs in four primary areas: foundation, management system, delivery system, and accountability. In 2014, ASCA replaced the National Standards for Students (2004) with the ASCA Mindsets & Behaviors for Student Success. The ASCA Mindsets & Behaviors for Student Success list 35 standards, including the specific attitudes, knowledge, and skills students should demonstrate as a result of a comprehensive, data-driven school counseling program (ASCA, 2014).

Given the current climate of accountability and educational reform, school counselors should not be complacent by only developing programs based on comprehensive models but should also present results that show positive student outcomes. So the question is reframed from "What do counselors do?" to "How are students different because of what school counselors do?" (ASCA, 2012b, p. 17). As Brown and Trusty (2005) suggest, "If school counselors expect to be credited with raising student achievement, they must provide clear-cut evidence that this occurs because of their interventions" (p. 13). Demonstrating outcomes such as increased graduation rates, improved standardized test scores, and decreased behavior referrals are important to mark yearly progress and are often included in schoolwide improvement goals. However, data must clearly establish that the results are linked to counseling interventions. Mixed methods of data collection and analysis—such as observations, document analysis, focus groups, and multiple assessments—may offer school counselors additional support in terms of substantiating effectiveness. School counselors need to make efforts to become familiar with evidenced-based practices through professional development, trainings, and collaboration with allied professionals, such as school psychologists and special education coordinators.

Evidenced-based practices will be more fully explored later in the book. However, Exercise 1.4 asks you to form small groups and discuss the following question:

EXERCISE 1.4

SMALL GROUP DISCUSSION

What do you know about evidence-based practices? What are some examples of evidence-based interventions that can be used by school counselors and delivered through classroom guidance programming that may contribute to student achievement (i.e., increased school engagement, increased attendance, a decrease in behavior referrals, or a decrease in suspensions)? Think about Brown and Trusty's (2005) charge for school counselors.

Current Focus on School-Based Prevention Programs

Schools and those individuals that have access to students in a school are in optimal positions to identify programs and provide outreach efforts that are preventative in nature. Those in the helping professions, such as school counselors, can also collaborate with other school-based professionals or community professionals in these prevention efforts. It is noticeable that prevention-oriented practices are evident in several fields from medicine (i.e., health screenings and flu shots) to computer science (i.e., virus detection programs) to automotive technology (i.e., inspection interval schedules). As school counselors, have we exempted ourselves from prevention practices out of the necessity of dealing with crisis situations or because we have not been trained on how to use and assess preventative programs? Perhaps both?

School-based prevention programs can positively impact a range of outcomes related to social/emotional development, behavior, academic success, and various short-term crisis situations. Unfortunately, the current climate of accountability measures pressures schools to focus on the immediate needs as related to student achievement. Schools are being managed to develop interventions during the school year that are often based on data from the previous year, such as matriculation and graduation rates, attendance rates, suspension rates, and so on. With schools and districts complying with mandates from NCLB and Race to the Top, administrators and staff must respond to data from the previous year with remedies and are not able to effectively review two- or four-year trends or rolling averages.

Two categories of school-based interventions exist: universal and targeted. Universal programs are usually implemented schoolwide, are affordable, aim to reduce a variety of risk factors, and promote a broad range of protective factors that will maintain order and sustainability (Greenberg, 2010). On the other hand, targeted interventions are usually delivered to a group of students because they have characteristics that place them at eventual risk or because some sort of crisis has occurred that is affecting their current functioning. A brief perusal of federal websites such as those of the Centers for Disease Control and Prevention or the National Institute of Health provides several examples of current grants and research initiatives related to preventative care and school-based prevention. This clearly provides evidence of the direction of school-based interventions and the areas of need. To sustain the school counseling profession and for school counseling interventions to remain effective and demonstrate impact, programs need to be developed that address issues beforehand that are identifiable and measurable. Comprehensive school counseling programs and lessons generated from the school counseling core curriculum can be focused on prevention, with interventions at the universal and targeted levels, and can be delivered through classroom guidance programming.

CLASSROOM GUIDANCE AS A DELIVERY SERVICE

The ratio of school counselors to students will range from state to state and also within each state from district to district. ASCA reports that the average school-counselor-to-student ratio for the United States is 1:471 (ASCA, 2011). The national range therein exists from 1016 students being served by one school counselor in California to 200 students being served by one counselor in the state of Wyoming. ASCA recommends a counselor-to-student ratio of 1:250. For school counseling trainees to understand, it is safe to assume that an approximate student caseload will be around 500. It is also safe to assume that families of those 500 students are also included in potential services. How can school counselors reach 500 students and possibly their families? How can school counselors develop and offer programs and services that are both preventative and evidence based to reach students and families?

The ASCA National Model (2012b) recommends that school counselors spend 80% or more of their time providing direct and indirect services to students. As part of the delivery system, classroom guidance programming consists of the school counseling core curriculum and includes structured lessons to help students gain competencies and also provides all students with developmentally appropriate knowledge and skills to help them be successful. Examine the chart in Exercise 1.5. It includes information as to school-based prevention areas that can be delivered through classroom guidance programming. The chart is far from complete. Work with a peer and identify additional topics areas and related evidenced-based practices.

EXERCISE 1.5

EXAMPLES OF EVIDENCE-BASED PRACTICES PER STUDENT DEVELOPMENTAL DOMAIN

	Academic	Career	Social/Emotional
Topic	Improve student academic and social competencies	Increase career decision-making and self-efficacy	Enhance social and emotional learning
Evidence-Based Practice	Student Success Skills (Brigman, Webb, & Campbell, 2007)	DISCOVER program (Maples & Luzzo, 2005)	The Incredible Years programs (The Incredible Years, 2013)

Levels of Prevention Model

Leavell and Clark (1958) proposed a model that describes varying levels of prevention. This model has been very influential in the public health sector. While this model examines disease and views disease on a continuum from health on one end to advanced disease on the other, the first two levels of prevention can be viewed through a sociocultural context and applied to the delivery of classroom guidance programming. The first two levels of prevention, according to Leavell and Clark, include *primordial* and *primary* prevention.

Primordial prevention is described as a lack of risk factors that has not appeared in a given population, and efforts in this level are directed toward discouraging harmful behaviors. In this scenario, primordial prevention in classroom guidance programming can be viewed as delivery of content that is psychoeducational in nature, such as Child Help/Speak Up/Be Safe (formerly the Good Touch/Bad Touch program) at the elementary level and reviewing graduation requirements or launching a career exploratory program at the high school level.

The next level is described as *primary prevention*. Primary prevention is described as having some risk factors of a social concern noted in the community, and actions being taken prior to allowing the community to become susceptible to the effects. At this level, primary prevention at the high school level may include school counselors delivering classroom guidance sessions on pathways to postsecondary opportunities if school data suggest low college attendance rates. A classroom guidance session at an elementary school operating from a primary prevention level may help prepare fifth graders for the transition to middle school in response to subpar first-quarter grades of current sixth graders.

Exercises 1.6a and 1.6b below are provided so you can better understand the very early stages of prevention and how they can be incorporated into comprehensive school counseling programs. Form small groups and identify classroom guidance programming topics for each level of prevention for all three levels of school (elementary, middle, and high school) and relate the intervention to the academic, career, and social/emotional domains.

EXERCISE 1.6A

UNDERSTANDING THE VERY EARLY STAGES OF PREVENTION (PRIMORDIAL PREVENTION)

Primordial prevention: psychoeducational content delivered to all students to contribute to their academic, career, and social/emotional development	*Elementary School*	*Middle School*	*High School*
Academic			
Career			
Social/Emotional			

EXERCISE 1.6B

UNDERSTANDING THE VERY EARLY STAGES OF PREVENTION (PRIMARY PREVENTION)

Primary prevention: psychoeducational content delivered to all students; some risk factors may be present in population	*Elementary School*	*Middle School*	*High School*
Academic			
Career			
Social/Emotional			

Developmental Guidance Programming

ASCA formed the first definition of *developmental guidance* in 1979. The very early hints of prevention in this definition described developmental guidance as facilitating the integration of several components of a student's life, such as personal/social, career, emotional, moral, and cognitive aspects (ASCA, 1979). Note that the personal/social domain has now been changed to social/emotional (ASCA, 2014). Along with the definition from ASCA, several early models of school counseling programming included a developmental/preventative approach as well as a guidance curriculum delivery system that was designed for all students (Gysbers & Henderson, 2006; Myrick, 1997). A developmental guidance curriculum is delivered in the classroom, can be psychoeducational in nature, teaches new skills, and is tied to the larger school-based curriculum. Myrick (1997) proposed a model of developmental guidance that has the following components:

1. Reaches all students

2. Includes a curriculum that is organized and planned

3. Remains sequential and flexible, based on the needs of the school and students

4. Becomes integrated in the total educational process

5. Actively involves teachers and other professionals

6. Allows students to learn new, helpful information

7. Supports the role of the school counselor as the professional providing specialized services

In today's schools, the developmental guidance curriculum would tie into the larger academic program by connecting units and sessions to content standards such as the common core curriculum. Evaluation procedures that measure student outcomes and objectives of the developmental guidance program and report these findings to stakeholders are also integral components of current practices in classroom guidance programming.

Operating under the premise that children need support and guidance as they pass through developmental stages, classroom programming provides a platform for access to all students and promotes growth in academic, career, and social/emotional areas. As experts on child and adolescent growth, school counselors can easily connect student standards and competencies to developmentally appropriate content. Campbell and Dahir (1997) suggest that school counselors can use developmentally appropriate standards as a guide and identify specific competencies for each grade level in the areas of academic, career, social/emotional development.

Developmental guidance programming—including sessions and units that are grounded in standards, based on the needs of the school and students, are evaluated, and have the outcomes reported—meets the very definition of primary prevention. Exercise 1.7 provides an outline for you to follow to help you better connect state educational standards to classroom guidance programming.

EXERCISE 1.7

CONNECTING STATE EDUCATIONAL STANDARDS TO CLASSROOM GUIDANCE PROGRAMMING

Think about how developmental guidance programming can look different at the elementary, middle, and high school levels. Consider bullying prevention. How can a session on bullying prevention be tied to the larger school curriculum and meet standards? In what content areas could a session on bullying prevention be included? Look at your state's Department of Education website and review the student learning standards. Complete the activity below.

Developmental guidance programming session on bullying	Elementary School	Middle School	High School
Describe the developmentally appropriate content and supporting activity for each session.			
In what content area/class could this session be presented?			
List the student/content standards for your state that are aligned with your lesson.			

PROFESSIONAL IDENTITY OF SCHOOL COUNSELORS

Council for Accreditation of Counseling & Related Educational Programs (CACREP) Standards

Hundreds of counseling programs in the United States are accredited by CACREP. The CACREP standards are designed to help students gain proficiency in learning counseling content and using skills effectively. Over 250 standards are included in the 2009 revision (CACREP, 2009) and the school counseling specialty includes more standards than any other program area. The following standards pertain to the development and implementation of the school counseling curriculum and classroom guidance programming:

- Provides . . . classroom guidance to promote the academic, career, and personal/social development of students (IV.D.2)
- Understands curriculum design, lesson plan development, classroom management strategies, and differentiated instructional strategies for teaching counseling and guidance related material (IV.K.3)
- Implements differentiated instructional strategies that draw on subject matter and pedagogical content knowledge and skills to promote student achievement (IV.L.3)

Several additional school counseling specialty standards are directly related to the development, delivery, and assessment of classroom guidance programming. In developing, delivering, and evaluating these sessions and units, the following topic areas are included in the standards to ensure that optimal training experiences exist for school counseling students:

- Ethical and legal considerations
- Student learning and development
- Cultural considerations and competence
- Transition programs
- Group dynamics
- School climate
- Parent and family engagement
- Needs assessment
- Assessment information
- Program evaluation
- Counseling outcomes/measurable outcomes
- Use of data
- Family/school/community collaboration
- Administrators, teachers, staff, community members collaboration
- Peer programming interventions

American School Counselor Association (ASCA)

Mindsets & Behaviors for Student Success: K–12
College- and Career-Readiness Standards for Every Student

ASCA replaced the National Standards for K–12 Students with the Mindsets & Behaviors for Student Success in 2014. In response to swift educational reform that followed the mandates of the NCLB legislation, accountability measures began to be implemented throughout school systems. Potential outcomes of the NCLB legislation focused on teacher preparation and achievement rates but failed to recognize potential barriers to student success, such as those pertaining to emotional and physical health, school safety, and the social and economic realities of youth and families. The ASCA National Standards for Students, first introduced in 1997, provided an initial framework that all school counselors can use. By operating from this framework, counselors have been able to identify and prioritize knowledge and skills that students should exhibit from participating in comprehensive school counseling programs. The current ASCA Mindsets & Behaviors for Student Success (ASCA, 2014) has been expanded from the initial framework and is based on research and best practices in student achievement.

The ASCA Mindsets & Behaviors for Student Success can be integrated with other professional standards such as teacher preparation, social work, and school psychology. These integrations can be condensed into charts and discussed with educational stakeholders such as teachers, administrators, parents, and community members. Providing an interdisciplinary system conveys to stakeholders that counseling interventions are tied to the larger academic curriculum, content standards, common core standards, and student learning outcomes. Discussions and data findings can provide evidence as to how school counseling programs enhance student learning and success and the ways in which student outcomes are different by actively participating in comprehensive school counseling programs. The ASCA Mindsets & Behaviors for Student Success serve as a foundation for the ASCA National Model and comprehensive school counseling programs. Exercise 1.8 will help you integrate CACREP national standards (CACREP, 2009) with the ASCA Mindsets & Behaviors for Student Success. The intended outcome of this activity is for you to better understand how accreditation standards and professional association standards influence your learning and practice.

EXERCISE 1.8

INTEGRATING CACREP NATIONAL STANDARDS WITH THE ASCA MINDSETS & BEHAVIORS FOR STUDENT SUCCESS

Examine the ASCA Mindsets & Behaviors for Student Success (2014). Notice the three domains (academic, career, and social/emotional) and related strategies and skills. Identify a guidance unit/session for each domain. Also, match a few CACREP national standards (2009) to these activities. Remember that school counselors must show evidence as to how students are different because of the counseling-related service or intervention. Be sure to note the title of the session, content to be covered, supporting activity, and evaluation.

School Counselor Competencies

ASCA designed school counselor competencies to provide a uniform framework that outlines the knowledge, attitudes, and skills that practitioners must possess to meet the demands of a school setting and the needs of its students. Counselor educators, school counselors, school counseling students, and administrators/supervisors can utilize these competencies in the following ways:

1. For training purposes in graduate education to ensure that students are equipped with the skills necessary to develop accountable, comprehensive programs

2. For self-evaluation purposes by practicing school counselors as professional development plans are designed and implemented

3. For evaluation purposes by district supervisors who have an understanding of the school counseling profession

The framework of the ASCA School Counselor Competencies (2012a) is similarly structured to the ASCA National Model except for the first section on school counseling programs. Each section presents standards related to knowledge, abilities and skills, and attitudes. The five components of the ASCA School Counselor Competencies include school counseling programs, foundations, management, delivery, and accountability. The delivery system of classroom guidance is interwoven in all five components but especially pertains to the delivery section. School counselors should exhibit the abilities and skills necessary to deliver classroom guidance programming through a core curriculum that is aligned with the ASCA Mindsets & Behaviors for Student Success. More information on the school counseling core curriculum will follow in Chapter 6. Exercise 1.9 is provided to help you better understand your own personal strengths and challenges in implementing classroom guidance programming.

EXERCISE 1.9

UNDERSTANDING YOUR PERSONAL STRENGTHS AND CHALLENGES IN IMPLEMENTING CLASSROOM GUIDANCE PROGRAMMING

Review the ASCA Mindsets & Behaviors (ASCA, 2014). In order to implement the school counseling core curriculum, it is suggested that practitioners use existing student data, develop materials and instructional strategies to meet student and school needs, encourage staff involvement, use a variety of technology, manage student behavior, include program assessments, and understand and be sensitive to multicultural and pluralistic trends. Based on your previous professional experiences, identify an area from those listed above that would be challenging for you. Then identify an area where you feel confident about your abilities. Discuss these areas with a peer.

The ASCA National Model

The ASCA National Model (2005) was designed to simply help counselors "do more counseling." The model provides a framework as to the components of a comprehensive, data-driven school counseling program that promotes student achievement. Based on ongoing data collection and integrating standards related to student development in the academic, career, and social/emotional domains, the model promotes the following: access and equitable educational practices for all students, outcomes of student knowledge and skills that provide evidence of comprehensive school counseling program effectiveness, delivery of a program that is systematic by design, decision making influenced by data, and services and interventions offered by a credentialed school counselor. Stakeholders of comprehensive school counseling programs include parents, teachers, administrators, students, and community members. These stakeholders meet as part of a team, are of additive value, and remain involved in the process of continuous program improvement and refinement. Four components comprise the framework of a comprehensive school counseling program and include the areas of foundation, management, delivery, and accountability.

The foundation of the comprehensive school counseling program is built upon a focus. The program focus includes school counselors' beliefs in program effectiveness and influence on student achievement. The beliefs then inform the program's vision of the future by influencing student outcomes. Finally, the mission of the comprehensive school counseling program is aligned with the school's at-large mission statement and describes the ways the vision and mission statements will be assessed. The ASCA Mindsets & Behaviors for Student Success and the ASCA School Counselor Competencies are also components of the foundation of comprehensive school counseling programs.

Management of comprehensive school counseling programs consist of organizational artifacts such as measurements, agreements, and other forms of data that clearly reflect the foundation that they rest on. Calendars reveal time spent on a weekly and monthly basis. Assessments related to counselor competencies and program outcomes are completed throughout the year. Annual agreements that identify program goals are reviewed and approved by administrators and a program-specific advisory council provides input and recommendations for continuous improvement. Data that examine the results of the program and action plans related to the developmental guidance programming and small group planning help gauge impact and outcomes.

The delivery of the comprehensive school counseling program is through direct and indirect student services. Not only are students served under this model but parents, administrators, teachers, and community members are also brought into the counseling process. Direct services include individual student counseling and programming, group counseling, responsive services, and the school counseling core curriculum. Making referrals, providing consultation, and collaboration comprise indirect services (ASCA, 2012b). It should be noted that classroom guidance programming provides a *direct* service to students.

Ethical Codes

In order to protect the clients counselors serve, a uniform set of dispositional and behavioral guidelines were developed by organizations to help guide professional practice. Counseling graduate students who are training to work in the schools should become familiar with both the ethical codes and standards of practice established by the American Counseling Association (ACA) and ASCA. Additionally, CACREP requirements specify that counseling students must obtain professional liability insurance prior to field placement. Professional liability insurance can be obtained through counseling organizations such as the ACA and ASCA, often at a reduced student rate.

Ethical dilemmas in who is defined as the client, confidentiality issues with minors, and dealing with student records will always be a part of working in schools. Not only do both sets of frameworks include ethical standards and codes of conduct that need to be followed, a decision-making process is also presented to guide school counselors who are dealing with ethical dilemmas. Review both the ACA Ethical Codes and Standards of Practice guidelines and the ASCA Ethical Standards for School Counselors on their respective websites. Pay close attention to the ethical codes pertaining to working with children and practicing in a school setting. Identify the ethical standards involved and use the ASCA ethical decision-making model (ASCA, 2010) in order to practice responding to situations in a fair and consistent manner. In Exercise 1.10, you will be asked to identify the ethical standards of the case and apply the standards to practice as it relates to classroom guidance programming.

EXERCISE 1.10

IDENTIFYING ETHICAL STANDARDS

Identify the ethical standards that relate to classroom guidance programming, counseling minors, and confidentiality. Consider this scenario: Jessica is a new counselor at Clarke Shoals High School, located in an urban city in the southeast. Jessica has three co-counselors and covers ninth-grade through twelfth-grade students with the last name beginning with the letters P–T. The four counselors divided the ninth-grade classes and presented a one classroom guidance session of a four-session unit to each homeroom. This particular session covered high school graduation requirements and the number of credits needed to matriculate from grade to grade. During the session, Jessica asked students to write questions they would like answered on a sheet of paper before the session ended. Jessica received a note from a student who was not on her caseload. The note indicated that the student is pregnant and needs help finding health services without her parents knowing. How would you proceed?

When delivering classroom guidance programming, school counselors must act in an ethical manner and ensure that the curriculum is developmentally appropriate and culturally relevant to the students. Just as counselors who provide therapy to clients meet their cognitive, social, and linguistic needs through a culturally sensitive lens, so should the design and delivery of the school counseling curriculum be. Hermann, Remley, and Huey (2010) discuss the five moral principles that serve as the cornerstone of our ethical guidelines. These moral principles are included in ethical considerations, as not all dilemmas may be addressed by ethical codes. However, the moral principles of autonomy, nonmaleficence, beneficence, justice, and fidelity can be used to help guide discussions and to better understand the conflicting issues of the dilemma. Review each of the five moral principles that serve as a foundation to our profession's ethical guidelines. For each principle, identify a situation that may arise from delivering developmental classroom guidance programming. Further identify a resolution to the ethical dilemma.

KEYSTONES

- The school counseling profession began as vocational guidance at the turn of the century.
- Classroom guidance was expanded to include personal/social concerns along with career development soon after.

- School counselors may or may not be former teachers. The delivery system of classroom guidance is often presented later in a training program, frequently in practicum and internship. Practice with classroom guidance needs to occur throughout a training program, as the task itself is developmental in nature.
- Accountability measures and educational reform as of late have prompted counselors to examine the question, *How are students different because of what school counselors do?* (ASCA, 2012b, p. 17)
- Classroom guidance programming is an ideal delivery system for programs that are rooted in prevention.
- Our national accreditation standards (CACREP) and professional organizations (ACA, ASCA) influence learning outcomes of counseling trainees and contribute to the professional identity of school counselors.

SUMMARY

In this chapter, readers were presented a brief overview of the history of counseling and the roots of the school counseling specialty. How the profession has transformed over the years as well as accountability measures and future trends such as prevention-based programs were further discussed. Accreditation and professional standards and ethical codes pertaining to developmental classroom guidance programming were also provided so that readers might become more knowledgeable about how school counselors inform their work and how counselor professional identity is formed.

REFERENCES

American Counseling Association (ACA). (2005). *ACA code of ethics.* Alexandria, VA: Author.

American School Counselor Association (ASCA). (1979). *Standards for guidance and counseling programs.* Falls Church, VA: ASCA.

American School Counselor Association (ASCA). (2004). ASCA National Standards for Students. Alexandria, VA: Author.

American School Counselor Association (ASCA). (2010). *Ethical principles for school counselors.* Retrieved March 22, 2015, from http://www.schoolcounselor.org/asca/media/asca/Resource%20Center/Legal%20and%20Ethical%20Issues/Sample%20Documents/EthicalStandards2010.pdf

American School Counselor Association (ASCA). (2011). *Student-to-school-counselor ratios 2010–2011.* Retrieved March 22, 2015, from http://www.schoolcounselor.org/asca/media/asca/home/Ratios10-11.pdf

American School Counselor Association (ASCA). (2012a). *ASCA school counselor competencies.* Retrieved March 22, 2015, from http://www.schoolcounselor.org/asca/media/asca/home/SCCompetencies.pdf

American School Counselor Association (ASCA). (2012b). *The ASCA national model: A framework for school counseling programs* (3rd ed.). Alexandria, VA: Author.

American School Counselor Association (ASCA). (2014). *Mindsets and behaviors for student success: K–12 college- and career-readiness standards for every student.* Alexandria, VA: Author.

Brigman, G., Webb, L., & Campbell, C. (2007). Building skills for school success: Improving the academic and social competence of students. *Professional School Counseling, 10*(3), 279–288.

Brown, D., & Trusty, J. (2005). The ASCA national model, accountability, and establishing causal links between school counselors' activities and student outcomes: A reply to Sink. *Professional School Counseling, 9*(1), 13–15.

Campbell, C. A., & Dahir, C. A. (1997). *The national standards for school counseling programs.* Alexandria, VA: American School Counselor Association.

Council for Accreditation of Counseling & Related Educational Programs (CACREP). (2009). *2009 standards for accreditation.* Alexandria, VA: Author.

Education Trust. (1997). *Working definition of school counseling.* Washington, DC: Author.

Greenberg, M. (2010). School-based prevention: Current status and future challenges. *Effective Education, 2*(1), 27–52.

Gysbers, N. C., & Henderson, P. (2006). *Developing and managing your school guidance program* (4th ed.). Alexandria, VA: American Counseling Association.

Hermann, M., Remley, T., & Huey, W. (2010). *Ethical and legal issues in school counseling.* Alexandria, VA: American School Counselor Association.

Herr, E. L., & Erford, B. T. (2011). Historical roots and future issues. In B. T. Erford (Ed.), *Transforming the school counseling profession* (3rd ed., pp. 19–43). Columbus, OH: Pearson Merrill Prentice Hall.

House, R. M., & Martin, P. J. (1998). Advocating for better futures for all students: A new vision for school counselors. *Education, 779*, 284–291.

Leavell, H. R., & Clark, E. G. (1958). *Preventative medicine for the doctor in his community: An epidemiologic approach.* New York, NY: McGraw-Hill.

Maples, M. R., & Luzzo, D. A. (2005). Evaluating DISCOVER's effectiveness in enhancing college students' social cognitive career development. *Career Development Quarterly, 53,* 274–285.

Myrick, R. D. (1997). *Developmental guidance and counseling: A practical approach* (3rd ed.). Minneapolis, MN: Educational Media Corporation.

Paisley, P. O., & Hayes, R. L. (2003). School counseling in the academic domain: Transformation in preparation and practice. *Professional School Counseling, 6,* 198–205.

Paisley, P. O., & McMahon, H. G. (2001). School counseling for the 21st century: Challenges and opportunities. *Professional School Counseling, 5,* 106–115.

Parsons, F. (1909). *Choosing a vocation.* Boston, MA: Houghton Mifflin.

Sink, C. (Ed.). (2005). *Contemporary school counseling: Theory, research, and practice.* Boston, MA: Houghton Mifflin/Lahaska.

The Incredible Years. (2013). [website]. Retrieved March 26, 2015, from http://incredibleyears .com/programs/

Ziomek-Daigle, J., McMahon, H. G., & Paisley, P. O. (2008). Adlerian-based intervention for professional school counselors serving as both counselors and educational leaders. *Journal of Individual Psychology, 64*(4), 450–467.

Chapter 2

The Three Broad Domains: Academic, Career, and Social/Emotional

Jolie Ziomek-Daigle
University of Georgia

> *Professional school counselors are uniquely trained and qualified to address all students' academic, career, and social/emotional developmental needs by designing comprehensive school counseling programs.*
>
> (American School Counselor Association, 2004)

At the conclusion of this chapter, readers will be able to

- understand the three broad domains (academic, career, and social/emotional) that school counselors address to enhance K–12 student development;
- describe research and outcome studies related to evidence-based school counselor interventions interwoven throughout the presentation of the three domains; and
- review the American School Counselor Association (ASCA) Mindsets & Behaviors for Student Success so that readers will understand that the work of school counselors is intentional and tied to national and professional standards.

Historically, school counselors have provided services and interventions to K–12 students under three broad domains. The goals are for students to develop thorough knowledge and skills; mastery in the areas of academic success; career and college understanding; and social/emotional growth. The three domains of academic, career, and social/emotional development are embedded in all frameworks generated by ASCA to guide counselors in developing comprehensive programs. Formerly the ASCA National Standards for Students (2004) and currently the ASCA Mindsets & Behaviors for Student Success (2014) serve as frameworks for the ASCA National Model (2009). The model and frameworks further define the roles and responsibilities of the school counselor, promote student academic success, and situate counseling programs as integral components of student learning.

ATTENDING TO THE NEEDS OF K–12 STUDENTS IN THREE DEVELOPMENTAL DOMAINS

The ASCA Mindsets & Behaviors for Student Success

The ASCA Mindsets & Behaviors for Student Success (2014) highlight three broad domains of student development: academic, career, and social/emotional. "These domains promote mindsets and behaviors that enhance the learning process and create a culture of college and career readiness for all students" (ASCA, 2014). The framework includes 35 standards that can be applied to all three domains based on outcomes of needs assessments and student learning. The standards can also be applied through individual counseling, small group counseling, and classroom guidance programming.

Academic Domain

The ASCA National Model and its focus on the academic development of K–12 students clearly emphasizes the importance of school counselor action in this domain. Not only is academic development positioned first most often in school counseling literature and in professional development, the subsequent domains (including career and social/emotional) are often tied to enhancing student academic achievement. It is no surprise as to why. School counselors are trained as both practitioners and educators and provide services and interventions to K–12 students. Further, through movements such as the Transformed School Counseling Initiative and educational reform measures such as No Child Left Behind (NCLB) Act (U.S. Department of Education, 2001), academic achievement is very much on the radar of those who make decisions to fund school counselors, such as policy makers, federal and state education officials, superintendents, and administrators. The ASCA National Model not only emphasizes strategies to increase academic achievement but also challenges counselors to advocate for social change and to work to close achievement gaps for all students.

Even with the rigorous accountability measures of the last decade, achievements gaps among student learners have not closed; in fact, the gaps have widened. Most notably, gaps continue to increase between student race and ethnicity and across socioeconomic status and include students with disabilities. The passage of NCLB placed a spotlight on the failing U.S. educational system but, at the same time, created rigid policies that often punished students through retention and teachers through unsound evaluations in some of the neediest schools (U.S. Department of Education, 2001). To this end, academic *development* for students falls under the oversight of the school counselor. But, at the same time, teachers and administrators are charged with the academic *instruction* of the students. Nonetheless, through comprehensive, data-driven school counseling programs and a well-developed school counseling curriculum, counselors can attend to the academic needs of *all* students. Exercise 2.1 is provided to help you think through the school counselor's role in academic development and the difference between *instruction* and *enhancement*.

EXERCISE 2.1

THINKING THROUGH THE SCHOOL COUNSELOR'S ROLE IN ACADEMIC DEVELOPMENT

Take a moment and think about the school counselor's role in academic instruction. Teachers (and multiple teachers at the middle school and high school levels) provide classroom instruction based on grade level (elementary) or content areas (math, social studies). Elementary teachers teach all academic content for multiple grade levels. Teachers in middle school and high school teach content by subject. However, counselors are expected to enhance the academic development of all students. What are the primary differences between academic instruction and academic enhancement? How are the two related? You may want to consult relevant research. Discuss your thoughts and findings with a peer.

The charge for school counselors is to ensure the academic development and success of all students in the building. By the definition of *all students*, this includes groups of students who may have attendance problems, students with behavioral disabilities, students attending in-school suspensions, students who may be receiving services through homebound programs, students who are English language learners, and students whose disabilities may be more appropriate for a self-contained classroom. School counselors must reach all students at certain checkpoints during the school year. Classroom guidance programming is a delivery system that provides access to all students in a classroom setting. Research findings indicate that classroom guidance programming, as a means to promote academic development, has been largely effective (Sink, 2005b).

Showing evidence of the school counselor's effectiveness in improving the academic lives of students is complicated. Brown and Trusty (2005) argue that school counseling programs entail much more than just academic interventions, and teasing out which components aid academic achievement may prove challenging. Further, teachers and administrators are often charged with shaping the academic culture at a school, not counselors. It remains unclear to many how school counselors directly impact student achievement. Unfortunately, the current lack of outcome studies in this area is occurring at a time when important conversations are convening regarding educational reform and curriculum design. Research findings clearly indicate that the single most important school-related influence on academic achievement and student learning is classroom instruction (Galassi & Akos, 2012). How can school counselors improve student outcomes in areas related to academic development and achievement?

Very few programs exist that promote academic achievement in Grades K–12 and are delivered through classroom guidance. The Student Success Skills (SSS) intervention is a counselor-led classroom guidance programming unit that addresses academic achievement (Brigman, Campbell, & Webb, 2004; Campbell & Brigman, 2005). The SSS intervention has resulted in student improvement in math and reading test scores at both local and state levels. The intervention enhances students' academic, social, and self-management skills, including the micro skill sets of goal setting, progress monitoring, and active learning. Additional academic enhancement programs (i.e., Succeeding in School, Solution Shop) have yielded very limited findings but are worthy of further exploration and research.

Sink (2005b) suggests that classroom guidance programming that emphasizes student cognition strategies will help students learn self-regulation, self-management, and self-monitoring and lead to improved academics (see Student Success Skills, described in Exercise 2.2). Additional activities that could enhance the academic domain would include exercises in memory and retainment of information, organization, and study habits. As students are learning academic self-regulation skills, counselors should incorporate social/emotional development content as well. Research indicates that classroom guidance programming grounded in key interpersonal and relational skills undergirds academic achievement and learning (Campbell & Brigman, 2005; Sink, 2005b). The following constructs not only enhance academic success and learning but become characteristics of a psychologically healthy individual: motivation, self-efficacy, problem solving, active listening, understanding of self and others, cooperation, engagement, and empathy (Nicoll, 1994; Sink, 2005a). Galassi and Akos (2012) discuss a study in which school counselors provided study skills and test-taking interventions to underachieving students in small group or classroom guidance activities. However, as the authors suggest, many school counselors lack an understanding of the broader conceptualization of the psychology behind those behaviors (i.e., study skills) that, at the core, include self-regulation and learning skills. Exercise 2.2 references a useful article for you to review and serves as an evidence-based practice pertaining to student success.

EXERCISE 2.2

ARTICLE REVIEW:
EVIDENCE-BASED PRACTICE AND STUDENT SUCCESS

Student Success Skills (SSS)

The SSS program is an example of a school counseling intervention that supports student academic achievement. Learn more about this program by reviewing the 2011 article entitled "Student Success Skills: An Evidence-Based School Counseling Program Grounded in Humanistic Theory" by Villares, Lemberger, Brigman, and Webb in the *Journal of Humanistic Counseling.*

The development of the academic domain is not only tied to psychological health as stated earlier (i.e., social/emotional development) but also to the preparation of students in becoming career and college ready. Breaking down the micro skills (i.e., motivation, self-efficacy, active listening, etc.) of self-regulation and learning for students will provide a foundation for them to become lifelong learners and successful in the workforce. Students must understand the process of learning, experience academic success, and learn skills (such as how to rebound after academic failures) if they are to create a vision bridging current academics to a future career. Attesting to the need to provide relevant academic and postsecondary planning, research demonstrates that the particular courses school counselors recommend to students, such as advanced mathematics or an applied science course (i.e., geology), increase the likelihood of attaining a bachelor's degree (Trusty & Niles, 2003).

Motivation is one of the most important psychological constructs to discuss when considering classroom guidance programming for students in the academic domain. Academic motivation as it relates to school success should be included in the delivery of classroom guidance programming to all students. Research findings suggest that the lack of motivation often leads to student disengagement, under-achievement, and dropping out (Rowell & Hong, 2013; Ziomek-Daigle & Andrews, 2009). Further, other influences have an impact on academic motivation, such as the school climate, educators' perceptions of achievement, family support, and the educational attainment of families (Eccles, 2007).

Rowell and Hong (2013) identified several motivational constructs, such as one's beliefs/perceptions, goals, and values, that impact student learning as well as the level of how one is motivated either intrinsically or extrinsically. Students' beliefs and perceptions of their learning can be attributed to their level of self-efficacy or their belief in their ability to perform and accomplish certain tasks (Bandura, 1997). Research indicates that students who do not believe in their abilities to achieve (i.e., self-efficacy) will avoid tasks, quit when frustration arises, and avoid additional efforts (Weiner, 1986). Students who set academic goals then develop a process that can be monitored or altered and that produce feelings of competence and mastery when tasks are achieved. School counselors are in unique positions to provide feedback to students on whether they are on the right track to achieve goals (Rowell & Hong, 2013) by providing classroom guidance programming in the academic domain at certain checkpoints throughout the school year. Further, student values concerning learning are often connected to engagement in the subject matter and what they stand to gain from work in school and at home. For example, homework matrices (i.e., tic-tac-toe chart) are becoming more useful in allowing students to decide what homework tasks need to be completed in a particular subject matter. Finally, the level of engagement with the subject matter will provide cues as to whether the student is intrinsically or extrinsically motivated. In later childhood and adolescence, students who are intrinsically motivated are more successful in achieving goals. Students who are engaged in the classroom and subject matter and learn in an autonomous-supportive classroom environment tend to develop intrinsic motivation (Rowell & Hong, 2013).

The domain of academic development includes standards that are embedded in school counseling programs alongside strategies used and activities offered to support and encourage students' learning. Standards focused on academic development are more visible within Category 2, the behavioral standards. Behavior standards are grouped into three categories and are often those more commonly associated with student success. The three subcategories include learning strategies, self-management skills, and social skills. Take a look at Exercise 2.3 to explore how you can develop appropriate student learning outcomes.

EXERCISE 2.3

DEVELOPING STUDENT LEARNING OUTCOMES RELATED TO THE ASCA MINDSETS & BEHAVIORS FOR STUDENT SUCCESS (ACADEMICS)

Based on the research presented under the academic domain section *and* after reviewing the ASCA Mindsets & Behaviors for Student Success pertaining to academics, construct three to four learning outcomes for K–12 students related to classroom guidance programming. One example follows: Students will meet Standard A.1–3 and identify attitudes and behaviors that lead to successful learning by understanding what motivates them.

Career Domain

As discussed in Chapter 1, our roots in counseling emerged with the vocational outreach of Frank Parsons at the turn of the 20th century. Helping students understand their career interests and skills through testing, matching desired careers to postsecondary programming, and building school-to-career partnerships in communities has been a part of the scope of professional school counseling for over 100 years. No doubt that advancement in the area of career development has occurred over the decades, yet professional school counselors continue to devote their energies to helping students connect their interests and abilities to the world of work.

Challenges with the U.S. economy along with changes in immigration, demographics, and technology have increased awareness in this area and call on professional school counselors to develop and integrate career activities at the elementary, middle, and high school levels. By integrating career development in the earlier grades, a message is being sent to students that career building and success occur across a lifetime. Further, the advancement of globalization and technology is changing curriculum at the high school and postsecondary levels at a very rapid pace. Some examples include virtual education, career academies, and dual enrollment. Fostering career development and keeping abreast of career trends is an important consideration in managing comprehensive counseling programs and delivering classroom guidance programming in the present day.

A shift in career development theory occurred when Super (1957) proposed that career is a developmental process, with abilities and interests changing throughout the lifespan. Niles and Harris-Bowlsbey (2013) discussed career development over the lifespan and theorized that it includes adjusting to life roles and that managing the transition in and out of these roles is necessary, especially when unexpected workforce trends occur. The ASCA Mindsets & Behaviors for Student Success in the career area emphasize that counselors should assist students in developing the knowledge and skills for selecting and implementing a career choice and should also guide students to develop life-role readiness. Specific questions to include in career activities that promote life-role readiness thinking for students include "What skills do I need for success as a student, employee, and community member?" and "What knowledge and skills do I need to accomplish my career aspirations and adapt to change throughout my life?" (Akos & Niles, 2007).

With respect to the most recent federal and state goals and initiatives to improve postsecondary participation for all students, the career domain is visibly linked to postsecondary participation and planning. Unfortunately, a lack of research exists supporting the school counselor's effectiveness in providing career content and college planning (Dahir & Stone, 2009). Counselors in the schools often find themselves curtailing crisis situations and meeting the immediate day-to-day needs of the students, teachers, and administrators. Many of these remedial activities pertain to dropout prevention, academic support, bullying/peer relationships, mental health concerns, and family support. Increasing career awareness and postsecondary planning delivered proactively through classroom guidance and as a result of developing comprehensive counseling programs to all students would situate school counselors in moving students along the K–16 continuum, with the career foundation built prior to entering college and ensuring success in postsecondary completion. K–16 represents the continuum from kindergarten through bachelor's degree completion. These activities, in turn, would address Dahir and Stone's (2009) concern that very little outcome data link the work of school counselors to K–12 student postsecondary success.

The stunt in economic growth in the last decade has propelled educators and policy makers to reconsider career and college planning as a need for all students. A clear link exists between students receiving career knowledge and enrolling in postsecondary institutions. Belasco (2013) found that students who had access to college-related information and who met with the counselor in increasing frequency approaching graduation had an increased likelihood of attending postsecondary institutions, particularly four-year universities. Further, students from families with low socioeconomic status are often unaware of and intimidated by college campuses and lack support for their college aspirations. These students often benefit from increased access to college-related information and an ongoing relationship with a counselor. Families with more affluence are able to provide outside resources, such as a contracted college counselor, to their children. This process only results in increasing the college-attending culture of this subgroup. School counselors need to pay particular attention to increasing opportunities for career and postsecondary readiness for all students, including those who may be of low socioeconomic status. Research findings indicate that sustaining the national economy's growth and competiveness is undeniably tied to increasing the educational attainment of individuals with lower socioeconomic status (Belasco, 2013).

The career development domain includes standards embedded in school counseling programs and activities to help students connect school to the world of work, to begin to plan for a successful transition from school to postsecondary education, and to anticipate work transitions throughout their life span. The career development standards are visible throughout ASCA's behavior standards and across the subcategories of learning strategies, self-management skills, and social skills (see Exercise 2.4).

EXERCISE 2.4

DEVELOPING STUDENT LEARNING OUTCOMES RELATED TO THE ASCA MINDSETS & BEHAVIORS FOR STUDENT SUCCESS (CAREER)

Based on the research presented under the career domain section *and* after reviewing the ASCA Mindsets & Behaviors for Student Success pertaining to career development, construct three to four learning outcomes for K–12 students related to classroom guidance programming. One example follows: Students will meet Standard B.1–3 and demonstrate knowledge of the career-planning process by identifying local training programs or college majors in their interest areas.

Social/Emotional Domain

As discussed earlier, accountability measures of the last two decades have brought about changes in standardizing common core elements of the K–12 curriculum and measuring outcomes of student learning. A missing component of many present-day discussions on what qualities a successful K–12 student should possess (i.e., academic success, career and college readiness, and self-confidence) are most likely the aspects of a psychologically healthy person. The late educational reform movement has placed an inordinate amount of attention on student achievement outcomes through test scores, outcome measures, and teacher quality and has neglected the needs a child may have to develop emotionally, personally, and socially. Additionally, the reform movement overemphasized the growth of personnel (i.e., additional administrators, curriculum coaches) and funding (i.e., rewarding an increase in test scores) for what, in theory, would help improve academics. This direction toward growth in personnel and resource allocation has not yielded an improvement in achievement and has subsequently moved attention away from holistic, multilayered student development, including social/emotional growth.

Half of all the school counseling outcome studies published in the 1980s and 1990s fell under the umbrella of remedial responsive services, which may have been (and continue to be) a true reflection of a school counselor's time. Sink (2005a) hypothesized that the focus on remediation matters and response to crisis is, in fact, a realistic portrayal of daily school counseling work. School counselors often feel that they are responding to the crisis of the day due to the lack of proactive, preventative programming in all areas, especially in the area of student social/emotional development.

In the past, the little time left to promote student development in the social/emotional domain that was not of the immediate nature was usually delivered through classroom guidance programming. Often, these units were linked to programs focused on the areas of affective education, character education, and moral education (Nicoll, 1994). Some critics of character education programs have argued that many programs have been developed through a very narrow lens that often excludes cultural norms, traditions, and behaviors. Further, no one character education program seems to capture the traits and characteristics most commonly agreed upon as promoting social and emotional growth. Nicoll (1994) identified the following social skills in eight of the more popular affective education programs: understanding self and others, empathy, communication, cooperation, and responsibility. In Barna and Brott's (2011) study examining how counselors spend their time, "meeting academic standards" was identified by counselors as "most important." However, participants in the study identified that the principles of character were more relevant to the social/emotional standards and provided an overall link to improving academic achievement. When designing classroom guidance, programming focused on social/emotional student development should be individualized enough to reflect the present-day challenges of youth but broad enough to appeal to and meet the needs of all intended audiences.

It remains clear that academic achievement is purely measured through outcomes such as grades, test scores, and graduation rates. However, these academic measures are not indicators as to how well-rounded a student is or will be in the future. Social/emotional traits for K–12 students that may contribute to current and future success in the areas of academics, career, and college include motivation, engagement, intentionality, and self-efficacy. Common challenges such as aggression, anxiety, and inattention/hyperactivity act as roadblocks to positive self-growth traits such as the ones listed above (Barna & Brott, 2011). Intentional classroom guidance programming can provide the psychoeducational content to assist student interpersonal growth, meet standards, and produce outcomes linking the work of school counselors to K–12 student success.

Very few programs exist that deliver information on social/emotional development through classroom guidance. Thompson, Robertson, Curtis, and Frick (2013) presented several school-based intervention programs for childhood anxiety that may be delivered through classroom guidance programming. One program, FRIENDS for Life, aims to prevent anxiety symptoms through a cognitive behavior lens. Through a comparison of pre- and posttest scores, children who participated in the FRIENDS for Life program demonstrated fewer anxiety symptoms than children in a control group. Similarly, studies related to the Coping Cat Curriculum (Kendall, 1994) revealed from pre- and posttest data that 64% of children enrolled in the program no longer met the diagnostic criteria for anxiety after a follow-up one year later. Exercises 2.5 and 2.6 are provided below to provide you with opportunities to peruse research related to evidence-based practices and how such programs are aligned with the ASCA Mindsets & Behaviors for Student Success.

EXERCISE 2.5

EVIDENCE-BASED PRACTICES ALIGNED WITH THE ASCA MINDSETS & BEHAVIORS FOR STUDENT SUCCESS (FRIENDS FOR LIFE)

Peruse the web and locate information on the FRIENDS for Life anxiety prevention program. Identify which ASCA Mindsets & Behaviors for Student Success in the social/emotional area would be met should a school counselor implement this program.

EXERCISE 2.6

EVIDENCE-BASED PRACTICES ALIGNED WITH THE ASCA MINDSETS & BEHAVIORS FOR STUDENT SUCCESS (COPING CAT CURRICULUM)

Peruse the web and locate information on the Coping Cat Curriculum. Identify which ASCA Mindsets & Behaviors for Student Success in the social/emotional area would be met should a school counselor implement this program.

School counselors can balance the developmental domains of students by placing emphasis on social/emotional growth as it relates to academic achievement. Classroom guidance programming can be initiated at the beginning of each academic year to promote the social/emotional characteristics needed for achievement and success. Sessions, for example, can be based on the principles of character such as understanding, empathy, communication, cooperation, and responsibility. Social/emotional characteristics that keep students focused and interested in academics include motivation, engagement, intentionality, and self-efficacy. Developing classroom guidance programming with these constructs in mind provides a one-two punch for student outcomes in the academic and personal/social domains. Finally, addressing anxiety reduction and identifying coping mechanisms prior to high-stakes testing periods through classroom guidance may be beneficial for all students. Lessons focused in this area may provide a skill set to serve a lifetime of challenges and transitions in the personal and professional worlds.

The social/emotional domain includes standards embedded in school counseling programs that help students manage emotions and gain interpersonal skills. The standards are based on several noncognitive factors (Farrington et al., 2012) and include many of the social/emotional characteristics described above: persistence, resilience, goal setting, help seeking, cooperation, self-efficacy, self-regulation, self-control, motivation, effort, organization, and learning strategies. The standards pertaining to social/emotional development are included in both Category 1 (mindset standards) and also in Category 2 (behavior standards). The psychosocial beliefs and attitudes students have about themselves comprise the mindset standards. See Exercise 2.7 for more information.

EXERCISE 2.7

DEVELOPING LEARNING OUTCOMES RELATED TO THE ASCA MINDSETS & BEHAVIORS FOCUSED ON STUDENT SUCCESS (SOCIAL/EMOTIONAL)

Based on the research presented under the social/emotional domain section *and* after reviewing the ASCA Mindsets & Behaviors for Student Success pertaining to social/emotional development, construct three to four learning outcomes for K–12 students pertaining to classroom guidance programming. One example follows: Students will meet Standard C.2 by learning about the differences between appropriate and inappropriate physical contact by attending the Child Help/Speak Up/Be Safe (formerly the Good Touch/Bad Touch prevention education program) psychoeducational sessions.

Exercise 2.8 is provided to help you understand the power and importance of collaboration with parents and community members as you build comprehensive school counseling programs grounded in promoting students' academic, career, and social/emotional development.

EXERCISE 2.8

UNDERSTANDING THE POWER OF COLLABORATION WITH PARENTS AND COMMUNITY MEMBERS

Although school counselors make substantial efforts to develop comprehensive counseling programs and deliver effective classroom guidance programming, a family/school/community partnership should also be evident in the activities. Helping students academically achieve, become career and college ready, and sustain social/emotional growth is also the work of teachers, administrators, parents, and community members. These areas of development need to be reflected in the school's mission and vision statements and school improvement plan. School counselors can actively promote development in these areas by improving relationships with parents; collaborating with teachers and administrators to develop comprehensive counseling programs; and partnering with community agencies, service organizations, and local businesses and industries. Research on school counselor collaboration clearly demonstrates that a team approach in delivering comprehensive programs ensures that services and interventions are tailored and systematically delivered to meet the needs of all students (Sink, 2005a).

KEYSTONES

- School counselors have historically provided programs, services, and interventions that address three broad domains of student development: academic, career, and social/emotional.
- The ASCA National Model (2009) and the ASCA Mindsets & Behaviors for Student Success (2014) provided specific standards for K–12 learning, further defined the roles and responsibilities of the school counselors, promoted student academic success, and situated counseling programs as a central component to student achievement.
- School counselors enhance the academic curriculum in schools and infuse counseling-related material into the larger academic curriculum.
- Motivation is an important psychological construct and is related to academic achievement.

- Activities related to career awareness, exploration, and development can be included in classroom guidance programming across grades and levels. Many states are now mandating the completion of career activities across K–12 levels to help build the workforce.
- Creating a college-attending culture and improving college readiness through classroom guidance programming can help close achievement, attainment, and opportunity gaps.
- Attention to students' social/emotional development has declined over the last few decades as a result of academic accountability and educational reform.
- Counselors need to remember that students' social/emotional needs must be met before success can be seen in academics and interest can become apparent in career and college activities.

SUMMARY

In this chapter, readers were presented the three broad domains (academic, career, and social/emotional) that guide school counselors' work. Research studies related to each of the three domains were discussed so that readers would have a better understanding of interventions that may be used by school counselors when attending to a specific developmental domain. Finally, the ASCA Mindsets & Behaviors for Student Success were included in this chapter so that readers might gain knowledge as to the expectations of every student.

REFERENCES

Akos, P., & Niles, S. G. (2007). Promoting educational and career planning in schools. In B. Erford (Ed.), *Transforming the school counseling profession* (2nd ed., pp. 195–210). New York, NY: Prentice Hall.

American School Counselor Association (ASCA). (2004). *ASCA national standards for students.* Alexandria, VA: Author

American School Counselor Association (ASCA). (2009). *The American school counselor national model: A framework for school counseling programs.* Alexandria, VA: Author.

American School Counselor Association (ASCA). (2014). *Mindsets & behaviors for student success: K–12 college- and career-readiness standards for every student.* Alexandria, VA: Author.

Bandura, A. (1997). *Self-efficacy: The exercise of control.* New York, NY: Freeman.

Barna, J. S., & Brott, P. E. (2011). How important is personal/social development to academic achievement? The elementary school counselor's perspective. *Professional School Counseling, 14*(3), 242–249.

Belasco, A. S. (2013). Creating college opportunity: School counselors and their influence on postsecondary enrollment. *Research in Higher Education, 54*(7), 781–804.

Brigman, G., Campbell, C., & Webb, L. (2004). Student success skills. Helping students develop the academic, social, and self-management skill they need to succeed. *Classroom Guidance Manual.* Boca Raton, FL: Atlantic Education Consultants.

Brown, D., & Trusty, J. (2005). School counselors, comprehensive school counseling programs, and academic achievement: Are school counselors promising more than they can deliver? *Professional School Counseling, 9,* 1–8.

Campbell, C., & Brigman, G. (2005). Closing the achievement gap: A structured approach to group counseling. *Journal for the Specialists in Group Work, 30,* 67–82.

Dahir, C., & Stone, C. (2009). School counselor accountability: The path to social justice and systemic change. *Journal of Counseling and Development, 87,* 12–20.

Eccles, J. C. (2007). Families, schools, and developing achievement-related motivations and engagement. In J. E. Grusec & P. D. Hastings (Eds.), *Handbook of socialization* (pp. 665–691). New York, NY: Guilford.

Farrington, C. A., Roderick, M., Allensworth, E., Nagaoka, J., Keyes, T. S., Johnson, D. W., & Bechum, A. (2012). *Teaching adolescents to become learners: The role of noncognitive factors in shaping school performance. A critical literature review.* University of Chicago Consortium on Chicago School Research.

Galassi, J. P., & Akos, P. (2012). Preparing school counselors to promote academic development. *Counselor Education and Supervision, 51,* 50–63.

Kendall, P. (1994). Treating anxiety disorders in children: Results of a randomized clinical trial. *Journal of Consultation and Clinical Psychology, 62,* 100–110.

Nicoll, W. G. (1994). Developing effective classroom guidance programs: An integrative framework. *The School Counselor, 41*(4), 360–364.

Niles, S. G., & Harris-Bowlsbey, J. (2013). *Career development interventions in the 21st century* (4th ed.). Columbus, OH: Merrill Prentice Hall.

Rowell, L., & Hong, E. H. (2013). Academic motivation: Concepts, strategies, and counseling approaches. *Professional School Counseling, 16*(3), 158–171.

Sink, C. A (2005a). Comprehensive school counseling programs and academic achievement. A rejoinder to Brown and Trusty. *Professional School Counseling, 9,* 9–12.

Sink, C. A. (2005b). Fostering academic development and learning: Implications and recommendations for middle school counselors. *Professional School Counseling, 9*(2), 128–135.

Super, D. (1957). *The psychology of careers: An introduction to vocational development.* New York, NY: Harper.

Thompson, E., Robertson, P., Curtis, R., & Frick, M. H. (2013). Students with anxiety: Implications for professional school counselors. *Professional School Counseling, 16*(4), 222–234.

Trusty, N., & Niles, S. (2003). High school math courses and completion of the bachelor's degree. *Professional School Counseling, 7,* 99–107.

U.S. Department of Education. (2001). *No Child Left Behind* (ERIC Document No. ED 447 608). Washington, DC: Author.

Weiner, B. (1986). *An attributional analysis of achievement motivation.* New York, NY: Springer.

Ziomek-Daigle, J., & Andrews, P. G. (2009). Dropout prevention in the middle grades. *Middle School Journal, 40*(5), 54–60.

PART II

DEVELOPMENTAL AND CONTEXTUAL CONSIDERATIONS FOR CLASSROOM GUIDANCE

Chapter 3

THE ELEMENTARY SCHOOL

JOLIE ZIOMEK-DAIGLE
University of Georgia

CHRISTY W. LAND
University of West Georgia

> *"Thank you for helping this school get along and be fair. I liked all the activities you did with the whole class. My favorite activity was five ways to handle a bully. I like your puppets. I like coming to your room, it is fresh in there. We are all working together to be friends. You are a great counselor!"*

The above quote was written by an elementary school student to her school counselor and highlights the importance and complexity of the role of the school counselor at the elementary level. New directions for practice in elementary school counseling have emerged in the school counseling literature, with a strong focus on comprehensive programming, collaboration, and preventative measures and are central tenets of the American School Counselor Association's (ASCA) national model of school counseling (ASCA, 2012; Walsh, Barrett, & DePaul, 2008). ASCA has implemented 35 mindset and behavior standards, organized into three domains (academic, career, and social/emotional development) that guide and enhance the learning process for all students with a focus on career and college readiness (ASCA, 2014). After reading the chapter on the elementary student and school environment, you will be able to

- understand the physical, social/emotional, and cognitive needs of elementary-age students,
- understand the role of a strengths-based professional school counselor at the elementary level,

- understand a comprehensive school counseling program at the elementary level,
- identify prevention programs and counseling interventions with elementary school students, and
- see which of the ASCA Mindsets & Behaviors for Student Success standards should result from a comprehensive school counseling program.

The gap in research in the school counseling literature is most noticeable in the area of elementary counseling. Perhaps this is due to our attention to crisis situations or remedial education at higher levels, but nonetheless, elementary school counseling lacks sound evidence-based practices and steady state funding for counseling positions. To take case in point, at the elementary level, one may find no counselors, half-time counselors, or counselor-to-student ratios of 1:700 across school districts in the United States. There is an obvious landscape difference between counseling at the elementary level compared to counseling programs at the middle school and high school levels. One may ask, "Why is this the case?" Evidence-based prevention programs are plentiful for the elementary grades, and young people ages 4–12 are developmentally situated to initiate behavior changes and academic remediation. Is it that more serious issues may occur in the later grades, such as dropping out, disengagement, pregnancy, or bullying? Or is it plausible to consider that the elementary ages of 4–12 have considerable developmental differences in language, cognition, and behavior than older children and adolescents, which may baffle educators and counselors alike? ASCA notes that elementary school counselors are "truly jacks-of-all trades" (ASCA, 2012, p. 75) and must work to find an appropriate balance in the delivery component of their school counseling program.

Almost 100 years ago, in 1928, William Burnham became the first advocate for counselors in the schools by expressing a need that mental health interventions for young children were necessary. Formal education in the United States often begins with preschool and prekindergarten programs. However, attendance is not mandated in these early childhood programs and funding for such programs remains inconsistent. In fact, Wright (2012) reports that preschool funding differs from state to state and that the United States is the only Western country lacking a universal preschool program. Many states provide the funds for preschool education in high-needs areas where the federal government does not, and the inconsistency between state budgets from year to year can wreak havoc on programs producing outcome data. In contrast, Head Start and Early Start programs are mostly funded by the federal government and aim to provide early education to children of low-income families and children with disabilities. Head Start programs have steadily provided evidence of catching children up to the performance level of middle- and upper-class peers at the kindergarten level. Though research has indicated that Head Start programs improve the academic and social skills of poor students and students with disabilities (Wright, 2012), the target population is still quite narrow, and needy children that do not meet the criteria or families that have not been identified may go without these services. Many learning disabilities and behavioral problems can be identified early on and also remediated, therefore preschool and prekindergarten programs remain a true investment in education, children, and society.

CASE STUDY

John suffered from asthma and allergies as an infant and young toddler, which often resulted in ear infections. As a consequence, John's hearing was impacted, compromising his speech and language development. When John began to talk, his words were often jumbled and hard for others to understand, making it difficult for John to effectively communicate. As John's vocabulary and understanding of the world around him continued to grow, John often became frustrated at his inability to clearly communicate with his peers and the adults in his life. John lived in a state that offered a state-funded prekindergarten program, which he began to attend at the age of four. His parents and teachers recognized the impact that his speech and language development was having on his learning and social interactions. John was found eligible to receive supportive services and began to see a speech pathologist once a week to help address his areas of deficits. In fact, John continued to see a speech therapist throughout prekindergarten, kindergarten, and first grade. Due to the early identification of his speech and language challenges, John is beginning second grade and no longer requires additional supportive services. John's speech and language development is on target with his peers, and he is flourishing both academically and socially.

ELEMENTARY SCHOOL STUDENTS

The elementary school setting includes the most grade levels (i.e., prekindergarten through Grade 5, on average) and the largest range of student ages. Some elementary schools begin with prekindergarten classes—possibly even preschool, with Head Start programs—and go through fifth or sixth grade. The ages of children at the elementary level may range from three (at Head Start or preschool) through eleven or twelve. Whereas school counseling interventions may not need to be tailored according to the developmental level of students at the middle school or high school levels, there is no doubt that elementary school counselors will need to adapt lessons based on the ages of the students. The next section will present developmental considerations and characteristics of early childhood. Developmental considerations and characteristics need to be understood and applied to any interventions focused on prevention or counseling.

Physical Development

Physical growth is slower during the childhood years as compared to the infant, toddler, and adolescent stages of growth. Early childhood (4–8 years old) is a time period when gross motor skills, such as running and climbing, and fine motor skills, such as using utensils, are developing slowly. However, these skills are acquired and mastered by the later childhood years. Bodies become more toned and mature during this time, with muscle groups forming and body hair becoming more apparent. Younger children will, at times, skip meals and not display overt signs of being hungry. This is most likely due to their body slowing down. This changes, however, as the child approaches adolescence. Older children (10–11 years old) may be approaching or may have entered puberty and feelings of self-consciousness may emerge. If not detected at an earlier age, chronic illness may emerge at this stage of development. Many elementary-age children attend school with chronic illnesses such as asthma, diabetes, and anemia. By kindergarten, children have probably lost a tooth and permanent teeth are filling in.

Cognitive Development

Early childhood marks a period of imagination, concrete thinking, and self-centeredness. Piaget's theory of cognitive development may be a useful framework for elementary school counselors to consider in their work with children during this developmental time period. Throughout the elementary years, young children are making the transformation from preoperational thought to concrete operational thought, allowing students to begin to think in a more logical manner (Myers, Shaffner, & Briggs, 2002). Additionally, cause and effect is blurred and, as Vernon (2010) illustrates, a child has a difficult time assigning identities to one person, such as a teacher who is also a parent. During early childhood, parents might find that their child is finding their voice, talking back, and offering opinions. Impulsivity is still present but can be better controlled. Later childhood brings higher-order thinking, extended conversations, and an understanding of logical consequences. During this time, older children begin to see differences between themselves and others, such as being short, having red hair, or having emerging acne. Vocabularies grow to include more than 40,000 words (Vernon, 2009) and basic vocabulary and grammar are obtained. The brain grows to 90% of its full weight and children experience an increase in memory due to a greater ability to encode, store, and retrieve information (Lightfoot, Cole, & Cole, 2009).

Social/Emotional Development

Play is the center of most learning during childhood. Though younger children do begin to take turns and share, some arguing during play will ensue. The vocabulary of young children is still growing, so expressions will be revealed through behavior. Managing behavior during this age range will be a struggle for parents and educators. Most children only know a few emotions, such as mad, sad, happy, and scared, which can restrict their communication with others. The stereotype of boys and girls is apparent for the most part, with boys liking rough and competitive play and girls preferring nurturing and cooperative play. You also see same-sex grouping of play during this time as play becomes segregated. As children mature, friendships and peer groups become paramount in life. Older children are more empathic and understand differences among people and worldviews. They are more social and engage in more cooperative activities in the classroom and outside of school. Young childhood fears of monsters become more legitimate and fears of real-life issues such as death, failing school, and becoming involved in a car accident are on their minds. This is the age in which children begin to understand their ethnic identity. Parents at this age may tend to overschedule their child in after-school and weekend activities. Parents may believe that the structure provided by activities will enrich a child's talents in the sports or arts. Parents may need to be reminded that free play encourages creativity, imagination, and independence. Play can be a time to fantasize, experience emotional relief, and create control in their world. Parents need to keep in mind that play had been reduced in the schools due to an increase in academic rigor. This playtime should be promoted in the home in the afternoons and on the weekends. Additionally, children this age still require 10 or more hours of sleep per day and may need a calming transition from afternoon to evening and dinner to homework to bed, so overly scheduled activities (rather than free, relaxed play) may be more taxing on children.

STRENGTHS AND CHALLENGES OF ELEMENTARY SCHOOL STUDENTS

As with all populations of students, elementary-age students will provide their parents, teachers, and counselors with unique challenges. However, much satisfaction can be achieved by seeing a young child improve and excel academically and behaviorally/socially as a result of counseling interventions. Elementary school counselors are situated to develop counseling interventions that are rooted in prevention and encompass strengths-based theories. Access to parents is more available at the elementary level due to the higher level of needs this group presents. Parents are usually present during pick-up and drop-off times, need to be available for report card conferences, and are more active with parent/teacher organizations and school-based activities. The academic material at this level is not as challenging for parents, and parent involvement with homework and projects is at an all-time high during the elementary grades.

Strengths-Based Counseling

Strengths-based counseling (SBC) should be understood and used by counselors at the elementary level. The elementary ages are important years; children need help dealing with problematic behaviors by understanding and building on their individual strengths and resilience. SBC allows children to fully understand the gifts they possess to manage challenging times. Individual strengths help enhance coping skills and add positive dimensions to the self. As a form of primary prevention, school counselors need to move away from providing deficit-reduction services to a smaller percentage of high-needs students and encourage managing programs that promote successful academic, career, and social/emotional skills and the individual strengths of students (ASCA, 2012; Galassi, Griffin, & Akos, 2008).

As Galassi et al. (2008) discuss, one of the primary functions of the school counselor is to focus on problem prevention and problem reduction. Dealing with crisis situations and offering remedial services will inevitably be a part of a school counselor's day. However, data-driven, systematic, comprehensive school counseling programs should seek positive development in the academic, career, and social/emotional domains. Characteristics of comprehensive school counseling programs grounded in promoting student strengths, positive psychology, prevention, and wellness will include a promotion-oriented delivery, incorporate evidence-based practices, and create successful partnerships through advocacy, leadership, and collaboration. Harris, Thoresen, and Lopez (2007) contended that incorporating strengths-based work in counseling programs may provide a foundation for an individual and have more lasting effects than any one specific strategy. See Exercise 3.1 for an example of a strengths-based approach to a bullying problem.

EXERCISE 3.1

CASE CONCEPTUALIZATION FROM A STRENGTHS-BASED APPROACH

Bobby is a fourth-grade student who attends an urban elementary school. Bobby is sent to the school counselor's office because his teacher notices that he looks teary-eyed after coming in from recess. After speaking with Bobby, the school counselor is

(Continued)

(Continued)

able to ascertain that many of the kids in his classroom have been making fun of his weight; this could even be considered a bullying situation. While it sounds like this teasing has been going on for some time, in previous years, Bobby has not reported or shown signs of being picked on. The counselor has known Bobby for several years and is aware that he is in the gifted program, he has a supportive and involved family, and he is very interested in theater and drama. In fact, Bobby was selected for a lead in the upcoming school play. The school counselor is concerned, as she dealt with a similar situation with another student in the same classroom just last week. From a strength-based prospective, consider the following questions:

- How could the school counselor work to help Bobby cope and manage this teasing utilizing his individual strengths?
- How could the school counselor address these incidents within the same classroom proactively?
- Are there preventative measures that the school counselor may want to consider?

COMPREHENSIVE SCHOOL COUNSELING PROGRAMS AT THE ELEMENTARY LEVEL

As discussed in earlier chapters, the introduction of the ASCA National Model allowed counselors to develop data-driven, systematic programs. As being a part of the team of school staff, credit may be given to the work of school counselors for an increase in academic achievement and test scores as well as levels of career and college readiness. Specifically at the elementary school level, young students should be able to understand the connection between school and the world of work (ASCA, 2014). However, if counselors truly want to show their contribution to student development, direct interventions and services tied to comprehensive school programs are imperative. As Sink and Stroh (2003) discuss, research providing direct implications to comprehensive school counselors' programs for enhancing student academic achievement and social/emotional development is scarce. In the first study that attempted to directly correlate an outcome of student achievement to comprehensive school counseling programs, several findings emerged (Stink & Stroh, 2003). First, a gain in academic achievement and a movement to close achievement gaps occurred even for early elementary-age children (Grades 3–4) with a "less than totally engaged comprehensive school counseling program" as compared to students in a control group over a two- to three-year time period (p. 220).

Additionally, children of all socioeconomic statuses benefitted academically and socially by attending schools with a well-established comprehensive school counseling program. Overall, the study found that younger students (i.e., lower elementary grades) performed better on standardized tests and academics at schools with comprehensive school counseling programs than at those without a program in existence.

Research findings indicate that elementary-age students greatly benefit from data-driven, systematic school counseling programs. It would behoove elementary school counselors to implement programs that align outcomes to direct interventions and services. Vernon (2009) suggests that classroom guidance programming should be designed to target academics at the elementary level. Sink and Stroh (2003) present an example of a guidance curriculum entitled "How to Succeed in School." The guidance lessons include study skills, organization and planning tips, positive behaviors in the classroom, test-taking strategies, improved writing, and homework completion tasks. In fact, ASCA (2014) developed 35 mindset and behavior standards to prioritize and identify specific knowledge, beliefs, and skills that students should acquire from access to a comprehensive school counseling program. Use Exercise 3.2 to consider how to create your own classroom guidance lesson.

CASE STUDY

A professional elementary school counselor addresses the academic domain in her biweekly classroom guidance lessons. Her last classroom lesson for second grade was on organization. To ensure that the lesson was developmentally appropriate, engaging, and meaningful, she utilized creative platforms to help her second graders understand the importance of organization. For example, she opened the lesson on organization by reading *The Bernstein Bears and the Messy Room* by Stan and Jan Bernstein. The book is a developmentally appropriate way to introduce the concept of organization to young students as well as hook them into the lesson. After discussing the importance of organization, the school counselor brought out a tray of school supplies that was disorganized and messy. She gave the students thirty seconds to look at the disheveled items on the tray, put the tray out of sight, and asked the students to write down as many items as they could remember from the tray. Next, the school counselor showed the students a tray with organized school supplies for 30 seconds and again asked them to write down as many items as they could remember. The school counselor facilitated a discussion on the difference between the two trays and closed the lesson by summarizing the importance of organization.

EXERCISE 3.2

CREATING A CLASSROOM GUIDANCE LESSON

You are a school counselor at an elementary school that houses students in kindergarten through fifth grade. The state that you work in has mandated a standardized writing test for all fourth-grade students. While the fourth-grade students are familiar with taking standardized assessments, this is the first year that they will be given a writing test. The test will require students to respond to a writing prompt, and their writing will be scored and assessed in several areas. The fourth-grade teachers have asked you to conduct a classroom guidance lesson to assist the students in preparing for this upcoming writing test. Considering the following:

- What developmental considerations will you need to think about when planning your lesson?
- What will be the objectives of your classroom lesson?
- How will you design your lesson (i.e., What activities will you implement?)?

CASE STUDY

To address the career development domain, one elementary school counselor organizes a monthly "Career Café." This involves the school counselor inviting a professional into the school building to talk about their job specifications during the students' lunch time. The school counselor organizes the schedule so that each class in the school is able to attend four Career Café presentations throughout the school year. In addition, the school counselor organizes a Career Day for all students in the school each spring.

Counseling Interventions with Elementary School Students

Counselors need to understand that there exists quite a range in the cognitive and language development of children at elementary schools. Younger children, enrolled in prekindergarten through third grade, will probably respond best through the use of play therapy and expressive arts. With age and further development, older children will be able to think through questions and respond appropriately. However, research indicates that the use of play therapy skills (i.e., tracking, returning responsibility) and expressive arts is useful across the lifespan (Vernon,

2008) and with various populations such as small groups, couples, siblings, and families. Counselors do need to keep in mind that, even with growth in cognition, older children are still spontaneous and impulsive and have difficulty in seeing possible consequences to their actions.

Overarching challenges for younger children in the school will be the inability to engage in cooperative play and understand multiple perspectives. Learning differences may exist twofold for this age group: (1) Academic success in reading, writing, and reasoning may range due to a lack of exposure to preschool education, the parents' educational attainment level, and the family's socioeconomic status. Children are usually able to catch up to normal ranges by the second or third grades. (2) Learning difficulties may not be detected and supports may be delayed during this "catching up" period; more teachers of this age group report the existence of waiting periods before referring a child to testing.

Older children enrolled in Grades 3–5 are more likely to experience great success in school and to excel in some or all classes. Others may have academic experiences such as low grades, low standardized test scores, teacher conflict, and low overall school engagement that subsequently affect their sense of self. Older children are also more dependent on peer relationships and approval and these factors also affect one's sense of self. Older children are transitioning to middle school and, for some, the perfect storm of lagging academics and school engagement as well as dependence on peer approval may be the reality.

The next section will discuss common interventions to problems that counselors will help alleviate at the elementary level. Though some of these school-based challenges may exist across elementary, middle, and high school levels (such as bullying), others will be presented and fitted for work with young children.

CASE STUDY

A school counselor is facilitating a changing family's small group to offer support to students experiencing some type of family change (i.e., divorce, separation, relocation). Due to the number of children referred and scheduling purposes, the school counselor includes students ranging from second to fourth grade in the small counseling group. Therefore, when planning for the group sessions, the school counselor must carefully select activities that will be developmentally appropriate for the age range of students in her group. The school counselor utilizes expressive art activities

(Continued)

(Continued)

throughout the group, as not only is the approach effective with elementary-age students but such activities can be modified based on the developmental level of the students. For example, during one of the early sessions, the group members were given materials and asked to paint a family portrait. Details and quality of the paintings ranged based on the ages, however, the activity was developmentally appropriate for all of the students in the group. As the group members shared about their family portraits, all of the group members were able to benefit from hearing developmentally appropriate explanations of the other family units.

Primary Prevention

The counseling profession is easily distinguished from other allied fields due to its focus on prevention. While there have been increased efforts in providing interventions rooted in prevention, more evidenced-based programs are available that enhance student academic, career, and social/emotional development. Prior to any enhancements in the three domains of student development, behavior must be managed in a systematic manner. Positive behavior interventions & supports (PBIS) programs have been in existence since 2000. Sugai and Horner (2009) contend that PBIS programs will look different from school to school but that five basic components exist: (1) a leadership team; (2) a brief, overarching schoolwide philosophy or framework; (3) specific behavior guidelines for areas of the school such as classroom, bathroom, lunchroom, and buses; (4) individual classroom guidelines; and (5) specific strategies for students who need additional support. Additionally, data are collected along the way that provide the documentation to the leadership team for decision making.

More attention has been given to PBIS in recent years due to its positive outcomes at all three levels in Grades K–12 and also includes evidence of successful outcomes in juvenile justice programs (Curtis, Van Horne, Robertson, & Karvonen, 2010). PBIS is being discussed at the national level and accepted as an evidence-based practice for many federal and state educational grants. Though limited research exists on the outcomes of PBIS in the elementary school setting, the existing results are favorable. Outcomes range from school to school but a compilation of the research reveals a decrease in behavioral problems and suspension by 20%–60% (Sugai & Horner, 2009). The decrease in suspensions is significant for educators, administrators, and policy makers, as school attendance rates are closely monitored and tied to funding. Exercise 3.3 illustrates how to use PBIS in the school.

EXERCISE 3.3

IMPLEMENTING AN EFFECTIVE POSITIVE BEHAVIOR INTERVENTIONS & SUPPORTS (PBIS) PROGRAM

You have been offered your first counseling job at an elementary school. In preparation for the school year, you begin to review school data and collaborate with staff members and stakeholders and have come to the conclusion that this elementary school would benefit tremendously from a PBIS program. Considering the five components of all PBIS programs, discuss the steps that you would take to begin to implement an effective PBIS program in your school.

Bullying Prevention

Most people would report being bullied during their childhood years. More are not as open to admitting playing the role of the bully. Bullying prevention efforts gained momentum in the early 2000s. This may be fueled, to some degree, from reports issued after the series of tragic school shootings in the 1990s. These reports indicated that the shooters had been chronically bullied (Vossekuil, Fein, Reddy, Borum, & Modzeleski, 2002). In fact, 67% of all school shootings were completed by individuals who had experienced significant childhood bullying (Wright, 2012). Individuals also view acts of bulling differently, which may change how bullying is identified and treated. Bullying comments may be centered on sex/gender, race/ethnicity, disability, sexual orientation, and appearances that may go noticed or unnoticed by adults in the building due to their own early experiences and permissiveness on how others should be treated.

Bullying will become more aggressive both physically and verbally as children age. Physical bullying becomes increasingly more common from third grade on (Wright, 2012). Children who bully enjoy the power and lack empathy. Children who are bullied often disengage from school and do not participate in small groups during class activities, lunch, and outside activities. Another form of bullying, which parents and counselors probably have not experienced, is cyberbullying. Cyberbullying should be treated in the same manner as in-person bullying. Social media outlets include Facebook, Twitter, YouTube, Pinterest, and Tumblr, and children can contact other children with threatening and harassing comments and stalking. These acts, along with hacking and identity theft, may all take the shape of bullying and violate state and federal laws. Parents and counselors also have to consider that children may text and send messages through e-mail that may be bullying behavior. Bullying prevention efforts need to include acts of cyberbullying. Bullies may find more power and freedom by remaining masked behind technology.

CASE STUDY

A professional school counselor working at the elementary level understands the importance of developing a schoolwide definition of bullying as well as a uniform system for reporting and addressing incidents of bullying. The school counselor visits each classroom during the first month of school to educate her students on the definition of bullying, ways to handle incidents of bullying, and the schoolwide reporting procedure. These early lessons ensure that the students understand what bullying is, how to handle bullying, and how they should report bullying. Additionally, students will understand consequences that may incur if they are involved with bullying. The school counselor also speaks at staff meetings on the definition of bullying and reporting procedures. The school counselor makes posters with their schoolwide definition of bullying that teachers are required to visibly post in their classroom. These initial lessons are instrumental in comprehensively, collaboratively, and proactively addressing bullying at the elementary school level.

WHAT IS AN ELEMENTARY SCHOOL LIKE?

In your typical elementary school exists a sense of excitement and energy that an individual feels upon walking through the front doors. Often, school lobbies and front offices are adorned with colorful pictures and motivational sayings and are visually enticing. Hallways throughout the school display student work, giving an elementary school an at-home feel. The chatter of little voices can be heard as one walks the hallways. Visitors may observe teachers engaging students through a variety of teaching methods and young students are captivated by the learning process. One may watch young students playing on the playground, conversing with friends at lunch, playing in the gymnasium during P.E., or learning to play the recorder in music class. The onlooker may see a young student in tears because his or her mom has gone for the day and, on the next hallway over, observe an eleven-year-old who is headed off to middle school in a few short months.

While there is no doubt that most elementary schools appeal to young students through fun and play, there has been a shift in the last decade to a standards-driven academic curriculum at all grade levels, beginning in kindergarten. Therefore, an elementary school student's days are structured and scheduled with the aim of providing a balance of both academic and social learning. Younger students may have a difficult time adjusting to this structure and may need additional support in order to successfully meet school expectations. Older students may be dealing with issues related to transitioning to middle school or managing stress. Additionally, there will be school-specific and community issues related to factors such as socioeconomic status and ethnicity to consider. Therefore, a critical first step for any school counselor who is preparing to implement a comprehensive school counseling program is to analyze school data and tailor interventions and programs based on such data.

KEYSTONES

- New directions for practice in elementary school counseling have emerged in the school counseling literature with a strong focus on comprehensive programming, collaboration, and preventative measures and are central tenets of the ASCA's national model of school counseling (ASCA, 2012; Walsh et al., 2008).
- Whereas school counseling interventions may not need to be tailored according to the developmental level of students at the middle school or high school levels, there is no doubt that elementary school counselors will adapt lessons based on the ages of the students.
- Elementary school counselors are situated to develop counseling interventions that are rooted in prevention and encompass strengths-based theories.
- In order for school counselors to truly show their contribution to student development, direct interventions and services tied to comprehensive school programs are imperative.
- Research findings indicate that elementary-age students greatly benefit from data-driven, systematic school counseling programs. It would behoove elementary school counselors to implement programs that align outcomes to direct interventions and services.
- Counselors need to understand that there exists quite a range in the cognitive and language development of children in elementary schools. Younger children (enrolled in prekindergarten through third grade) will probably respond best through the use of play therapy and expressive arts. With age and further development, older children will be able to think through questions and respond appropriately.
- While there have been increased efforts in providing interventions rooted in prevention, more evidenced-based programs are available that enhance student academic, career, and social/emotional development.

REFERENCES

American School Counselor Association (ASCA). (2012). *ASCA national model: A framework for school counseling programs* (3rd ed.). Alexandria, VA: Author.
American School Counselor Association (ASCA). (2014). *Mindsets & behaviors for student success: K–12 college- and career-readiness standards for every student*. Alexandria, VA: Author.

Curtis, R., Van Horne, J. W., Robertson, P., & Karvonen, M. (2010). Outcomes of a school-wide positive behavioral support program. *Professional School Counseling, 13*, 159–164.

Galassi, J., Griffin, D., & Akos, P. (2008). Strengths-based school counseling and the ASCA national model. *Professional School Counseling, 12*(2), 176–181.

Harris, A. H. S., Thoresen, C. E., & Lopez, S. J. (2007). Integrating positive psychology into counseling: Why and (when appropriate) how. *Journal of Counseling and Development, 85,* 3–13.

Lightfoot, C., Cole, M., & Cole, S. R. (2009). *The development of children.* (6th ed.). New York, NY: Worth Publishers.

Myers, J. E., Shaffner, M. F., & Briggs, M. K. (2002). Developmental counseling and therapy: An effective approach to understanding and counseling children. *Professional School Counseling, 5*(3), 194–202.

Sink, C. A., & Stroh, H. R. (2003). Raising achievement test scores of early elementary school students through comprehensive school counseling programs. *Professional School Counseling, 6*, 352–364.

Sugai, G., & Horner, R. H. (2009). Responsiveness-to-intervention and school-wide positive behavior supports: Integration of multi-tiered approaches. *Exceptionality, 17,* 223–237.

Vernon, A. (2010). *Counseling children and adolescents.* (4th ed.). Denver, CO: Love Publishing.

Vossekuil, B., Fein, R., Reddy, M., Borum, R., & Modzeleski, W. (2002). *The final report and findings of the safe school initiative: Implications for the prevention of school attacks in the United States.* Washington, DC: U.S. Department of Education.

Walsh, M. E., Barrett, J., & DePaul, J. (2008). Day-to-day activities of school counselors. Alignment with new directions in the field and the ASCA national model. *Professional School Counseling, 10*(4), 370–378.

Wright, R. J. (2012). *Introduction to school counseling.* Thousand Oaks, CA: SAGE.

Chapter 4

THE MIDDLE SCHOOL

SAM STEEN
George Washington University

JOY ROSE
Columbia Heights Education Campus

KRISTIN AVINA
Truesdell Education Campus

DANA JENKINS
Chicago Public Schools

Middle school counselors are professional educators with a mental health perspective who understand and respond to the challenges presented by today's diverse student population. Middle school counselors do not work in isolation; rather they are integral to the total educational program.

(American School Counselor Association, 2012)

Professional school counselors are charged with demonstrating an understanding of the broader counseling profession and all of its complexities in our global society. School counselors are also expected to possess the requisite skills that can be applied to school settings where the emphasis is on promoting academic, career, and social/emotional development of all prekindergarten–12 students. School counselors must also examine numerous external factors that may impact a school environment, such as community issues and pressing trends. Preservice school counselor candidates complete a certain number of internship hours fulfilling roles that many school counselors are performing in actual practice (Council for Accreditation of Counseling & Related Educational Programs [CACREP], 2009). In some cases, school counselors may have completed internships in a rural elementary school or a suburban high school during their master's program. Other school counselor candidates may have gained both public and private school setting experience in an urban community. However, the roles that the school counselor is required to fulfill within their first school counseling job might very well not resemble any of their prior experiences. Essentially, each school district, school community, school administration, faculty, and so forth is uniquely different. Preparing school counselors to perform specific roles required in comprehensive, developmental counseling programs and to apply these functions appropriately within the respective context may be an overwhelming endeavor.

In this chapter, adolescent development (i.e., physical, cognitive, social development) will be explored. Next, a discussion on the middle school setting and the complexities and opportunities associated with this level of school will follow. An in-depth discussion of classroom guidance programs and strategies to think about when creating and implementing these programs is included. Additionally, a reflective case illustration is presented. In this case, the reader is given the opportunity to reflect on how they might function in the presented situation. Further, responses from two current middle school counselors about their experiences with similar situations are provided. Last but not least, a variety of examples of classroom guidance lessons are included. In summary, a number of developmental factors to be considered with adolescents typically attending a middle school will be discussed, and these factors will serve as a backdrop to what middle school students may be thinking, feeling, or doing during this stage of their lives and how school counselors can use classroom guidance programming efforts to help pave the way to student success.

After reading this chapter about middle school classroom guidance and student development, the reader will be able to

- identify key aspects of adolescent development,
- understand the dynamics of middle school settings, and
- understand the application of classroom guidance programming in middle schools.

ADOLESCENT DEVELOPMENT

Physical Development

Aside from infancy, no other phase of life is characterized by greater, more rapid, and more diverse development than early adolescence (ages 11–14). As part of adolescents' growth and development, they often need endless food, physical activity, and sleep. Additionally, they can be restless and energetic. There are growth spurts that occur for both sexes, and girls may begin to menstruate (Northeast Foundation for Children, 2005).

It goes without saying that the changes associated with puberty can be difficult, but this difficulty is compounded for students who mature either early or late, compared to their peers. The complexity that is faced by a school counselor serving students who are maturing early can be seen in the case study below.

CASE STUDY

Mrs. Dominique, a sixth-grade counselor at a school that serves students in Grades 5–9, would often have to deal with students who were physically maturing earlier than their peers. One challenge that she faced in particular in working with boys and girls was planning the conversations she would have with the students so they would be useful to those who were maturing faster (in order to help normalize their experience) as well as for others who were not overly zealous about their physical changes. More specifically, Mrs. Dominique discovered that it was more socially beneficial for boys to mature early in relation to their peers; however, the young girls who matured physically earlier than their peers were often the recipients of teasing or even bullying in school from other boys and girls. However, boys who mature late physically compared to their peers were also suffering from similar insults. Given these realities, Mrs. Dominique decided to create a special classroom guidance lesson in order to more fully discuss and explain the emerging changes experienced during puberty. Another purpose of the lesson was to address the negative experiences that some students were experiencing and the impact that additional teasing and bullying may have on these students. She co-taught this lesson with the health education teacher so standards in both areas (health promotion, counseling) could be met.

Cognitive Development

In general, "cognitive development in adolescence is mixed with important advances and remaining limitations" (Wigfield, Lutz, & Wagner, 2005, p. 113). While gains in areas such as self-reflection and the ability to make hypotheses are observed, an elevated likelihood to undertake risky behaviors highlights apparent deficits in the decision-making process of adolescents. These cognitive challenges could impact how others perceive these students during this stage of development. For example, students may begin to experiment with more risky behavior, such as binge drinking. In the event that a student is associated with the wrong crowd by attending parties where this is occurring, the student's experience at school may be altered, because others may have a hard time seeing this student favorably if this information surfaces. Academically, according to the Northeast Foundation for Children (2005), students might exhibit any number of characteristics that are more intellectually oriented during these phases of development. For example, their cognitive development allows adolescents to think abstractly. They are now able to set reasonable goals and concentrate well. These students often write better than they speak, and they need short, predicable homework assignments to build good study habits. Further, middle school students may begin to excel at a certain subject or a skill, such as drawing. It is important to note that these cognitive abilities may manifest themselves in any number of ways; these are just a few features that may be typical for students in these age ranges.

Social Development

Students who are approximately 11 to 14 years of age undoubtedly display a wide range of social behaviors. According to a commonly accepted theory, identity versus role confusion intersects during this stage of development (Erikson, 1965). Therefore, it would be appropriate for middle school counselors to address the difficulty students may face when making decisions based on personal impulses (i.e., impulse control, anger management, organization) or alignment with a certain social group membership (i.e., friendship groups, conflict resolution, bullying prevention). For instance, these students may be quick to anger but are also quick to forgive. They tend to be quite competitive, but they are also known for being very cooperative. At the same time, these students often worry about who's "in" and who's "out." Students during the middle school years often argue, challenge rules, and test limits (Wood, 2005).

Early adolescence is characterized as a period in which there is increased desire for autonomy and self-determination by the students. These aspirations manifest themselves in students possibly being self-absorbed and self-conscious. At the same time, students might also battle identity issues and compete for their peers' attention (Eccles et al., 1993).

Adolescent development is recognized as a very difficult life stage for both the adolescent and the surrounding adults. In fact, adolescents are *necessarily* engaged in fighting against adult domination and resent any situation that seems to resemble the parent-child struggle with which they are battling both externally and internally, such as in the classroom. Although early adolescence is a time when students will attempt to distance themselves from their parents, they often want to fill this space through close relationships with other peers and, in some cases, other adults. Efforts students make to assert their autonomy often cause conflict with adults regarding rules about dress, language, music, preference for friends, and academic performance.

In school settings, it is commonly accepted that the basic task of preadolescence is to develop a realistic sense of identity inclusive of strengths and weaknesses and ideals of self-worth and movement toward respected vocational choice and/or post-secondary options. However, these internal struggles are inevitably compounded by a myriad of environmental factors from the surrounding school community (Bryan, 2005). For example, many students who have recently immigrated to our country are experiencing challenges that are not always easy to identify. These students—whether navigating underfunded, wealthy, or rural public school systems—face numerous barriers and difficulties to accomplish these developmental tasks. The added stress experienced by new immigrants, especially under hostile conditions, can be seen in the following case study.

CASE STUDY

Manuel is in the seventh grade at a public middle school. He recently came to the U.S. with his mother from El Salvador. Though Manuel was attending school in his home country, he has had a nine-month interruption in his education while he and his mother were traveling. Manuel's teachers have noticed that he is adjusting well to his new school, and he has not had any trouble making friends. He is a little behind in his math skills but has shown improvement after just a week of after-school tutoring. One area of concern with Manuel is the way he interacts with his male teachers. He seems to disregard anything they say to him and is often blatantly disrespectful to them. Through some individual conversations with Manuel, the school counselor learns that his father has been absent from his life since he was five years old and Manuel is harboring a lot of animosity toward him. Additionally, during the course of their travels from El Salvador, Manuel and his mother had several unpleasant interactions with some of the men who were traveling in the group with them. These things have combined to cause Manuel to really distrust men and that is playing out in his relationships with his teachers. After discussing it with Manuel, the school counselor sets up meetings for Manuel and his mother with each of Manuel's male teachers. The goals of these meetings were to establish open communication between Manuel and his teachers as well as between the teachers and Manuel's mother. Additionally, Manuel was able to share with the teachers a little bit about his experiences and through this sharing, the foundation for a trusting relationship was laid. Changes did not happen overnight, but over time, Manuel was able to learn that all of his teachers truly wanted the best for him and this changed his attitude, which in turn showed in his classroom performance and academic achievement.

More specifically, schools still continue to struggle with how to reach the needs of more racially, ethnically, and culturally diverse populations as evidenced by lower test scores and performance outcomes in many geographical areas. Further, this diversity expands beyond simple race and ethnicity and includes socioeconomic status, sex, gender, sexuality, spirituality and religion, cognitive abilities, mental health status, physical ability, and citizenship as seen in the illustration above. During the middle school years, it is imperative that school counselors are open to addressing a wide range of issues due to the constantly changing and developing identities of middle school students, their families, and communities.

Check for Understanding

✓ Other than infancy, preadolescence may be a time that provides the most robust and rapid developmental challenges.

✓ Though preadolescence is a time period when students may distance themselves from their parents, they are often looking to fill these spaces with other caring adults.

✓ During preadolescence, students place high worth on the opinion of their peers as they search for independence and autonomy.

THE MIDDLE SCHOOL

During the time period that students are transitioning into middle school, they are navigating the mental and physical changes that come with the transition into early adolescence. Adolescents "who cannot find even a small like-minded group in which they feel comfortable are in distress" (Cohen, Reinherz, & Frost, 1994, p. 49). A small subgroup may be as large a group as some adolescents can handle. A unique value of the middle school student population is that groups have been found to be instrumental in "one another's growth and struggle for self-understanding" (Corey & Corey, 1982, p. 235).

Schools are social environments that do not always respond to the developmental needs of students. Ideally, middle school environments furnish students with enough structure for their current levels of maturity and yet provide an equally challenging environment to move them toward higher levels of academic achievement and social maturity (Akos, 2005). Moreover, for middle schools to be successful, their students must be successful. For students to be successful, the school's organization, curriculum, pedagogy, and programs must be based upon the developmental readiness, needs, and interests of young adolescents. Instead, however, many middle schools are preoccupied with control of behavior rather than engaging students in problem solving that might foster responsible and independent behavior.

The middle school years are perhaps the first time in students' lives that they are making independent and autonomous choices that may significantly shape their developmental paths. And yet, Eccles et al. (1993) found that middle school students often made fewer decisions regarding their learning than elementary students. Students often suggest they are treated like babies when there is no differentiation between rules for sixth and eighth graders. Adolescents need an environment that is both reasonably safe and intellectually challenging. Students are less likely to do well if the social environment does not meet their developmental needs and social expectations (Eccles et al., 1993).

Additionally, the educational structure, teaching strategies, and learning environment need to be congruent with students' learning and developmental needs. Some of the negative psychological changes associated with adolescent development result from a mismatch between the developmental needs of adolescents and the available opportunities that their social and/or school environments provide. For example, when adolescents are in settings (school, home, or community) that are not attuned to their needs and emerging independence, they can lose confidence in themselves. This may cause them to slip into negative behavior patterns such as truancy, disengagement, and dropping out (White & Kelly, 2010).

The role and responsibility of the school counselor in dropout prevention is receiving more attention in the literature, especially for the elementary and middle school settings as compared to the high school setting (White & Kelly, 2010). Schools can no longer wait until high school to address dropping out and disengagement because the data are clear that by middle school, there are a number of indicators that correlate with future dropout rates. Absenteeism and truancy are two of the highest predictors of dropping out, along with suspensions, behavioral referrals, and low scores in math and English/language arts. Additionally, nearly 25% of all students are not graduating on time or at all (Ziomek-Daigle & Andrews, 2009). Further, those individuals who do drop out continue to have the highest rates of unemployment (White & Kelly, 2010). Therefore, middle school classroom guidance programs that are comprehensive and developmentally appropriate seem to be an effective way to reach a large number of students facing any host of issues, such as family problems, peer pressure, truancy, and absenteeism (Bryan, Steen, & Day-Vines, 2010). These factors, in turn, have been associated with dropping out during the transition between middle and high school (Prevatt & Kelly, 2003).

Check for Understanding

✓ All aspects of schools need to be appropriate for students' developmental levels.

✓ Students at the middle school level need environments that are both structured and challenging in order to foster their independence and autonomy.

✓ Middle school may be the first time that students are making independent choices that will affect their developmental paths.

✓ By meeting the cognitive, developmental, and emotional needs of students, school environments can prevent negative behavior patterns such as truancy and dropping out.

CLASSROOM GUIDANCE PROGRAMMING: THE ESSENTIAL COMPONENT OF COMPREHENSIVE SCHOOL COUNSELING PROGRAMS IN MIDDLE SCHOOL

In light of the difficulties that many students face during their preadolescent years, school counselors, accreditation bodies (e.g., CACREP) and the American School Counselor Association (ASCA) must demonstrate that school counseling programs have a positive effect on student academic, career, and social/emotional development (ASCA, 2012). ASCA, the flagship organization for professional school counseling members, emphasizes these broad components of student development within the ASCA National Model. Recently, ASCA revised a position statement specifying that comprehensive school counseling programs designed and facilitated by school counselors aim to promote student achievement and are developmental, preventative, and multifaceted.

The ASCA National Model for School Counseling Programs (ASCA, 2012) generally defines classroom guidance programming as part of the delivery system with an emphasis on providing direct services for students to prevent the onset of mental health issues, for students in crisis, or for students in transition. ASCA also recommends that direct services include presenting psych education in the classrooms to a large number of students.

School Counseling Core Curriculum

This curriculum consists of structured lessons designed to help students attain the desired competencies and to provide all students with the knowledge, attitudes and skills appropriate for their developmental level. The school counseling core curriculum is delivered throughout the school's overall curriculum and is systematically presented by professional school counselors in collaboration with other professional educators in K–12 classroom activities.

(ASCA, 2012)

Classroom guidance programming is imperative for school counselors who are responsible for addressing issues related to academic, career, and social/emotional development for all students. It is believed that it would be nearly impossible to resolve all of the needs of so many students utilizing individual counseling or small groups as the primary modes of service. These classroom guidance programs may revolve around character education with monthly themes; current initiatives mandated by central office; building-level administrative programs (e.g., bullying prevention or social skills); or critical needs that are evident in the school (i.e., career awareness), unique to the local student body (i.e., dropout prevention), or a combination of any or all of these (Bryan et al., 2010).

BENEFITS OF CLASSROOM GUIDANCE

Although the CACREP standards (2009) and the ASCA National Model for School Counseling Programs (ASCA, 2012) might suggest that school counselors make proactive efforts to attend to all of the needs of students, no one can argue the reality that a special emphasis is placed on academic achievement. The current dialogue among educational policy stakeholders (Steen & Noguera, 2010) centers on the ability of school counseling programs to directly influence student achievement outcomes. This impact may be direct or proximal in nature (e.g., by following the classroom guidance program for study skills, students will be able to communicate their academic goals more clearly) or indirect or distal (e.g., at the conclusion of the classroom guidance program on social skills, students will increase their overall grade point average by a percentage). It has been found in the academic literature that professional school counselors can indeed support the efforts that teachers and administrators are making in schools to increase academic achievement by using carefully crafted, targeted, and implemented strategic interventions (Brown & Trusty, 2005). A local school counselor serving for only two years in an urban school district highlights such an intervention that aims to increase academic achievement in the following case study.

CASE STUDY

A professional school counselor working at a public middle school in Washington, DC implemented a set of classroom guidance lessons focused on organizational, time-management, and study skills. These lessons were implemented after the first quarter, when a pattern of tardiness and low grades in English and math had been noticed by teachers and administration. The purpose of these lessons was to help students better understand how being organized would help them in school, how time management skills could help them get their homework done and still have time for what they wanted to do, and how good study skills could lead to incremental success.

The case illustration describes a strategic intervention that clearly links the needs of the students, the intended outcomes, and the intervention that is selected for comprehensive school counseling programs. At first glance, this may simply mean choosing interventions that are related to the problem they are trying to address. However, in addition to being clear about the purpose, goals, and objectives of the interventions or programs, it is also necessary to narrowly define what the outcomes are for the intervention or program, even if more information beyond these expected outcomes are explored. In the age of accountability, counselors need to be sure to link these outcomes to the goals and objectives of comprehensive school counseling programs. Additionally, it is imperative that school counselors choose interventions that are developmentally appropriate for the students they are working with.

For example, a school counselor can use classroom guidance programming to help students who are transitioning from one grade level to the next. The classroom guidance program can be a single session or a unit made up of multiple sessions. Typically, classroom guidance curricula consists of units with four to six lessons (Bryan et al., 2010). In this session or sessions, the goals may be to learn strategies for successfully transitioning from the seventh to eighth grade. The objectives of the program may be to learn how to communicate one's learning style to one's new teacher, to learn how to self-advocate in writing, and to learn how to monitor one's daily schedule and responsibilities. Essentially, this program attempts to meet the objectives of the session(s). However, these sessions will also generate tangential discussions that are by-products. This is important to note, because the overall goals and objectives may have been met and these tangential benefits that include academic or personal success may not be obvious at first.

That being said, classroom guidance is ideal because of the following:

- The peer group is one of the most powerful influences in adolescent development and classroom lessons may provide opportunities for students to normalize their experiences.
- Students during this stage of life are often unclear about their own feelings and values; therefore, they turn to peers to help explore aspects about themselves. The classroom structure can offer a chance to learn content while also processing how students make sense of this newly acquired information.
- Students can be taught decision-making processes and how to apply these skills in their unique situations. (Bryan et al., 2010)

In other words, classroom guidance programming can serve as an appropriate venue to promote positive peer interactions, especially during a time when students' peer groups tend to reinforce existing strengths and weaknesses rather than to change adolescents' characteristics. Research has shown that adolescents perform better academically, have more achievement-oriented goals, and think more about the future when they have access to supportive networks that include their peer group and caring adults.

Classroom guidance programming also provides an environment that may mirror the manner in which students often are required to relate to one another. This mode of delivery can be used to teach skills that are useful in life, not just in the classroom. This mechanism could also help the students dissect realistic situations and scenarios and provide several sources of feedback to gain insight, increase self-esteem, or gain a sense of accomplishment that comes about through helping others (Shechtman, Bar-El, & Hadar, 1997).

PLANNING CLASSROOM GUIDANCE

Assessment

As a first step, school counselors should develop and provide a needs assessment prior to planning classroom guidance programming and should also review data from the previous school year. The outcome of the assessment data is used to design guidance curricula that could meet specific developmental, social/emotional, and academic needs of the students. If the classroom guidance program is preventative in nature, then the needs assessment can also illuminate which topics might be of interest to the students. For example, topics such as friendships, healthy relationships, and getting along with your parents may be of interest to preadolescent students.

Another way to identify student needs is to examine existing data that is regularly being collected. For example, there are a number of data sources available, such as standardized tests, grades, attendance, behavior referrals, and suspensions. These sources are reliable and readily available to school counselors on databases such as SASI. Also, teachers and other school faculty and staff are valid sources of data. Their input can also be instrumental in developing precise programs. Using this information will help to create classroom guidance programs that are able to address needs that are systemic in nature. Below, please see Figure 4.1, which is an example of an outline that can be used to plan for a classroom guidance lesson/unit.

Classroom Guidance Goals and Objectives

Establishing clear goals and objectives are important. After identifying the students' needs through assessment or through reviewing existing data, school counselors can use this information to help determine appropriate goals and objectives for the classroom guidance program. Typically, goals are recognized as general statements about what the students will be able to do following the guidance unit or lesson. The objectives are stated as specific and measurable behavioral changes that are anticipated following the program and should be written in a manner in which they can be evaluated.

Some possible goals might include teaching students how to identify and express their feelings (such as appropriate coping skills) or strategies that students can use to handle stressful events that may occur (such as stress management

Figure 4.1   Classroom Guidance Lesson Plan

Classroom Guidance Lesson Plan

- Lesson Name/Topic
- Goal and Objectives
- Materials Needed
- Time
- Classroom Activities

  o Introduction/Review
  o Teaching
  o Processing
  o Closing

- Evaluation Strategies
- Homework/In-Between Lesson Activity (if applicable)

skills). Regardless of the overall goals, it is important that the objectives include knowledge and skills that are readily linked to student achievement. Examples of objectives that could be used to frame these lessons are "to define effective communication," "to learn effective communication strategies (e.g., speaking, writing, advocacy)," and "to practice these strategies." These objectives can also include "to discuss cultural considerations in effective communication." Communication can easily be applied to student achievement, especially when having the students utilize these skills with their teachers and families. Next, school counselors should develop guidance curricula that take into consideration the ASCA National Standards for School Counseling Programs, relevant state standards, or specific school improvement goals. For example, a school improvement plan might include a goal related to increasing student attendance. In this case, school counselors can develop a classroom guidance program that addresses the barriers some students may face when coming to school and provides strategies for overcoming these barriers. The ASCA National Model and National Standards for School Counseling Programs (ASCA, 2012) provide useful frameworks for producing lessons that are data driven and relevant. School counselors should find resources to generate ideas for activities and materials for lessons. Many resources are available in print or on the web. The resources can also be found in school counseling journal articles, on professional counseling websites (e.g., ASCA website [http://www.schoolcounselor.org]), and at professional development venues (e.g., state and national counseling conferences and local workshops). Delucia-Waack (2006) has incorporated numerous resources for leading adolescents in large group formats, including a resource guide of books, videos, and games.

School Counseling Facilitation and Leadership Skills for Classroom Guidance

School counselors can use some of the following skills to facilitate classroom guidance programs. These skills include a way of being—for example, caring, warmth, empathy, support, positive regard, acceptance, and genuineness—as well as specific opening and closings that can be used to deliver information, generate discussion, or process the information that is being explored. These skills are key elements to building a safe environment in the classroom in which to help students want to participate in the activities, especially for middle school students. School counselors can provide some structure and expectations ahead of time. More importantly, these expectations should be coupled with the co-creation (with student input) of classroom norms, goals, and appropriate student dispositions. In addition to establishing a cohesive and safe environment, the school counselor should help the students make meaning of the information and ideas generated during the class sessions and to explore the learning that may emerge. In particular, stimulating the students emotionally can help them make a personal connection to what they have learned or experienced in the session. This can be done by having the students connect and explore their feelings and the connection to their behaviors. A Venn diagram on strategies to engage students is provided for review in Figure 4.2.

It is important to note that school counselors are competing with widespread media (e.g., visual and auditory stimuli) and other emerging informational technology when working with middle school students. Regardless, school counselors will need to facilitate classroom lessons in ways that maintain student attention.

Figure 4.2 Venn Diagram

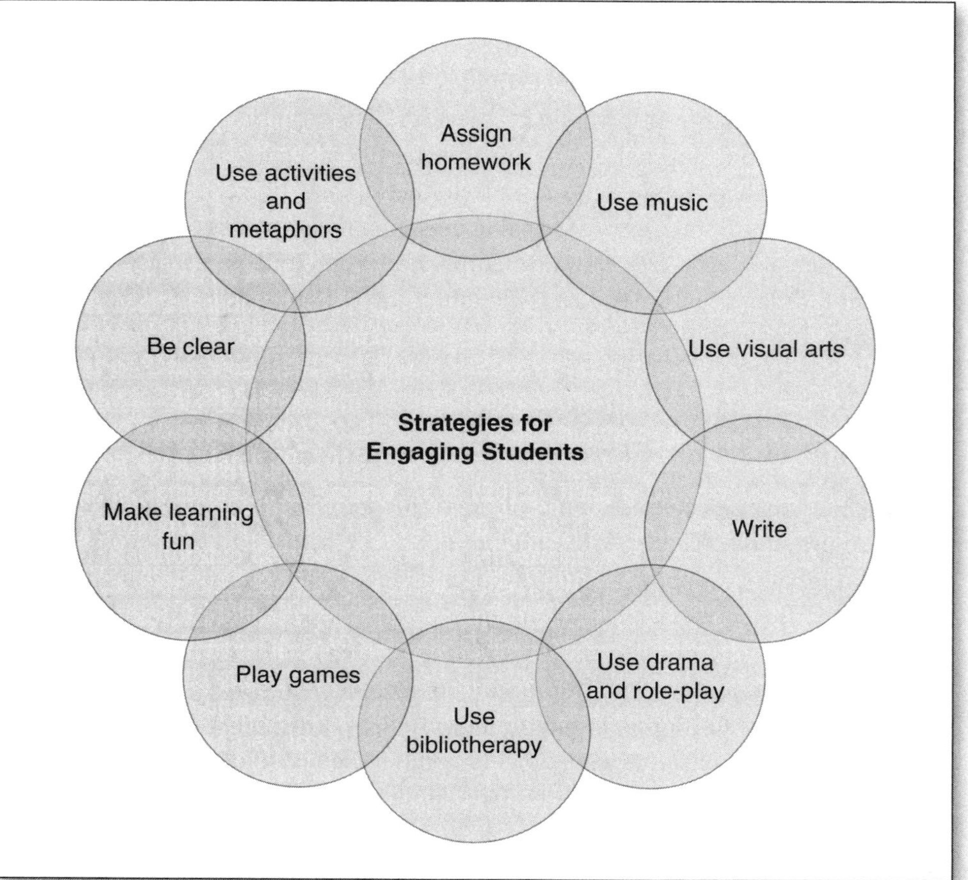

Assign homework

Use activities and metaphors

Use music

Be clear

Use visual arts

Strategies for Engaging Students

Make learning fun

Write

Play games

Use drama and role-play

Use bibliotherapy

As such, having enthusiasm about the subject matter and providing encouragement to the students can help to create a space that values students' opinions. Using various media and formats when presenting information could help to engage students. In fact, activities could be facilitated in a way that incorporate visual, auditory, and tactile stimulation (as one example, a middle school counselor might use a talk show format with some students functioning as the show host, others as panelists, and the other students asking questions as members of the audience; Davis, 2005). If students are engaged, the chances are increased that the lesson will promote critical thinking and foster an environment that makes the information meaningful for them (Brown & Trusty, 2005). Below, you will find an example of a classroom guidance session on goal setting.

CASE STUDY

Ready, Set, Goals Classroom Guidance

Possible Classes and Performance Standards to Be Integrated: English/language arts, math, social sciences, science, world languages

Goals: (try to be specific in terms of information learned, new behaviors or skills, thoughts, or feelings)

1. Students will learn the difference between short- and long-term goals.

2. Students will learn how to set SMARTR goals for themselves, specifically when they pertain to their academic achievement.

3. Students will explore and discover the strategies necessary for reaching the goals that they set for themselves.

Objectives: ASCA Mindsets & Behaviors for Student Success

Category 2: Behavior Standards

Learning Strategies

Demonstrate critical-thinking skills to make informed decisions.

Identify long- and short-term academic, career, and social/emotional goals.

Estimated Time Length: 45 minutes

Materials: large stars cut out of construction paper, markers or colored pencils, colored index cards, hole punch, yarn

(Continued)

(Continued)

Introduction

Share with students that in this session, we will be discussing short-term and long-term goals. Students will learn what short- and long-term goals are and then set goals to be achieved this school year. Ask for student volunteers to share how they would define short-term goals. One definition for a *short-term goal* is a goal that you will achieve in the near future (e.g., in a day, within a week, or possibly within a few months). Next, have students share how they would define *long-term goals*. One definition for a long-term goal includes a goal that you will achieve over a longer period of time (e.g., one semester, one year, five years, or twenty years). Once the definitions have been explained and are understood by all, introduce students to the idea of creating SMARTR goals.

S–specific

M–measurable

A–achievable

R–results focused

T–time bound

R–reevaluate

Ask students to brainstorm one short-term academic goal and one long-term academic goal that they would like to achieve over this school year. Remind students that we want to try and set SMARTR goals for ourselves. Allow students time to think and discuss with their peers.

Activity

Provide each student with a cut-out star to write down the goals that they developed. Have students write their long-term academic goal on one side and their short-term academic goal on the other side of the star. Next, give students four to five colored index cards that have been cut in half. Ask them to write one strategy on each that will represent a step toward reaching their goal. Also, give the group members yarn in order to connect the index cards to the star. Ask for volunteers to share one or both of the goals they came up with, as well as the steps they think it will take to reach their goals. If students are willing, hang up the stars in your office for display.

Processing Questions

* What was it like for you to set specific goals for this school year?

* How did you go about choosing the steps it would take to reach your goals?

* What can we do, as a class, to help each other be successful in reaching our goals this year?

Finally, allow students to compliment each other's ability and willingness to honestly engage in the discussions on setting goals and discovering strategies to accomplish them.

Student Extension Activity

* Have students identify and connect with one person in the school via e-mail, school postal system, or in person. Encourage the students to contact this person before the next lesson to share their goals with them and to be prepared to share the interactions that occurred.

Adaptations: The conversation could be adapted to focus on personal goals or career goals as well as more specific academic goals.

Suggestions on how to integrate into core curriculum: This activity could be integrated into the core curriculum by having students focus their goal-setting on specific subject areas. The teachers could then be given the goals for their classroom and follow up with student progress throughout the year.

Evaluation Strategies

Due to the emphasis that ASCA places on the need for school counselors to include both formative and summative evaluations of their school counseling programs, it is essential that classroom guidance lessons are evaluated. Classroom guidance lessons can be shown to have a high level of efficacy for teaching students what they need to learn, and evaluation strategies are necessary to measure this process.

There are three types of data that can be used to evaluate the effectiveness of school counseling programs and guidance lessons in particular. These include process, perception, and outcome data. Process data answer the question, "What did you do and for whom?" whereas perception data answer the question "What do people think they know, believe, or can do?" and finally, outcome data answer the question "So what?" (ASCA, 2012). An example of perception data for a classroom guidance lesson on test-taking strategies could involve collecting pre- and post-assessment data that determine whether or not students improved in their ability to successfully prepare for midterms or final exams. Making evaluation an important part of your guidance program will increase your chances of delivering successful guidance lessons.

**Additional Classroom Guidance Lesson Examples
Based on the ASCA Mindsets & Behaviors for Student Success**

Classroom Guidance Lesson Example One

Unit	Bullying Prevention (Social Skills)
Lesson	Changing Negative Words to Positive Words
ASCA Mindsets & Behaviors for Student Success	Category 2: Behavior Standards Social Skills 2. Create positive and supportive relationships with other students. 6. Use effective collaboration and cooperation skills. 9. Demonstrate social maturity and behaviors appropriate to the situation and environment.
Objectives	Students will learn how it makes others feel/react when hurtful, negative things are said about them. This lesson is intended to teach students that they are a part of a greater world, where their actions have consequences. The students will also learn how positive phrases/words can have a much better impact than negative ones.
Materials	• Backpack • Books of different sizes • Post-its (different colors)
Time	20–30 minutes
Activity	1. Ask for a student volunteer who might be "comfortable being uncomfortable." Ask the student to put on the empty backpack. 2. Discuss how this backpack represents the invisible backpack we all wear each day—our self-esteem (how we feel about who we are and our self-worth). 3. Give the student a post-it and ask the student to jump up as high as he or she can, sticking the post-it to the wall. 4. Ask students in the class to describe times when they have witnessed bullying behavior. For every incident cited, students should add a book into the backpack. Each book represents one negative comment/behavior. 5. Once all books are in the backpack, the student is asked again to jump up as high as he or she can, sticking the post-it to the wall. 6. Discuss why this post-it didn't go as high as the last one. 7. Students are then asked to share words of encouragement and praise about the student. For every positive shared, a book is taken out of the backpack. 8. Ask the student to jump one last time as high as he or she can, sticking the last post-it to the wall.

	9. Point out that the third sticker is higher than the other two. Discuss why and the following:
	
	    a. How do negative words impact us?
	    b. How can positive words impact us?
	    c. How can we foster a more positive school climate?

Closing	Review the impact positive and negative phrases/words can have. Discuss what students have learned from the activity.
Homework	Challenge students to share five words of encouragement or praise with friends and family over the next week. Students should keep track of how they felt after sharing encouragement/praise and what kind of an impact it had on the other person.
Evaluation Strategies	Process: How many lessons are in the unit? How many students received each lesson? Perception: Pre- and post-surveys assess the students' knowledge about positive and negative words. Outcome: Compare the number of the discipline referrals related to verbal bullying before and after the guidance lesson.

Classroom Guidance Lesson Example Two

Unit	Tools for School and Learning (Self-Management Skills)
Lesson	Task Management
ASCA Mindsets & Behaviors for Student Success	Category 2: Behavior Standards Self-Management Skills 2. Demonstrate self-discipline and self-control. 3. Demonstrate the ability to work independently. 8. Demonstrate the ability to balance school, home, and community activities.
Objectives	Students will be able to effectively manage upcoming tasks to help them be successful in school. Through the lesson, students will learn how to prioritize important tasks and eliminate unrealistic tasks that they plan to accomplish over the next week. Students will also plan ahead for tasks that need to be completed.
Materials	• White board • Dry erase markers • Paper • Pencils

(Continued)

(Continued)

Time	35–45 minutes

Activity	1. Start out by asking students, "What do you always make time to do every week that's really important to you?" Record the responses on the board
	
	2. Direct students to individually create a to-do list for the week.
	
	3. Introduce the PREP tips for task management. As each letter is presented, encourage students to review and rework their to-do lists. Use the responses that were previously recorded on the board as examples.
	
	  • **Prioritize**—Sort the tasks into three groups; label each to-do task with #1, #2, or #3:
	
	    1. Absolutely essential for having a productive, successful week at school (e.g., completing homework, studying for a test).
	
	    2. Important for your relationships with family and friends or your physical or mental health (e.g., going to the movies, eating dinner together, exercising).
	
	    3. Everything else (e.g., playing video games, watching TV).
	
	  • **Reorganize**—Predict how much time the most important tasks will take. Write in a day of the week next to each #1 and #2 task. These are the things each day that you must do. If you have multiple tasks that take significant amounts of time, spread them out.
	  • **Eliminate**—Cross out two things or more from the list that are either unrealistic expectations for the week or things that will not have a negative impact your life if they do not get done.
	  • **Plan ahead**—Forecast three important to-do tasks that you know you will need to schedule time for next week (e.g., science fair project).

Closing	Ask students to share out some of their top priorities for the upcoming week.
Homework	Students will need to keep a time log of how they spend their time for one week to be used in the lesson on time management.
Evaluation Strategies	Process: How many lessons are in the unit? How many students received each lesson? Perception: Pre- and post-surveys assess the students' knowledge about the PREP tips for task management. Outcome: Track students' homework completion rates before and after the lesson.

Classroom Guidance Lesson Example Three

Unit	College and Career Development (Learning Strategies)
Lesson	High School Planning Vocabulary
ASCA Mindsets & Behaviors for Student Success	Category 2: Behavior Standards Learning Strategies 5. Apply media and technology skills. 6. Set high standards of quality. 9. Gather evidence and consider multiple perspective to make informed decisions.
Objectives	Students will become familiar with terms frequently used in high school and college course planning. In the lesson, students will learn the importance of these terms and will demonstrate their gained knowledge by completing an activity using technology.
Materials	• White board • Dry erase markers • Pencils • Computers • Handout **Handout Example** High School Planning Vocabulary Activity 1: Definitions | Credits:	
Graduation Requirements:	
Prerequisite:	
AP:	
Elective:	
GPA:	
Career Cluster:	
STEM:	
Extracurricular Activities:	
4-Year Plan:		

(Continued)

(Continued)

Activity 2: Internet Research				
# Graduation Credits:		Elective:		
Required Course:	1.	Extracurricular Activity:		
	2.	Same Career Cluster:	1.	
	3.		2.	
Physics Prerequisite:		STEM Course:		
AP Course:		Extracurricular Activity:		

Time	35–45 minutes

Activity	1. Before the lesson begins, list the following vocabulary terms on the white board: credits, graduation requirement, prerequisite, AP, elective, GPA, career cluster, STEM, extracurricular activity, and 4-year plan.
	
	2. Review the definition and importance of each term with student input. Instruct students to fill in the definition of each term on the vocabulary handout.
	
	3. Students will use the Internet to find the following on a high school's website:
	
	  o amount of credits required for graduation
	  o three required courses
	  o prerequisite for physics
	  o one AP course
	  o one elective
	  o one extracurricular activity
	  o two courses within the same career cluster
	  o one STEM course

Closing	Discuss why being familiar with high school planning vocabulary is important. Ask students to share one thing they will take away from the lesson.
Homework	Students will add the completed vocabulary handout to their career-planning portfolio.
Evaluation Strategies	Process: How many lessons are in the unit? How many students received each lesson? Perception: Use an exit ticket at the end of each lesson to assess whether students understood the high school vocabulary. Outcome: Track high school progress (course grades, successful completion of ninth grade compared to past students).

Classroom Guidance Lesson Example Four

Unit	Transitioning to High School
Lesson	Lesson 1 of 3: What Are Your Options?
ASCA Mindsets & Behaviors for Student Success	Category 2: Behavior Standards Learning Strategies 5. Apply media and technology skills. 9. Gather evidence and consider multiple perspectives to make informed decisions.
Objectives	Students will learn about the high schools in their area that are options for them. This lesson is intended to present individual high schools and the different things they have to offer students. Students will begin thinking through which school would be the best choice for them and why.
Materials	• White board • Dry erase markers • Computers • High school choices worksheet • Pencils
Time	35–45 minutes
Activity	1. Ask students to name all the high schools in the area that they know. Have a student volunteer write the list on the white board. If there are any school options that the students don't name, add them to the list when the students are finished. 2. Have the students work in groups of three on the computer to research the schools that are on the list. Assign one or two schools (depending on the length of the list) to each group of students and direct them to the school district website to find information on the schools. 3. Provide students with prompts to guide their research: What kinds of classes and programs are offered at the school? Where is the school located? What is the graduation rate at the school? What extracurricular activities and sports are offered at the school? 4. After the students have had time to research the schools, have each group share with the class on what they learned.
Closing	To close the lesson, have the students complete the high school choices worksheet based on the information they have learned about the different schools during the lesson.
Homework	Ask students to share their high school choices worksheet with their parents.

(Continued)

(Continued)

Evaluation Strategies	Process: How many lessons are in the unit?
	How many students received each lesson?
	Perception: Students complete the high school choices worksheet before and after the lesson to evaluate what knowledge they gained about the high schools in their area through the lesson.
	Outcome: Track the various types of high schools that the students will attend.

High School Choices Worksheet

My first choice of high school is _____.

The reasons this is the best school for me are

1. _____

_____

_____

_____

2. _____

_____

_____

_____

3. _____

_____

_____

_____

My second choice of high school is _____.

The reasons this is a good choice for me are

1. _____

_____

_____

_____

2. _____

_____

_____

_____

3. _____

_____

_____

_____

My third choice of high school is _____.

The reasons this is a good choice for me are

1. _____

_____

_____

_____

2. _____

_____

_____

_____

3. _____

_____

_____

_____

(Continued)

(Continued)

Unit	Transitioning to High School
Lesson:	Lesson 2 of 3: Building Your Time Management Skills
ASCA Mindsets & Behaviors for Student Success	Category 2: Behavior Standards Self-Management Skills 2. Demonstrate self-discipline and self-control. 3. Demonstrate the ability to work independently. 8. Demonstrate the ability to balance school, home, and community activities.
Objectives	Students will learn the importance of time management, specifically related to success in high school. This lesson is intended to give the students tangible examples of how to accomplish time management as they make the transition into high school. Students will learn how to prioritize their time in order to best reach academic success.
Materials	• Time budget worksheet • Sample high school class schedule • Pencils
Time	35–45 minutes

Activity	Facilitate a discussion about successful time management and the importance of this skill as they transition into high school.
	
	1. Explain to the students that in order to manage their time, they must
	   a. consider everything they have to do and want to do during the day,
	   b. understand how much time each activity in a day will take, and
	   c. make a plan that helps them get through the day.
	2. Give each student a copy of the time budget worksheet as well as a sample high school class schedule.
	3. Instruct students to complete the time budget worksheet based on the sample high school schedule they were given. Remind them to include in their time budget any extracurricular activities they might participate in next year in high school (sports, jobs, etc.)
	4. Discuss with students how their time budget worked out.
	   a. Were they able to fit everything they needed into the 24-hour period?
	   b. If not, is there anything on their list that can be removed in order to make their time budget work?

Closing	Close the discussion by stressing the importance of time management in terms of being successful at school.
Evaluation Strategies	Process: How many lessons are in the unit?
	How many students received each lesson?
	Perception: Use an exit ticket with tasks including defining have to and want to and examples of student scenarios where they must remove tasks to make the time budget work.
	Outcome: Tracking attendance and tardies at various periods following the classroom guidance lesson.

Your Time Budget Worksheet

Name_____

Your job is to balance your time budget!	
Total time spent:	24 hours

(Continued)

(Continued)

Unit	Transitioning to High School
Lesson	Lesson 3 of 3: What Supports Will There Be for You in High School?
ASCA Mindsets & Behaviors for Student Success	Category 2: Behavior Standards Self-Management Skills 9. Demonstrate the ability to manage transitions and to adapt to changing situations and responsibilities. Social Skills 3. Create relationships with adults that support success. 8. Demonstrate advocacy skills and the ability to assert self, when necessary.
Objectives	Students will learn what supports will be available to them in high school. This lesson is intended to encourage students as they transition into high school by outlining for them what their support system in high school will be like. Students will begin thinking through which school would be the best choice for them and why.
Materials	• List of high school counselors and other support systems
Time	35–45 minutes
Activity	1. To begin the discussion, define internal and external assets with the group. Ask students if anyone can provide a definition. One common definition for internal assets are aspects within oneself that are strengths (e.g., a sense of purpose, personal power). External assets are defined as aspects outside of oneself that enable one to be successful and are provided by the family, school, and/or community. Explain to students that this lesson will focus on external assets, including specific sources of support at the high schools they've been discussing. 2. Next, have students turn and talk to the person on their right to brainstorm a list of individuals/organizations who could serve as support networks inside the school community. Examples include school counselors, teachers, advisors, and mentors. 3. Have students regroup as a class and share the list/ideas they came up with.* *As the facilitator, the school counselor should come prepared with a list of supports that are active in the high schools. For example, prepare a list of the names of school counselors who work at the high schools that were the most often chosen on the students' high school choices worksheet.
Closing	Have students share with the group what they learned from today's lesson. Were they aware of all the supports that will be available to them in high school? How do they feel now about transitioning into high school?

Homework	In preparation for follow-up lessons, have students brainstorm the community supports that they know of in their own community.
Evaluation Strategies	Process: How many lessons are in the unit?
	How many students received each lesson?
	Perception: Have the students list a number of individuals that will be able to help them when they transition to high school.

Check for Understanding

- Classroom guidance provides school counselors with an avenue to reach a large number of students through a single intervention.
- As with the curriculum and instruction of classroom teachers, classroom guidance lessons must be developmentally appropriate in order to meet the needs of the students.
- It is advantageous for school counselors to involve classroom teachers in their guidance lessons. For example, adopting the classroom rules during the guidance lesson will provide useful consistency for students as well as using student performance standards.
- Classroom guidance lessons can help students learn from, and model for, their peers appropriate behaviors and decision-making patterns.

REFLECTIVE CASE ILLUSTRATIONS

Imagine you are a first-year school counselor in a middle school with a caseload of 300 seventh graders. Your school is located on the east coast in a middle-class community. In this community, numerous cultural backgrounds are represented, including recent immigrants and displaced families as well as a large population of military families. What are your thoughts and reactions to this scenario thus far? At the end of the first quarter, you are asked to meet with a few students individually who are dealing with some stressful events in their lives. The manner in which these youngsters attempted to deal with their problems was exacerbated by the powerful influence each of the peers had on each other. In other words, these students were not initially linked. But after meeting with them individually, it became apparent that their inappropriate coping mechanism (e.g., cutting oneself, substance issues, fighting) was not an isolated event. These students were aware of each other and the manner in which each student was attempting to handle his or her problems. It appeared as if they were influencing each other. In this case, what could you do?

Following brief individual sessions with a few students, you decide to consult with your school administration team. After this discussion, it was suggested a classroom guidance unit might be appropriate. What are some topics that might be useful to address these counterproductive behaviors?

After the consultation with the school administrators, you decide that the purpose and goals of this classroom guidance unit will be to explore and discuss stressful life events and discover productive strategies to deal with these issues if they arise. The objectives of this classroom guidance program are to

1. teach students the definition of *coping*,

2. describe four ways that students can appropriately cope with life's challenges, and

3. ask students to identify how they have coped in difficult situations in the past.

In light of these objectives, what are some specific lessons you can generate about this topic? What are some activities that you can use? What types of multimedia would you include? What are some strategies you can use to lead the sessions? Generate a few processing questions for the lessons. If students become unfocused, how will you handle these disruptions? What kind of extension lessons (homework) can you provide to ensure that the learning has long-term implications? How will you follow up with the teachers on these lessons? What is the evaluation? How will you know if you met the anticipated outcomes of your lessons?

Below, please find responses from two current middle school counselors about the case illustration listed above. The counselors respond to the questions as if they were facing the same scenario.

Joy Rose's Response

My first thought is that I would aim for facilitating three classroom guidance lessons around the issue of coping because this issue has manifested in enough students to warrant full classroom guidance as opposed to individual or small group; ideally, this would happen once a week for three weeks, with the fourth week used for makeup sessions due to any scheduling conflicts that may have arisen in the previous weeks. The first session would be a basic introduction to what coping is and the types of situations that may require good coping skills. For the largely Latino (first-generation English language learners) and African American population of students that I work with, we would have to start with a very clear, concise, and basic level to build rapport and work our way up from there.

Creative engagement activities would be essential in order to keep students focused—for example, using pair-and-share (defined as when students think about the prompt, then share their thoughts with the person beside them). This allows the students to brainstorm with a partner their own definitions of *coping*. Next, I would have a discussion as a larger group in order to establish the definition that we will all use for the classroom guidance lessons. Additionally, I would incorporate some team-building activities into the classroom guidance lessons to foster cohesion and create a safe space for sharing about what may be a sensitive topic for some students. For example, as part of the second session, I would start with an activity called "Fear in a Hat." This activity essentially solicits statements or completed sentence stems anonymously written that are placed in a small hat, box, or other container. Next, students take turns reviewing one of the statements and embellish what they believe the author of the comment was truly expressing. This simple yet engaging activity allows students to share fears that they have, but it is anonymous sharing, so students can feel more comfortable giving and receiving the reactions to the statements. The goal is to create normalized feelings that come as a by-product of knowing one is not dealing with these feelings alone or, at the very least, that these feelings are heard and understood. In other words, students will recognize things they have in common with their classmates that they may not have known before. In the third session, we would discuss the power and impact of peer influence as it relates to life stressors and coping. This lesson's objective would also help students identify positive coping skills that they can adopt in the future. The classroom guidance unit will be evaluated using a self-made pre- and posttest assessment tool (with five or six short questions) to determine the effectiveness of the program. Example questions on the assessment include *Can you define coping skills? Please provide examples of your current coping skills. Give three examples of positive coping skills. List three people you can go to when you need help.* The data would be used to make suggestions on improving the classroom guidance curriculum as well. Finally, I would draw from the information provided by the pre- and posttest data as well as from observations during the classroom guidance lessons in order to determine whether there are additional students who need individual interventions regarding coping, self-harm, and so on. I believe it is important to note that individual counseling sessions and group counseling interventions will continue as a way to supplement the preventative nature of this classroom guidance program.

Kristin Avina's Response

The first thing that comes to mind is the need to implement a few programs to support this population: year-round new student orientation (since it is likely that incoming new students will come throughout the year), a military family transition group (it may be

(Continued)

(Continued)

difficult for students, especially at this age, to move to a new school and make friends), and a newcomer to the country group (to familiarize students with the U.S. school system and give them a safe place to ask questions). To me, I think it would be important to find out which student first initiated the idea to self-harm and look into the reasons for resorting to cutting as a coping mechanism. Other students may not have begun cutting without the encouragement of their peers. In order to meet the objectives, lessons would be created around the following topics: healthy coping mechanisms, the importance of mental health, and discovering positive outlets for anger and stress. I would then create a number of different relaxation techniques to keep the students engaged throughout the lessons. Some of the processing questions I would use for the lessons include the following: *What would you do if you felt extremely stressed or sad? Who would you turn to if you felt extremely stressed or sad? What are factors of those individuals that would lead you to them? What if these people are not available? What would you do then?* Before implementing the classroom guidance lessons, I would think about which students I anticipate might have a strong reaction to the topic, or any serious topic, and let them know of the session information beforehand. Any students who did not receive the lesson with the larger group would receive the information in a small group setting or individually, if necessary. It would also be important to educate teachers on coping mechanisms and that, in this case, cutting is being used as a negative coping mechanism. Although one's first inclination is to think cutting is the problem, cutting is actually the way a student is dealing with another problem. I would also discuss warning signs of cutting (scabs/scratches that never seem to heal, hiding arms) and what to do if one suspects that a student is self-harming.

Before beginning the lessons, I would conduct a pre-survey with the students about their knowledge of coping mechanisms, whether they have an adult to turn to in a crisis, and how they handle a situation if they know of another student self-harming. Following the intervention, I would collect post-survey results and compare and contrast the findings. I would also include open-ended questions to get a general sense of what the students may have found useful in these lessons and things they may have felt were less effective.

KEYSTONES

In this chapter, an overview of adolescent development, the unique nature of the middle school setting, and strategies school counselors can use to implement classroom guidance lessons in a middle school setting were presented.

- Given the rapid and often challenging physical, cognitive, and social developmental changes that are associated with entering preadolescence, school counselors must be mindful of these developmental aspects and factors that may interrupt or influence this growth and development.

- During the middle school years, peer groups become much more meaningful to students as they push for independence and autonomous thinking. Students often begin to distance themselves from their parents in favor of other caring adults.
- It is imperative that classroom guidance programming is developmentally appropriate, engaging, and precise in attending to the unique needs of this student population. As the chapter revealed, a particular emphasis on the roles and functions school counselors play in relation to classroom guidance programs was discussed.
- It is essential to acknowledge the importance of being aware and knowledgeable of the developmental changes middle school students are experiencing while maintaining a flexible counseling disposition that allows room to adjust your programming efforts in appropriate and meaningful ways.
- Utilize data from needs assessments to plan effective classroom guidance programming that is linked to the needs of the students and the schoolwide goals and objectives.
- Classroom guidance provides a venue to promote positive peer interactions at a developmental period where peer groups are highly valued as well as to teach invaluable life skills.

ADDITIONAL RESOURCES

Print Resources

Jenson, W., Rhode, G., Ashcraft, P., & Bowen, J. (2008). *The tough kid bully blockers book.* Eugene, OR: Pacific Northwest.

Jenson, W., & Sprick, R. (2013). *Absenteeism & truancy: Interventions & universal procedures.* Eugene, OR: Pacific Northwest Publishing.

Muro, J. J., & Kottman, T. (1995). *Guidance and counseling in the elementary and middle schools: A practical approach.* Madison, WI: Brown & Benchmark.

Rhode, G., & Jenson, W. (2010). *The tough kid book* (2nd ed.). Eugene, OR: Pacific Northwest.

Scales, P. C. (2005). Developmental assets and the middle school counselor. *Professional School Counseling, 9*(2), 104–111.

Sink, C. A. (2005). Fostering academic development and learning: Implications and recommendations for middle school counselors. *Professional School Counseling, 9*(2), 128–135.

Tucker, C., Smith-Adcock, S., & Trepal, H. C. (2011). Relational-cultural theory for middle school counselors. *Professional School Counseling, 14*(5), 310–316.

Internet Resources

American School Counselor Association (ASCA): http://schoolcounselor.org
Association for Middle Level Education (AMLE): http://amle.org
National Office for School Counselor Advocacy (NOSCA): http://nosca.collegeboard.org
Region of Peel, Bullying Prevention Lesson Plans: http://peelregion.ca/health/bullying/

REFERENCES

Akos, P. (2005). The unique nature of middle school counseling. *Professional School Counseling, 9*(2), 95–103.

American School Counselor Association (ASCA). (2012). *The ASCA national model: A framework for school counseling programs* (3rd ed.). Alexandria, VA: Author.

American School Counselor Association (ASCA). (2014). *Why middle school counselors.* Retrieved March 31, 2015, from https://www.schoolcounselor.org/school-counselors-members/careers-roles/why-middle-school-counselors

Brown, D., & Trusty, J. (2005). School counselors, comprehensive school counseling programs, and academic achievement: Are school counselors promising more than they can deliver? *Professional School Counseling, 9,* 1–8.

Bryan, C. J. (2005). Advances in the assessment of suicide risk. *Journal of Clinical Psychology, 62*(2), 185–200.

Bryan, J., Steen, S., & Day-Vines, N. (2010). Psychoeducational groups in schools. In B. Erford (Ed.), *Group work in the schools* (pp. 207–224). New York, NY: Merrill/Prentice Hall.

Cohen, E. R., Reinherz, H., & Frost, A. K. (1994). Self-perceptions of unpopularity: Its relationship to emotional and behavioral problems. *Child and Adolescent Social Work Journal, 11*(1), 37–52.

Corey, M. S., & Corey, G. (1982). *Groups: Process and practice.* Independence, KY: Thomas Brooks/Cole Publishing.

Council for Accreditation of Counseling & Related Educational Programs (CACREP). (2009). *2009 standards for accreditation.* Alexandria, VA: Author.

Davis, T. E. (2005). *Exploring school counseling: Professional practices and perspectives.* Boston, MA: Houghton Mifflin.

Delucia-Waack, J. (2006). *Leading psychoeducational groups for children and adolescents.* Thousand Oaks, CA: SAGE.

Eccles, J. S., Midgley, C., Wigfield, A., Buchanan, C. M., Reuman, D., Flanagan, C., & Mac Iver, D. (1993). Development during adolescence: The impact of stage-environment fit on young adolescents' experiences in schools and in families. *American Psychologist, 48*(2), 90–101.

Erikson, E. (Ed). (1965). *The challenge of youth.* New York, NY: Doubleday Anchor Books.

Northeast Foundation for Children. (2005). *Eighth graders: Common developmental characteristics of 12, 13, and 14 year olds.* Retrieved March 31, 2015, from http://www.responsiveclassroom.org/sites/default/files/pdf_files/pamphlets/rc_pamphlet_cc8.pdf

Prevatt, F. F, & Kelly, F. D. (2003). Dropping out of school: A review of intervention programs. *Journal of School Psychology, 41,* 377–395.

Shechtman, Z., Bar-El, O., & Hadar, E. (1997). Therapeutic factors and psycho educational groups for adolescents: A comparison. *The Journal for Specialists in Group Work, 22,* 203–214.

Steen, S., & Noguera, P. (2010). A broader and bolder approach to school reform: Expanded partnership roles for school counselors. *Professional School Counseling, 14*(1), 42–52.

White, S., & Kelly, F. (2010). The school counselor's role in school dropout prevention. *Journal of Counseling & Development, 88,* 227–230.

Wigfield, A., Lutz, S. L., & Wagner, A. L. (2005). Early adolescents' development across the middle school years: Implications for school counselors. *Professional School Counseling, 9,* 112–119.

Wood, C. (2005). *Yardsticks: Children in the classroom ages 4–14* (3rd ed.). Turner Falls, MA: Northeast Foundation for Children.

Ziomek-Daigle, J., & Andrews, P. G. (2009). Utilizing identification and intervention strategies to prevent middle school dropout. *Middle School Journal, 40*(5), 54–60.

Chapter 5

THE HIGH SCHOOL

MELINDA M. GIBBONS
University of Tennessee

AMBER N. HUGHES
Lindsey Wilson College

Secondary school counselors enhance the learning process and promote academic achievement. School counseling programs are essential for students to achieve optimal personal growth, acquire positive social skills and values, set appropriate career goals and realize full academic potential to become productive, contributing members of the world community.

(American School Counselor Association, 2014)

This chapter describes the unique characteristics of high school students as they relate to classroom guidance programming at this setting. First, a general overview of high school classroom guidance programming is provided. Next, the chapter includes a summary of the various developmental and contextual facets of working with high school students. Then, the strengths and challenges of high school classroom guidance programming are presented, along with descriptions of various cultural issues related to adolescents. By the end of this chapter, you will have a better understanding of high school classroom guidance in general and of the unique characteristics of high school students in particular. The case of Jillian is presented at various points in the chapter to help illustrate the covered topics. At the end of this chapter, you will be able to

- understand the developmental and contextual issues related to high school students,
- identify general positives and challenges of providing classroom guidance programming to high school students,

- recognize how to address the cultural and systemic factors that affect high school students, and
- critically examine high school classroom guidance activities using guided exercises.

Although the goals of high school classroom guidance programming are similar to those for the elementary school and middle school levels, the delivery method and content focus are likely to be different. The Council for Accreditation of Counseling & Related Educational Programs (CACREP; 2009) requires counselors to frame counseling within a developmental lens and to address issues that may hinder school success. Therefore, it is imperative that high school counselors understand the students, families, and communities that comprise their schools.

High school students have varying perspectives on school counseling services. Gallant and Zhao (2011) surveyed urban high school students and learned that most were aware of school counseling services, with college preparatory and academic services being the most frequently noted assistance services. Only half of the participants, however, were aware of career services provided by school counselors and only 60% were aware of social/emotional services being available. In another large national study, most twelfth graders reported having some contact with their school counselors, mostly for college information (Bryan, Holcomb-McCoy, Moore-Thomas, & Day-Vines, 2009). African American and female students were more likely to visit their school counselor, as were students who believed their school counselor expected them to attend college. A small study of Latino students, however, noted themes of inadequate advisement, lack of availability, and low expectations related to school counselors (Vela-Gude et al., 2009). It is clear that some high school students utilize school counseling services, but demographic and perceived counselor expectation differences affect their participation levels. Based on research indicating a disconnect between students and counselors, high school counselors need to understand the variety of student perspectives about school counseling services.

One of the major challenges with providing classroom guidance programming at the high school level relates to scheduling. High schools are often on block or alternating-day schedules, making it difficult to easily reach all students in a specific grade level. Schools on block schedules typically offer four classes per semester, while schools using an alternating-day schedule might offer eight classes total but have four on one day and the other four on the next day, swapping for the entire school year. High school courses are also typically connected with end-of-course exams, which may lead to teachers being less willing to relinquish classroom time for counseling guidance activities. In addition, high school counselors may be kept busy helping students with postsecondary planning and academic monitoring tasks. Lastly, there may be a perception that classroom guidance programming is not as necessary for older students. Because of the focus on career and postsecondary planning, administrators, teachers, or parents may not understand the importance of continuing to meet the academic, career, and social/emotional needs of all students through classroom guidance.

SELLING CLASSROOM GUIDANCE

High school counselors need to be creative as they consider how to offer classroom guidance. The first step is gaining the support of your principal. Administrators respond well to data and facts. Provide relevant information about how a structured and sequential classroom guidance plan will enrich the lives of students and increase career and college readiness. Explain that high school students are primed to learn in groups and are cognitively ready to engage in perspective taking, decision making, and critical-thinking activities. Offer ideas on how you might provide classroom guidance without taking too much time away from classroom learning. For example, you can teach your lessons as part of the required PE or health class or work with teachers to integrate your lesson into an existing class topic (co-teaching). Once teachers and principals better understand classroom guidance, they might be more open to this type of intervention.

Check for Understanding

- Not all high school students utilize school counseling services. An apparent disconnect may exist between the high school counselor and the student.
- High school schedules and testing requirements can make classroom guidance challenging.
- Use data to garner support from administrators and teachers for increased counseling services.

CASE STUDY

Part I

Jillian is a school counselor at a midsized suburban high school in the southwestern U.S. The student population is diverse, with about 30% African American students and 30% Latino students, and 55% of all students qualifying for

(Continued)

(Continued)

free or reduced-price lunch. The school has 1,500 students divided alphabetically between the four counselors, giving Jillian a caseload of about 375 students. The counseling department is currently trying to integrate the American School Counselor Association's (ASCA) National Model (2012) into their program and, as a result, they are restructuring their offerings and overall organization. The results of a schoolwide and community-wide needs assessment indicated that more information on postsecondary attainment was desired, so the counselors have decided to increase their college- and career-preparation programming, with Jillian leading this initiative.

Currently, about 35% of the students continue their education at a four-year university and another 35% attend a community or technical college after high school. The remaining 30% enter the workforce or enlist in the military after graduation. Jillian's school district, similar to many across the U.S., is pushing for a postsecondary attendance rate of at least 90%. In addition, the needs assessment results indicated a desire from both parents and students for more college and career information earlier in high school.

With support from her administration and her fellow counselors, Jillian decides to create a four-year career- and college-readiness program focused on classroom guidance activities and supplemented with individual meetings as needed. She believes that classroom guidance is the best way to reach the entire school population and that a four-year process will give her time to guide all students in her school in reaching their postsecondary goals.

The main topic of her classroom guidance lessons will be on *transferable* or *soft* skills. In a nationwide survey, employers noted that the most important skills needed for workplace success were professionalism, oral and written communication, teamwork, and problem solving (Casner-Lotto & Barrington, 2006). Other important skills included self-direction, leadership, creativity, diversity appreciation, use of technology, and ethical behavior. Generally, high school and college students lack these skills, according to employers. Jillian plans to address one or two soft skills each year, with information about postsecondary options integrated into the lessons. She believes that the focus on both soft skills and concrete postsecondary information will influence the academic, career, and social/emotional needs of students, as suggested by the ASCA National Model (2012) and CACREP (2009).

Because time is limited and teachers are reluctant to allow counselors to use valuable class time, Jillian feels she must be both creative and succinct while still providing helpful lessons. She knows she must consider the physical, cognitive, and socioemotional development of high school students, the strengths and challenges of working with adolescents, and the typical needs of this population.

Discussion Questions

1. What are some other important topics that can be addressed in high school classroom guidance programming?

2. What has Jillian done well so far? What else do you think she needs to do in this situation?

DEVELOPMENTAL AND CONTEXTUAL CONSIDERATIONS

Physical Development

Adolescents go through many physical changes during high school. Mid-adolescence is characterized by continuation of puberty and changes in brain development (Blakemore, Burnett, & Dahl, 2010). Neuroendocrine changes in the brain start with the reactivation of the hypothalamic-pituitary-gonadal (HPG) neurons along with increased estrogen and testosterone secretion and sex organ development (Dorn & Biro, 2011). Although it is not fully known how hormonal changes affect the brain, we do know the two are linked (Blakemore et al., 2010). Aligned with these hormonal changes is sexual development.

Sexual development should be seen as a normal developmental process that includes behavior, identity, and social aspects. Sexual behaviors comprise a range of activities, from the choice to abstain all the way to sexual intercourse (Tolman & McClelland, 2011). By the end of adolescence, most teens have engaged in sexual intercourse; males, youth of color, and inner-city youth are reported to be more sexually active than their peers (Santrock, 2004). Sexual identity and orientation also develops during this time; these are discussed in more detail later in this chapter.

Adolescents experience other physical changes as well. Some health issues that may occur during the adolescence period include drug and alcohol use, pregnancy and sexually transmitted diseases, eating disorders, and suicide (Santrock, 2004). Many of these are associated with risky choices made by teens related to their physical well-being (Papalia, Olds, & Feldman, 2006). Relatedly, many teens lack a regular physical activity schedule, may not get enough sleep, and have increased body-image issues (Papalia et al., 2006). Girls are more likely to have low body image than boys, which may relate to higher levels of eating disorders in female teens (Perry & Pauletti, 2011). Though teens successfully navigate these physical changes, adults working with this population need to be aware of the many body changes occurring during this developmental stage.

Cognitive Development

Directly related to the hormonal changes mentioned above is the maturation of the brain during adolescence. The teenage brain shows a dramatic decrease in gray matter and increase in white matter, which is connected to increased cognitive functioning (Yurgelun-Todd, 2007). Called *neuroplasticity*, these brain changes relate to social and cognitive skill development, including increased executive functioning, social cognition, and perspective taking (Choudhury, Blakemore, & Charman, 2006). Executive functioning is associated with prefrontal cortex development and includes processing speed, memory, decision making, and risk-taking analysis. About one-third of adolescents begin to demonstrate *hypothetical-deductive reasoning*, or the ability to develop hypotheses about ways to solve problems rather than just using trial and error (Santrock, 2004). In addition, high school students show an increased ability to make decisions and engage in critical and abstract thinking (Steinberg, 2006).

With the brain development comes changes to the limbic system, affecting teens' abilities to contemplate risks and rewards when making decisions. In general, adolescents demonstrate more risk taking in actual situations than hypothetical ones (Albert & Steinberg, 2011). This difference suggests that although high school students may state appropriate behaviors when asked, they often behave differently in real-life situations, engaging in riskier behaviors. Researchers suggest that the connection between emotional processing and cognitive development may be the cause of risky decision-making behaviors (Yurgelun-Todd, 2007). In fact, Bradshaw, Goldweber, Fishbein, and Greenberg (2012) noted that "reward regions of the brain are more strongly activated when youth make risky decisions in the company of peers rather than alone" (p. S43).

Judgment and decision making in teens also may be affected by social context. Risk taking is influenced by a combination of cognitive reasoning, social context, and emotions, where direct experience alters decision-making abilities (Albert & Steinberg, 2011). We know that adolescents create their personal identities through social interactions, so a consideration of peer, teacher, school, and community contexts must exist when exploring decision making (Eccles & Roeser, 2011). Blakemore (2012) noted that how adolescents make choices is neurologically different, with teens using different parts of the brain to make decisions than they used during childhood. It remains important for high school counselors to understand the complex brain development that occurs during adolescence so they can design and deliver developmentally appropriate activities in their classroom guidance programming lessons.

Consider this example related to cognitive development: Jasmine is a high school counselor planning a career development program for the twelfth graders at her school. She wants to include a lesson on decision making because she is aware that the cognitive development of adolescents impacts their decision-making abilities. In a classroom guidance lesson, Jasmine introduces different styles of decision making and a step-by-step approach to making decisions. Jasmine knows that adolescents' decision making is impacted by their peers and emotions. So she has students practice making a decision using the step-by-step approach individually. She gives students time to apply the approach to an example decision and then asks students to share their decisions with the large group, giving them the opportunity to practice making decisions on their own before sharing those decisions with their peers.

Several other cognitive changes occur during high school. Adolescent *egocentrism* or social thinking develops during this time. Social thinking consists of two parts: (1) Teens tend to believe in an imaginary audience where they feel others are equally interested in them as they are in themselves and (2) teens create a personal fable or belief of invincibility and uniqueness (Santrock, 2004). Increased ability in perspective taking is influenced by mirror neuron development during the teen years. Egocentric bias affects this ability until sometime in adolescence, when teens ultimately become able to view both self-perspectives and other perspectives fairly accurately (Choudhury et al., 2006). All of these changes affect decision making, problem solving, and critical thinking during the high school years.

Check for Understanding

- High school students experience many physical changes related to adolescence.
- Increased cognitive functioning is a hallmark of development for high school students.
- High school students may struggle with decision making due to their focus on peers.

Discussion Questions

1. Based on your understanding of the cognitive and physical changes occurring in high school students, how can you create classroom guidance lessons that help promote executive functioning?

2. We know that decision making in teenagers includes a complex interaction of social, emotional, and cognitive reactions to a given issue. How might that influence how you teach decision making in classroom guidance lessons?

3. CACREP (2009) requires school counselors to apply "relevant research findings to inform the practice of school counseling" (p. 42). How does your understanding of cognitive and physical development inform your classroom guidance planning?

Social Development

The high school experience brings about certain social development considerations for adolescents. At this age, adolescents develop their identity, establish relationships with peers, and navigate changes in their relationships with parents and family members.

Identity Development

Identity is an individual's sense of self. Identity is an individual concept but also a social concept in that much of who we are depends on our interactions with others. Erikson (1980) identified the psychosocial crisis of identity versus role confusion as the primary task for adolescents. According to Erikson, teenagers make decisions about personal values and beliefs at this point in their lives. They develop or strengthen interests in sports, music, theater, others, or academics during the high school years. High school students may disagree with beliefs held by their parents as they begin to establish their own opinions on certain issues. Mild parent-child conflicts are a normative part of the adolescent identity development process as teenagers renegotiate their independent status within the family system (Steinberg, 2001). According to Erikson (1980), individuals successfully complete this stage when they have established a sense of self that is consistent with their beliefs. Individuals who experience problems at this stage develop role confusion. This may occur when teenagers fall victim to peer pressure and act in ways that go against their beliefs and values.

Yoder (2000) indicated that identity development was informed by social interactions and cultural beliefs and that this process resulted in a "personality with the realities of the social world" (p. 103). Marcia (1966) elaborated on Erikson's concept of identity. Marcia (1966) proposed four identity statuses based on an individual's exploration and commitment to different beliefs across life. These include foreclosure, identity diffusion, moratorium, and identity achievement. *Foreclosure* occurs when someone makes a commitment without exploration. *Identity diffusion* happens when an adolescent does no exploration and chooses not to commit to anything. With *moratorium*, a teenager explores an issue but does not commit. Finally, in *identity achievement*, an individual both explores an issue and commits to a certain belief on the topic. Meeus (2011) reviewed longitudinal research on Marcia's identity statuses. Meeus found that healthy identity development relates to an individual's positive outlook on life and also to accepting home environments. For example, a teenage girl with parents who support her desire to explore different styles of clothing and makeup will likely develop a style of her own. In another instance, a teenage boy who explores a variety of career and college options before deciding to attend a four-year university may have a more positive outlook on life. As adolescents navigate this psychosocial stage of development, they encounter opportunities to negotiate and renegotiate how they view themselves within their social world.

Peer Relationships

In high school, teenagers begin to establish closer relationships with peers while differentiating themselves from parents. Teens may no longer have confidence or trust in their parents and, at the same time, trust in their peers rises. Friends are now chosen based on interest commonality, but attention is also paid to social status and reputation. Groups become more stable during adolescence, no longer based only on proximity or parent friendships but also on common interest such as sports, religious beliefs, and hobbies. While they may no longer fully trust their parents, teens still need practical support (i.e., food and money) from parents (del Valle, Bravo, & Lopez, 2010). In terms of autonomy, teens seek independence in decision making on issues they consider personal. In the early adolescent years, some examples may include hairstyles and employability, and teenagers may continue to consult with parents on these matters. As teens age and begin to differentiate from their parents, the personal domain expands to involve issues such as morals and values (Daddis, 2011) as well as who they choose as friends.

Peer Pressure

Teenagers spend more time with peers and less time with parents as they transition through high school. Teens turn more toward their peers as confidants when they discuss personal problems and move away from sharing these issues with parents (del Valle et al., 2010). Thus, as teens navigate the sometimes-difficult issues adolescents face, they may be seeking advice and comfort from peers. For example, a fifteen-year-old girl, Sarah, is friends with her seventeen-year-old neighbor. This friend is pressuring Sarah to come to a party where there will be drinking and possibly drugs. Sarah is nervous about attending the party. However, rather than ask her parents for advice, Sarah asks her friend from math class. This friend is excited about the idea of attending a party for older students and encourages Sarah to go. In addition to seeking emotional support from peers, peers can provide pressure to do things. Higher levels of peer pressure may negatively impact self-esteem in teens (Kiran-Esen, 2012; Uslu, 2013). Peer pressure can also lead to bullying, drug use, and eating disorders. As with bullying, peer pressure can occur in a digital format. The National Center on Addiction and Substance Abuse at Columbia University (2012) found that 75% of teens surveyed were influenced to try drugs or alcohol after seeing pictures of peers experimenting on social media sites. Because of the importance and influence of peer relationships in adolescence, school counselors need to be attuned to this aspect of friendships for high school students.

Cyberbullying

Cyberbullying is the use of technology or social media to bully others. Cyberbullying includes sending cruel or insensitive text messages or e-mail, spreading rumors via text or social media, or sharing embarrassing pictures through social media or text. With the rise in technology availability and social media use, cyberbullying impacts many high school students. This type of bullying provides students with anonymity (Kowalski & Limber, 2007) and reduces feelings of responsibility and accountability (Juvonen & Gross, 2008; Mishna, Saini, & Solomon, 2009). Cyberbullying often occurs outside of the school building but directly affects the daily lives of students. Thus, cyberbullying may impact more students than counselors may anticipate and deserves special attention.

Here is an example of how to approach cyberbullying: Joseph, a high school counselor, has heard from several ninth-grade students about the rise in cyberbullying; students are posting racy and revealing pictures, edited to look like the bodies belong to certain students. Joseph decides to facilitate a classroom guidance lesson in all ninth-grade health classes to address this issue. He takes time to learn about the various computer programs and apps that students are using so that he can use them as examples in his lesson. During the lesson, Joseph asks students to discuss cyberbullying without naming perpetrators or victims and ensures that students are respectful of others during the discussion. He also introduces the various types of cyberbullying, such as denigrating others, exclusion, and harassment. He completes the lesson with a small-group activity where students create posters about preventing cyberbullying that can then be hung throughout the school. A short student survey reveals that the students felt heard and believed they better understood cyberbullying and its effects on others.

Romantic Relationships

Adolescence is marked by relationships with peers and social groups. Individuals may also develop romantic relationships in adolescence. Romantic relationships are mutually recognized, ongoing interactions that involve some form of attraction (Furman, Brown, & Feiring, 1999). Adolescent romantic relationships may be thought of as transitory and unimportant. However, recent research shows this may not be the case. Collins (2003) reviewed several studies related to adolescent romantic relationships and found that these relationships are important for adolescent functioning. Though the research is limited, Collins suggests that romantic relationships may impact identity development and other transitions from adolescence to adulthood. For example, Rochelle and Juan started dating in the eighth grade. They have maintained a strong relationship throughout their high school years. Rochelle and Juan have the same group of friends, though they spend most of their free time with one another. Both teens are applying to college and plan to attend the same four-year university. Juan, a first-generation college student, would likely not have thought to go to college if not for the influence of Rochelle and the help and guidance of her parents. These relationships may happen with the same gender, different gender, or a variation of both.

Sexuality

Adolescence is a time when individuals begin exploring sexuality. The role of peers, the media, and family create a social context from which adolescents develop their knowledge of sexual behaviors and beliefs (Tolman & McClelland, 2011). At this time, high school students may find themselves attracted to members of the same sex or might question their sexuality. Because of social stigma, teens may keep this attraction to themselves rather than share their developing feelings. This could lead to isolation and a lack of support from family and peers. Parents sometimes react with denial, guilt, or fear when their child discloses attraction to the same sex (Harrison, 2003). Additionally, students who identify as lesbian, gay, bisexual, transgender, or questioning (LGBTQ) may become socially isolated, have low self-esteem, and experience delays in other areas of identity development. Sexual orientation development may not fully form until young adulthood, especially for females (Saewyc, 2011). For some teens, sexual identity development is tied to higher rates of mental health issues, often due to stigma, bias, or other social issues.

Robinson and Espelage (2013) surveyed adolescents and compared responses from those who self-identified as LGBTQ versus youth that identified as straight. They found that LGBTQ youth were more likely to engage in risky sexual behavior than straight youth. Some of these differences can be explained by victimization by peers. However, when the researchers accounted for victimization, LGBTQ youth were still at greater risk for engaging in risky sexual behavior (Robinson & Espelage, 2013). In another study, researchers examined differences in drug use between LGBTQ students and straight students (Newcomb, Birkett,

Corliss, & Mustanski, 2014). The researchers determined that LGBTQ students reported more drug use than did the straight students.

Many developmental and contextual issues occur for high school students, including sexual identity development. Skillful high school counselors attend to these issues as they plan their comprehensive school counseling program activities. Considering the physical, cognitive, and social development of students can make classroom guidance programming more intentional and relatable.

Check for Understanding

- The search for identity is a key component of adolescent development.
- High school students focus much of their time and attention on friendships and romantic relationships and continue to differentiate themselves from their parents.
- Relationships can create complications for high school students, including peer pressure and sexuality issues.

Discussion Questions

1. Based on Marcia and Erikson's stages of identity development, how might you help students navigate the identity exploration process?

2. Think back to when you were a high school student. What do you wish your school counselor had discussed with you and your peers or what available programs would you have benefitted from?

3. Developing peer and romantic relationships are cornerstones of adolescence. How can you, a high school counselor, use classroom guidance programming as a way to help students navigate the challenges associated with these relationships? What, if any, are topics you would feel uncomfortable presenting to high school students?

CASE STUDY

Part 2

Jillian recognizes that she needs to consider the developmental level of her students in order to create an appropriate classroom guidance series. She knows that many of her ninth and tenth graders will still be developing their critical-thinking skills and that all of her students may struggle with decision-making abilities. Jillian also recognizes that her students are most influenced by their peers, so creating a positive peer culture is a critical component. Jillian also knows that many of her students have unique needs related to their cultural background and learning styles, so she cannot create a one-size-fits-all program.

Therefore, Jillian decides to start her four-year program by helping ninth-grade students develop lifelong learning characteristics. She believes that exploring how to be a successful student and postsecondary goal setting are developmentally appropriate focal points for classroom guidance. During her four guidance lessons for ninth graders, she will be sure to address cultural differences in her students and engage the entire grade level in creating a college-bound culture, which researchers describe as vital to helping students link postsecondary education to their own life goals (Usher, Kober, Jennings, & Rentner, 2012). She will wait to introduce critical thinking and problem-solving skills until eleventh grade, when students are developmentally more prepared.

Discussion Questions

1. What other developmental concerns does Jillian need to address in her planning?

2. How well do you believe most high school counselors address developmental and cultural considerations and why?

STRENGTHS AND CHALLENGES OF WORKING WITH HIGH SCHOOL STUDENTS

As is evident from the literature reviewed above, high school students are unique in many ways, especially with the surge of independence and identity development that occurs during this time. Working with this population presents both challenges and opportunities, and it is vital to recognize these characteristics in order to best meet the needs of the high school student.

Strengths

- *Increased abstract thinking*: Because the adolescent brain is rapidly evolving, high school students typically demonstrate increased ability to engage in critical and abstract reasoning. This characteristic is helpful for classroom guidance because students are likely to engage in group discussions about difficult topics facing teens today.
- *Enjoyment of group work*: High school students are deeply affected by their peers and often prefer the company of friends over others. Classroom guidance programming presents opportunities for students to engage with their classmates through activities, discussions, and group processing.

- *Increased focus on postsecondary planning*: Because high school students are nearing the end of their secondary education, they are naturally beginning to think about their futures. Building on this natural inclination to consider the future creates unique opportunities during classroom guidance programming.
- *Developing identity*: The primary psychosocial task for adolescents relates to identity development. Teenagers are already interested in learning about who they are and what they want from life. High school classroom guidance can connect with this innate desire.
- *Work experience*: Many teens work part-time during high school. They are becoming interested in the world of work because there are now tangible work activities in their lives. These initial work experiences provide bountiful examples that can be drawn on during classroom guidance.
- *Peer influence*: Adolescents are strongly influenced by their peers, and school counselors can use this influence to create a positive and college-bound schoolwide culture.

Challenges

- *Peer influence*: This influence can also be a challenge as high school students struggle to feel accepted by their peers. Relationship issues dominate much of the time for these students, while bullying and cyberbullying can negatively influence teen development.
- *Sexual exploration*: Although a natural and positive occurrence during adolescence, sexuality can also be rife with difficulties for teenagers. Personal decisions about sexual choices can have long-lasting effects for high school students, and school counselors often spend time helping students address these concerns.
- *Increased drug and alcohol use*: Due to increased risk-taking behaviors and peer influence, many high school students experiment with drugs and alcohol. Substance use by teens can interfere with future planning and decision making.
- *Preoccupation with self*: Teens are naturally focused on themselves and, as a result, may be unable to accept ideas presented as being universal to all adolescents. Their self-focus often makes them feel isolated or different from their peers.
- *Boundary testing and mood shifts*: High school students test limits as they explore their identity. Oftentimes, this boundary pushing, which way be moving away from the family unit, leads to problems for teens. Additionally, the hormonal and brain changes happening in adolescents can lead to moodiness and inconsistent dispositions.

- *Ability to leave school*: Students can choose to leave high school before graduation. The current national high school dropout rate is 26%, but the rate varies by ethnicity, family income level, ability status, and geographical location (U.S. Department of Education, 2013b). For ethnicity, Latino/a students have the highest rate (14%), followed by African American students (7%), and White students (5%). Differences by family income level exist as well, with students from the lowest-income quartile demonstrating the highest dropout rate at 13%, followed by 9% of the next lowest quartile (U.S. Department of Education, 2013b).

Discussion Questions

1. How will you navigate these challenges and build upon the strengths when developing your classroom guidance curriculum?

2. What challenge do you feel will be the most difficult for you to overcome and why?

CULTURAL CONSIDERATIONS

High school students go through physical, cognitive, and social development changes as they enter into adolescence. Development does not end there, however. Students may experience development in areas specific to their cultural, ethnic, or sexual identity. The American Counseling Association's Code of Ethics (2014) states that counselors of all specialties are required to be multiculturally competent. Thus, school counselors should be aware of identity development in all areas. Students of color experience ethnic identity development. This development, based on an individual's culture, occurs alongside other typical adolescent growth. Students who identify as LGBTQ may experience identity development related to their sexual orientation.

Adolescents who are students of color work through the stages of ethnic identity. Phinney and Ong (2007) reviewed research on ethnic identity models and conducted an analysis of ethnic identity using the Multigroup Ethnic Identity Measure (Phinney, 1992). Based on this research, they proposed that ethnic identity is composed of two components: exploration and commitment. These two variables are related but have distinct roles. Individuals must have some level of commitment in order to begin exploring. Additionally, this exploration may lead to even greater commitment. As teens enter high school, they may experience more diversity through larger classes than they were exposed to in elementary or middle school. Thus, high school students may begin exploring their ethnic identity rather than simply accepting the views of their parents (French, Seidman, Allen, & Aber, 2006). Attending to ethnic identity development may help high school students navigate this process.

Students who identify as LGBTQ may experience identity development specific to their sexual orientation. As with ethnic identity development, this may occur alongside or delay other typical development seen at this age. Degges-White and Myers (2005) proposed a model of lesbian identity development based on Marcia's (1966) theory of identity development and Cass's (1979) model of homosexual development. In their model, female adolescents who are identity diffused feel different from others their age, may be attracted to other females, and may be confused. In identity foreclosure, individuals may be attracted to individuals of the same sex but strongly identify as heterosexual. Adolescents in an identity moratorium may recognize their LGBTQ status but do not commit to the identity. These individuals may take on a more asexual identity. Finally, individuals who have achieved their LGBTQ identity respond positively to their feelings and outlook (Degges-White & Myers, 2005). In another study on identity development in LGBTQ youth, Rosario, Schrimshaw, and Hunter (2011) found that identity formation was not significantly related to psychological distress. They also noted that supportive relationships were related to better adjustment while negative relationships were related to poor adjustment.

Culture directly affects all people, including adolescents. High school counselors cannot assume a one-size-fits-all mentality and must consider the cultural groups represented by their students. Ethnic and sexual identity development typically begin in adolescence, so some high school students must face the challenges of adding these developmental concerns to the already-complex process of overall identity development. Classroom guidance activities need to factor in these developmental processes if they are to be relevant to all students.

CAREER DEVELOPMENT CONSIDERATIONS

Yet another developmental process that occurs during adolescence is related to future career choice. During high school, the primary career task is tentative decision making regarding next steps after graduation. Students have many options available to them, including two- and four-year colleges, technical schools, military, and the workforce. These choices may feel overwhelming for students, yet some students experience even more challenges beyond selecting a career path.

An example of how to address career development through classroom guidance can be found in the work of Mark, a high school counselor. Mark works primarily with the eleventh graders at his high school. In the past, he has provided information about how to select a college and has even had guest speakers from various colleges talk to students and their parents. He notes, however, that most of his students do not actually visit colleges before they apply, so they do not really understand what a college campus is like. Therefore, Mark decided to create a classroom guidance lesson about what life is like on a college campus. He searched online and found that most colleges offer a virtual tour of their campus. In his classroom guidance lesson, Mark used the BigFuture website to quiz students about what they want in a college. He then showed them several virtual tours of different types of postsecondary institutions. Students then worked in pairs to refine their understanding of what they want in a college. Students were given a homework assignment to write a paragraph on what type of college they hope to attend, and these were graded by the English teachers as part of a writing assignment.

Many high schools have access to online career programs to help students as they plan for their postsecondary options. Often, these programs are paid for by school districts or state Departments of Education, so access may be available free of charge. These include the following:

- http://www.ACT.org: ACT offers a complete career and college readiness program. Until June, 2014, this program was entitled Explore and Plan, but it is now called ACT Aspire. These computer-based programs offer assessments for elementary, middle, and high school students, providing information about their readiness and growth needs for postsecondary success. Explore and Plan both demonstrated high-quality materials with statistics representing the national population (Foster, 2013).
- http://www.official-asvab.com: The ASVAB, an aptitude battery developed by the military, can be combined with a career exploration option to help high school students understand potential career opportunities.
- http://www.kuder.com: The Kuder Career Planning System offers assessments, e-portfolios, and career and college information to help students plan for their future. One recent review of the Kuder system noted its strong normative support and ease of use (Gibbons, 2013).
- http://www.edits.net: The COPSystem Career Management Package includes various assessments and information that provide career-related guidance to students. According to a recent review of the assessments, reliability and validity information is sound and the program is recommended for use in secondary school settings (Bullock-Yowell & Osborne, 2013).

Other websites that may be helpful for career and college planning include the following:

- http://nces.ed.gov/collegenavigator: Sponsored by the National Center for Education Statistics, this website offers a user-friendly college search engine as well as links to the Occupational Outlook Handbook and Free Application for Federal Student Aid (FAFSA) websites.
- http://www.collegeboard.org: Home of the SAT and AP exams, this website includes college search and career information. It also includes BigFuture, a college exploration site.
- http://www.knowhow2go.org: Based on a national campaign to increase college attendance, this website offers a variety of information on postsecondary planning, specifically designed for early high school students.
- http://studentaid.ed.gov: Sponsored by the U.S. Department of Education, this website focuses on federal student aid for postsecondary education.
- http://www.whitehouse.gov/issues/education/higher-education/college-score-card: Sponsored by the U.S. Department of Education's College Affordability and Transparency Center, this site provides a comprehensive college search engine that ties affordability to the college selection process.
- http://www.collegeresults.org: Created by The Education Trust, College Results Online (CRO) offers a clearinghouse of data on postsecondary institutions. One unique aspect of this site is the ability to compare and contrast colleges on issues such as student success and value.

First-Generation College Status

In high school, students begin to explore their career options. This career exploration is impacted by parents, specifically the education level of parents. First-generation college students, or those whose parents did not attend college, have specific career needs. For example, first-generation college students report lacking academic skills in math, science, and writing (Reid & Moore, 2008) and are more likely to be of a student of color or to come from a low-income background (Terenzini, Springer, Yaeger, Pascarella, & Nora, 1996). Without intervention, first-generation college students are less likely to attend or complete college, often due to feeling less supported (Wang & Castaneda-Sound, 2008) or having lower college-attending self-efficacy (Gibbons & Borders, 2010). Helpful interventions include providing concrete information about college attendance, involving parents in postsecondary planning, encouraging students to enroll in advanced courses, and offering counseling services to address barriers to postsecondary success (Gibbons, 2007). Many of these activities can be completed through classroom guidance.

To address the unique needs of first-generation college-bound students, consider Lisa's story: Lisa is in her second year as a high school counselor at a diverse, mostly low-income school. Many of her students come from families without postsecondary experience, so Lisa wants to provide classroom guidance for the tenth-grade students about postsecondary options. Because these students often lack role models who have a college education, she asks previous graduates to return to the school to share their stories. She contacts those graduates who attend one of the local colleges and arranges for them to come to various classes. The graduates discuss their path to postsecondary education and highlight their successes and challenges. After the guest speakers, Lisa offers concrete information to students about postsecondary options along with financial aid and scholarship information. She ends by encouraging students to visit her office to further discuss their future plans.

High-Achieving Students

Students with higher academic abilities, often termed *gifted* or *advanced*, tend to get overlooked in terms of school support services. However, these students may face pressure from parents, peers, and the environment to fulfill high expectations. These pressures can lead to feelings of increased stress and compromised mental health (Suldo, Shaunessy, & Hardesty, 2008). Additionally, parents and school counselors may place more focus on academics than on other areas of adolescent development for these students who are naturally intelligent. In research on self-control and academic ability in high-achieving college freshmen, Honken and Ralston (2013) found that a lack of self-control in high school correlated with lower grades in college. The researchers concluded that students who are high achieving may not be forced to complete homework and engage in other behaviors requiring self-control because they are still able to perform well academically. This may lead to a lack of self-control in all areas once students move on to college.

Students with Disabilities

A significant number of high school students have a disability and, therefore, need special consideration for career development. In the 2010–2011 school year, 13% of students ages 3–21 had a disability (U.S. Department of Education, 2013a). Some of these students may transition to college, as about 11% of students in postsecondary institutions identified as having a disability (National Center for Educational Statistics, 2008). Those entering postsecondary schools typically have disabilities such as attention-deficit/hyperactivity disorder, specific learning disorders, mental health disorders, mobility impairments, or chronic illness (Raue &

Lewis, 2011). Other students with disabilities may enter the workforce. However, only 17.8% of individuals with a disability were employed in 2012 (Bureau of Labor Statistics, 2013). All students with an Individual Education Plan must receive transition planning, and students with disabilities have specific but varied career needs related to their disability. Thus, school counselors can work with them, and the special education teachers to help plan pathways beyond high school.

Check for Understanding

- Cultural issues such as racial and sexual identity development can complicate the already-difficult path to identity formation.
- Career-related and postsecondary planning concerns are at the forefront for high school students, and career decisions may be a critical need for students.
- Parent education level and student ability level can complicate career decision making.

Discussion Questions

1. What are some potential ethical issues related to addressing sexual and cultural identity development? How can high school counselors reduce the likelihood of ethical concerns?

2. How might you involve families in your classroom guidance activities? How would cultural differences affect your work with these families?

CASE STUDY

Part 3

Throughout her four-year classroom guidance plan, Jillian plans to address academic, career, and social/emotional needs as listed in the ASCA Mindsets & Behaviors for Student Success (2014). The standards she will address are listed in Figure 5.1. Table 5.1 provides an overview of the four-year classroom guidance programming plan. The classroom components are supplemented with in-class activities led by teachers, yearly parent meetings, and individual planning meetings as needed. Jillian also plans to use the lesson plan template provided by the ASCA National Model (2012). A sample lesson plan is included in Figure 5.2.

Figure 5.1 Transferable Skills and Corresponding ASCA Mindsets & Behaviors for Student Success

Critical Thinking

2.A.1 Demonstrate critical-thinking skills to make informed decisions

2.A.2 Demonstrate creativity

2.A.8 Actively engage in challenging coursework

2.A.9 Gather evidence and consider multiple perspectives to make informed decisions

2.B.1 Demonstrate ability to assume responsibility

2.C.5 Demonstrate ethical decision making and social responsibility

Teamwork/Collaboration

2.C.2 Create positive and supportive relationships with other students

2.C.3 Create relationships with adults that support success

2.C.4 Demonstrate empathy

2.C.6 Use effective collaboration and cooperation skills

2.C.7 Use leadership and teamwork skills to work effectively in diverse teams

2.C.8 Demonstrate advocacy skills and ability to assert self when necessary

Professionalism and Work Ethic

2.A.3 Use time-management, organizational, and study skills

2.A.5 Apply media and technology skills

2.A.6 Set high standards of quality

2.A.10 Participate in enrichment and extracurricular activities

2.B.3 Demonstrate the ability to work independently

Lifelong Learning/Self-Direction

2.A.4 Apply self-motivation and self-direction to learning

2.A.7 Identify long- and short-term academic, career, and social/emotional goals

2.B.4 Demonstrate the ability to delay immediate gratification for long-term rewards

2.B.5 Demonstrate perseverance to achieve long- and short-term goals

2.B.6 Demonstrate the ability to overcome barriers to learning

Note: Standards taken from ASCA Mindsets & Behaviors for Student Success (2014). Behavior Standards: A = Learning Strategies, B = Self-Management Skills, C = Social Skills.

(Continued)

(Continued)

Table 5.1   Four-Year Classroom Guidance Plan

Grade Level	Number of Classroom Guidance Sessions	Topic(s)	Behaviors Covered
Grade 9: Focus—Lifelong Learning			
9	1	Being a successful student and employee	2.A.4 2.B.6
9	1	Postsecondary goal setting	2.A.7
9	2	Achieving goals	2.B.4 2.B.5
Grade 10: Focus—Teamwork and Work Ethic			
10	2	Effective communication	2.C.4 2.C.7 2.C.8
10	2	Teamwork	2.C.2 2.C.3 2.C.6
Grade 11: Focus—Critical Thinking/Problem Solving			
11	1	How to make decisions	2.A.1 2.A.2
11	1	Consequences of decisions	2.A.9 2.B.1
11	1	Applying decision making to postsecondary plans	2.A.8 2.C.5
Grade 12: Focus—Postsecondary Goal Attainment			
12	2	Planning for your next steps	2.A.5 2.A.6 2.A.10

Note: See Figure 5.1 for descriptions of each behavior.

Figure 5.2a   Sample Lesson Plan

School Counselor: Jillian Smith

Activity: Specific, Measurable, Attainable, Realistic, and Timely (SMART) Goals

Grade: 9

Four-Year Classroom Guidance Plan: First year, Lesson 3

ASCA Behavior Standards:

2.A.7 Identify long- and short-term academic, career, and social/emotional goals.

2.C.6 Use effective collaboration and cooperation skills.

Learning Objectives

By the end of this classroom guidance lesson, students will

1. understand the SMART goals process,

2. use SMART goals to create postsecondary plans, and

3. work effectively in small groups to create plans.

Materials: SMART goals worksheet (see Appendix 5.1)

Procedure

1. Pretest on goal setting and SMART goals (Specific, Measurable, Attainable, Realistic, and Timely). See Appendix 5.2.

2. Introduce the concept of goal setting. Ask students about the importance of goals and how they achieved these goals in the past.

3. Discussion of various types of postsecondary options for students, including entering the workforce, military, two-year colleges, and four-year universities. Focus on providing concrete information about each option.

4. Introduce SMART goals and a discussion of how goals can be short or long term.

5. In small groups, have students create their own SMART goals. Each group creates goals for ninth grade, tenth and eleventh grade, and twelfth grade. Goals should be related to post-graduation plans (see Figure 5.2b).

(Continued)

Figure 5.2a (Continued)

6. Start a class discussion on using SMART goals to identify postsecondary plans and strengths and challenges in long-term planning. Discuss how to use the career assessments taken in high school (e.g., ASVAB, Kuder, ACT ASPIRE) to help achieve SMART goals.

7. Posttest on goal setting and SMART goals.

Plan for Evaluation

1. Process data: number of students in ninth-grade classes, number of classroom guidance activities

2. Perception data: pre- and posttests on goal setting, class discussions

3. Outcome data: assessment of SMART goal language when the ninth graders become tenth graders (e.g., Are students using SMART goals when discussing postsecondary plans? Do their parents know about SMART goals?), student graduation, and postsecondary education attendance rates.

Figure 5.2b   Sample SMART Goals

Jillian places Ricky, John, and Lucas together to determine SMART goals related to postsecondary planning. Ricky has always known he wanted to attend college and comes from a family where most of his relatives have postsecondary degrees. John and Lucas, however, are less certain about college and have few relatives with college experience. As they begin to discuss SMART goals, Ricky suggests they think about what is needed to succeed in college. He shares that academics alone are not enough and that they also need to consider extracurricular and leadership activities. Lucas mentions that he already holds a part-time job working at a local restaurant, and John describes his volunteer work at his church. Together, the three boys create the following SMART goals for ninth grade:

S: Add at least one new school-sponsored extracurricular activity to our current schedules. This activity will help us be more well-rounded.

M: Measured by attending at least one function (meeting, event) sponsored by the new group we each join.

A: To achieve this goal, we must explore the clubs and organizations available at our school. We can use the school website and talk to friends to learn about possible activities to join.

R: Yes, it is realistic. We can each find something that fits into our schedules. Activities will help us get into college. We do not think we need new skills; we just need to use our existing skills.

T: We have to join a club or organization by the end of the school year.

Using the same goal-planning activity sheet, the boys then create SMART goals for tenth, eleventh, and twelfth grades. They consider various options, each focused on postsecondary access and success, and ultimately include goals related to taking honors courses, looking at college-planning websites, and meeting with their school counselor to discuss college plans.

Jillian will also include ways to evaluate the effectiveness of her classroom guidance program. She plans to track the postsecondary choices that students make over the next few years as well as to examine the course choices students select to learn whether they are opting for college preparatory classes. She will also survey (i.e., perception survey) the students, teachers, and parents to collect feedback about the classroom guidance activities. Jillian knows that it will take time before she knows if her program is successful through tracking program data, but she believes that her attention to the general developmental and contextual issues of adolescents combined with attending to the unique needs of her student population will help her program be effective.

KEYSTONES

- High school students experience a variety of developmental changes throughout their four years, and these changes directly affect how they respond to classroom guidance programming.

- Classroom guidance programming in high school can be challenging, but it also is a time to build on the natural focus teens have on peer connections and postsecondary planning.

- High school classroom guidance programming requires sensitivity to cultural considerations and identity development, as they are core components in the lives of adolescents.

- School counselors can and should provide classroom guidance programming at the high school level, because the benefits to their students outweigh the challenges.

REFERENCES

Albert, D., & Steinberg, L. (2011). Judgment and decision making in adolescence. *Journal of Research on Adolescence, 21*, 211–224.

American Counseling Association. (2014). *ACA code of ethics*. Alexandria, VA: Author.

American School Counselor Association (ASCA). (2012). *ASCA national model: A framework for school counseling programs* (3rd ed.). Alexandria, VA: Author.

American School Counselor Association (ASCA). (2014). *ASCA mindsets & behaviors for student success: K–12 college- and career-readiness standards for every student*. Alexandria, VA: Author.

Blakemore, S. J. (2012). Imaging brain development: The adolescent brain. *NeuroImage, 61*, 397–406.

Blakemore, S. J., Burnett, S., & Dahl, R. E. (2010). The role of puberty in the developing adolescent brain. *Human Brain Mapping, 31*, 926–933.

Bradshaw, C. P., Goldweber, A., Fishbein, D., & Greenberg, M. T. (2012). Infusing developmental neuroscience into school-based preventative interventions: Implications and future directions. *Journal of Adolescent Health, 51*, S41–S47.

Bryan, J., Holcomb-McCoy, C., Moore-Thomas, C., & Day-Vines, N. L. (2009). Who sees the school counselor for college information? A national study. *Professional School Counseling, 12*, 280–291.

Bullock-Yowell, E. E., & Osborne, L. K. (2013). COPSystem career guidance program. In C. Wood & D. G. Hays (Eds.), *A counselor's guide to career assessment instruments* (6th ed.). Broken Arrow, OK: National Career Development Association.

Bureau of Labor Statistics. (2013). *Persons with a disability: Labor force characteristics summary*. Retrieved March 29, 2015, from http://www.bls.gov/news.release/pdf/disabl.pdf

Casner-Lotto, J., & Barrington, L. (2006). *Are they ready to work? Employers' perspectives on the basic knowledge and applied skills of new entrants to the 21st century US workforce (Final Report)*. Washington, DC: The Conference Board, Corporate Voices for Working Families.

Cass, V. C. (1979). Homosexuality identity formation: A theoretical model. *Journal of Homosexuality, 4*(3), 219–235.

Choudhury, S., Blakemore, S. J., & Charman, T. (2006). Social cognitive development during adolescence. *SCAN, 1*, 165–174.

Collins, W. A. (2003). More than myth: The developmental significance of romantic relationships during adolescence. *Journal of Research on Adolescence, 13*(1), 1–24.

Council for Accreditation of Counseling and Related Educational Programs (CACREP). (2009). *2009 standards for accreditation*. Alexandria, VA: Author.

Daddis, C. (2011). Desire for increased autonomy and adolescents' perceptions of peer autonomy: "Everyone else can; why can't I?" *Child Development, 82*(4), 1310–1326.

Degges-White, S. E., & Myers, J. E. (2005). The adolescent lesbian identity formation model: Implications for counseling. *Journal of Humanistic Counseling, 44*, 185–197.

del Valle, J. F., Bravo, A., & Lopez, M. (2010). Parents and peers as providers of support in adolescents' social network: A developmental perspective. *Journal of Community Psychology, 38*(1), 16–27.

Dorn, L. D., & Biro, F. M. (2011). Puberty and its measurement: A decade in review. *Journal of Research on Adolescence, 21*, 180–195.

Eccles, J. S., & Roeser, R. W. (2011). Schools as developmental contexts during adolescence. *Journal of Research on Adolescence, 21*, 225–241.

Erikson, E. H. (1980). *Identity and the life cycle* (Vol. 1). New York, NY: W. W. Norton & Company.

Foster, L. H. (2013). EXPLORE and PLAN. In C. Wood & D. G. Hays (Eds.), *A counselor's guide to career assessment instruments* (6th ed.). Broken Arrow, OK: National Career Development Association.

French, S. E., Seidman, E., Allen, L., & Aber, J. L. (2006). The development of ethnic identity during adolescence. *Developmental Psychology, 42*(1), 1.

Furman, W., Brown, B. B., & Feiring, C. (Eds.). (1999). *The development of romantic relationships in adolescence.* Chicago, IL: Cambridge University Press.

Gallant, D. J., & Zhao, J. (2011). High school students' perceptions of school counseling services: Awareness, use, and satisfaction. *Counseling Outcome Research and Evaluation, 2*, 87–100.

Gibbons, M. M. (2007). College preparation programming for prospective first-generation college students. *Tennessee Counseling Association Journal, 1*, 22–29.

Gibbons, M. M. (2013). Kuder Career Planning System. In C. Wood & D. G. Hays (Eds.), *A counselor's guide to career assessment instruments* (6th ed.). Broken Arrow, OK: National Career Development Association.

Gibbons, M. M., & Borders, L. D. (2010). Prospective first-generation college students: A social-cognitive perspective. *Career Development Quarterly, 58,* 194–208.

Harrison, T. W. (2003). Adolescent homosexuality and concerns regarding disclosure. *Journal of School Health, 73*(3), 107–112.

Honken, N. B., & Ralston, P. A. (2013). High-achieving high school students and not so high achieving college students: A look at lack of self-control, academic ability, and performance in college. *Journal of Advanced Academics, 24*(2), 108–124.

Juvonen, J., & Gross, E. F. (2008). Extending the school grounds?—Bullying experiences in cyberspace. *Journal of School Health, 78*(9), 496–505.

Kiran-Esen, B. (2012). Analyzing peer pressure and self-efficacy expectations among adolescents. *Social Behavior & Personality: An International Journal, 40*(8), 1301–1309.

Kowalski, R. M., & Limber, S. P. (2007). Electronic bullying among middle school students. *Journal of Adolescent Health, 41*(6), 22–30.

Marcia, J. E. (1966). Development and validation of ego-identity status. *Journal of Personality and Social Psychology, 3*(5), 551.

Meeus, W. (2011). The study of adolescent identity formation 2000–2010: A review of longitudinal research. *Journal of Research on Adolescence, 21*(1), 75–94.

Mishna, F., Saini, M., & Solomon, S. (2009). Ongoing and online: Children and youth's perceptions of cyber bullying. *Children and Youth Services Review, 31*(12), 1222–1228.

National Center for Educational Statistics. (2008). *Table 231: Number and percentage of students enrolled in postsecondary institutions, by level, disability status, and selected student characteristics: 2003–04.* Washington, DC: National Center for Education Statistics.

National Center on Addiction and Substance Abuse at Columbia University. (2012, August). *National survey of American attitudes on substance abuse XVII: Teens.* Retrieved March 29, 2015, from http://www.casacolumbia.org/addiction-research/reports/national-survey-american-attitudes-substance-abuse-teens-2012

Newcomb, M. E., Birkett, M., Corliss, H. L., & Mustanski, B. (2014). Sexual orientation, gender, and racial differences in illicit drug use in a sample of US high school students. *American Journal of Public Health, 104*(2), 304–310.

Papalia, D. E., Olds, S. W., & Feldman, R. D. (2006). *A child's world: Infancy through adolescence* (10th ed.). Boston, MA: McGraw-Hill.

Perry, D. G., & Pauletti, R. E. (2011). Gender and adolescent development. *Journal of Research on Adolescence, 21*, 61–74.

Phinney, J. S. (1992). The multigroup ethnic identity measure: A new scale for use with diverse groups. *Journal of Adolescent Research, 7*(2), 156–176.

Phinney, J. S., & Ong, A. D. (2007). Conceptualization and measurement of ethnic identity: Current status and future directions. *Journal of Counseling Psychology, 54*(3), 271.

Raue, K., & Lewis, L. (2011). *Students with disabilities at degree-granting postsecondary institutions* (NCES 2011-018). Retrieved March 29, 2015, from http://nces.ed.gov/pubs2011/2011018.pdf

Reid, M. J., & Moore III, J. L. (2008). College readiness and academic preparation for postsecondary education: Oral histories of first-generation urban college students. *Urban Education, 43*(2), 240–261.

Robinson, J. P., & Espelage, D. L. (2013). Peer victimization and sexual risk differences between lesbian, gay, bisexual, transgender, or questioning and nontransgender heterosexual youths in grades 7–12. *American Journal of Public Health, 103*(10), 1810–1819.

Rosario, M., Schrimshaw, E. W., & Hunter, J. (2011). Different patterns of sexual identity development over time: Implications for the psychological adjustment of lesbian, gay, and bisexual youth. *Journal of Sex Research, 48*, 3–15.

Saewyc, E. M. (2011). Research on adolescent sexual orientation: Development, health disparities, stigma, and resilience. *Journal of Research on Adolescence, 21*, 256–272.

Santrock, J. W. (2004). *Life-span development* (9th ed.). Boston, MA: McGraw-Hill.

Steinberg, L. (2001). We know some things: Parent-adolescent relationships in retrospect and prospect. *Journal of Research on Adolescence, 11*, 1–19.

Steinberg, L. (2006). Cognitive and affective development in adolescence. *TRENDS in Cognitive Sciences, 9*, 69–74.

Suldo, S. M., Shaunessy, E., & Hardesty, R. (2008). Relationships among stress, coping, and mental health in high-achieving high school students. *Psychology in the Schools, 45*(4), 273–290.

Terenzini, P. T., Springer, L., Yaeger, P. M., Pascarella, E. T., & Nora, A. (1996). First generation college students: Characteristics, experiences, and cognitive development. *Research in Higher Education, 37*(1), 1–22.

Tolman, D. L., & McClelland, S. I. (2011). Normative sexuality development in adolescence: A decade in review, 2000–2009. *Journal of Research on Adolescence, 21*, 242–245.

U.S. Department of Education. (2013a). *The condition of education 2013* (NCES 2013-037). Retrieved March 29, 2015, from http://nces.ed.gov/pubs2013/2013037.pdf

U.S. Department of Education. (2013b). *Digest of education statistics, 2012* (NCES 2014-015), Chapter 2. Retrieved March 29, 2015, from http://nces.ed.gov/pubs2014/2014015.pdf

Usher, A., Kober, N, Jennings, J., & Rentner, D. S. (2012). *What is the motivation and why does it matter?* Washington, DC: Center on Education Policy, George Washington University.

Uslu, M. (2013). Relationship between degrees of self-esteem and peer pressure in high school adolescents. *International Journal of Academic Research, 5*(3), 119–124.

Vela-Gude, L., Cavazos, J., Johnson, M. B., Cavazos, A. G., Campos, L., & Rodriguez, I. (2009). "My counselors were never there": Perceptions from Latino college students. *Professional School Counseling, 12*, 272–279.

Wang, C. C., & Castaneda-Sound, C. (2008). The role of generational status, self-esteem, academic self-efficacy, and perceived social support in college students' psychological well-being. *Journal of College Counseling, 11*, 101–118.

Yoder, A. E. (2000). Barriers to ego identity status formation: A contextual qualification of Marcia's identity status paradigm. *Journal of Adolescence, 23*, 95–106.

Yurgelun-Todd, D. (2007). Emotional and cognitive changes during adolescence. *Current Opinion in Neurobiology, 17*, 251–257.

APPENDIX 5.1

Smart Goals Worksheet

SMART GOALS

Specific, Measurable, Attainable, Realistic, and Timely

1. What is your specific goal?

    a. Who is involved?

    b. What do you want?

    c. What are the benefits to attaining this goal?

2. How is it measurable?

    a. How will you know when it is accomplished?

    b. How will you measure its effectiveness?

3. How is it attainable?

    a. What actions must you take to achieve this goal?

    b. What skills will you need to achieve this goal?

4. How is it realistic?

    a. Is your goal relevant?

    b. Do you have the skills needed to achieve this goal?

        i. If not, can you build these skills?

5. What is the time frame for you to reach this goal?

    a. How long, specifically, will it take to reach your goal?

APPENDIX 5.2

Pre- and Posttest

SMART GOALS CLASSROOM GUIDANCE

1. What do each of the letters in the SMART acronym represent?

    a. S

    b. M

    c. A

    d. R

    e. T

2. Why are SMART goals helpful?

3. How do SMART goals relate to your future plans?

PART III

PLANNING, EXECUTION, AND EVALUATION OF CLASSROOM GUIDANCE

Chapter 6

NEEDS ASSESSMENT AND UNIT/LESSON DESIGN

CLARE MERLIN
University of North Carolina

ANDREW J. KNOBLICH
Fairfax County Public Schools

Needs assessments help school counselors understand the needs of students according to stakeholders in their school community. Needs assessments are particularly beneficial in assessing the needs of underserved populations, such as students experiencing achievement gaps or differential access to resources.

(Erford, 2007)

The planning process is an essential component of establishing data-driven, comprehensive school counseling programs. In this chapter, how school counselors can design school counseling core curricula to guide the successful delivery and outcomes of school counseling services will be examined. To begin, the facets of a school counseling core curriculum will be explained. Next, the major planning components of developing a core curriculum will be highlighted. These components include conducting needs assessments, analyzing needs assessment data, creating curriculum units, writing learning objectives, and creating developmentally appropriate classroom guidance lesson plans. To facilitate an understanding of this process, several examples throughout the chapter have been incorporated. Furthermore, guided practice exercises within the chapter can be found that require consideration of real-life scenarios and how to address such situations in your current or future role as a professional school counselor. Designing a school counseling core curriculum is a vital part of comprehensive school counseling programs, and you are encouraged to continue to explore the topics highlighted in this chapter in order to address the needs of your particular student populations. The references included at the end of the chapter serve as a helpful resource for further investigation of the topics discussed herein.

After reading this chapter on needs assessments and lesson designs, you will be able to

- identify the importance of school counseling core curricula in comprehensive school counseling programs,
- create and implement needs assessments,
- use needs assessment data to identify standards for a core curriculum,
- organize curriculum standards into logical units and draft learning objectives for lessons,
- understand the value of a backward-design model in developing classroom guidance lesson plans, and
- understand developmental and multicultural considerations when designing classroom guidance programming lessons.

SCHOOL COUNSELING CORE CURRICULUM

The delivery component of the American School Counselor Association (ASCA) National Model addresses the ways in which school counselors impact students' academic, career, and social/emotional development using both direct and indirect student services (ASCA, 2012). Indirect student services include consultation, referrals, and collaboration, whereas direct student services include individual student planning, responsive services, and school counseling core curricula. School counseling core curricula provide the foundation for school counselors' classroom guidance lesson plans. The ASCA National Model defines this curriculum as one consisting of "structured developmental lessons designed to assist students" in attaining the competencies in the ASCA Mindsets & Behaviors for Student Success and that is "presented systematically through classroom and group activities K–12" (ASCA, 2012, p. 141). The ASCA Mindsets & Behaviors for Student Success identify specific skills, attitudes, and knowledge that students need to be successful in their academic, career, and social/emotional development and that students should be capable of demonstrating as a result of a comprehensive school counseling program (ASCA, 2014). These standards can serve as a guide to create a school counseling core curriculum that will help students achieve their highest potential (ASCA, 2012). See Table 6.1 for a sample of example ASCA Mindsets & Behaviors for Student Success.

Table 6.1   Examples of ASCA Mindsets & Behaviors for Student Success (ASCA, 2014)

Mindset	1.1 Belief in development of whole self, including a healthy balance of mental, social/emotional, and physical well-being
	1.3 Sense of belonging in the school environment
Learning Strategies	2.4 Apply self-motivation and self-direction to learning
	2.8 Actively engage in challenging coursework
Self-Management Skills	2.3 Demonstrate ability to work independently
	2.9 Demonstrate personal safety skills
Social Skills	2.3 Create relationships with adults that support success
	2.8 Demonstrate advocacy skills and ability to assert self, when necessary

Characteristics of Core Curriculum

Ideally, a school counseling core curriculum contains the following five components (ASCA, 2012):

1. *Planned*—School counselors benefit from designing school counseling core curricula prior to the beginning of the school year each year. Planning in advance allows school counselors to seek feedback from their program advisory council, administration, stakeholders, and other school counselors who have suggestions for improving programs.

2. *Preventative*—Planning a school counseling core curriculum in advance also allows school counselors to create a curriculum with a proactive rather than reactive focus. School counselors can outline how to best address the needs of their students in order to prevent crises and obstacles from arising during the school year.

3. *Written*—If school counselors would like to benefit most from a school counseling core curriculum, it is best if such a curriculum is written down and easily accessible. Writing down a school counseling core curriculum both solidifies the plans for a school counselor and allows the curriculum to be shared with school stakeholders such as administrators, teachers, parents, and other student support services specialists.

4. *Comprehensive*—School counseling core curricula are most helpful when they comprehensively address student needs. These needs fall into three domains: academic, career, and social/emotional.

5. *Developmental*—Developmental considerations of students must be taken into account when designing any part of a comprehensive school counseling

program, and the core curriculum is no exception. Lesson topics and methods for teaching the lessons should both be developmentally appropriate for students. Additionally, developmental considerations include variations between levels (elementary school, middle school, and high school) as well as within levels (e.g., first-grade students versus fifth-grade students, ninth-grade students versus twelfth-grade students).

When a school counseling core curriculum contains these five characteristics, it allows school counselors to facilitate a systematic delivery of lessons and activities to all students. These lessons and activities should also align with the school counseling program's goals, mission and vision, and outcomes related to student performance standards. School counselors use their school counseling core curricula to promote students' skills, attitudes, and knowledge by providing instruction about academic achievement, career development, and social/emotional growth (ASCA, 2012).

Implementing the Core Curriculum

School counselors implement school counseling core curricula through instruction and group activities. Instruction can be provided to students by individual teaching by school counselors, school counselors team teaching with other educators, or school counselors assisting in teaching other educators. It can include teaching the core curriculum, leading learning activities, or providing follow-up instruction to small counseling groups or individual students as needed. Group activities include planned events outside the classroom that promote student development, such as leadership workshops, team-building projects, college visits, community field trips, or college fairs (ASCA, 2012).

Action Plans for the Core Curriculum

The ASCA National Model recommends using an action plan template to deliver school counseling core curriculum (ASCA, 2012). The action plan template provides a tool for school counselors to use to design, document, and implement their school counseling core curricula. Using this template allows school counselors to create an efficient plan for helping students develop the skills, knowledge, and attitudes appropriate for their developmental level in the academic, career, and social/emotional domains (ASCA, 2012). Found under the management component of the ASCA National Model, the core curriculum action plan template consists of a chart in which school counselors can design and document the details of a lesson or activity (ASCA, 2012, p. 69). A detailed list of the core curriculum action plan template elements are highlighted in Table 6.2, and an example action plan is provided in Figure 6.1.

Table 6.2 ASCA National Model Core Curriculum Action Plan Template (ASCA, 2012)

- Grade level
- Lesson topic
- Audience
- ASCA domain, standard (mindset or behavior), and competency
- Curriculum and materials needed
- Projected start and end time
- Expected number of students impacted
- Type of perception data collection
- Type of outcome data collected
- Contact person

Developing a School Counseling Core Curriculum

The Council for the Accreditation of Counseling & Related Educational Programs (CACREP) requires that school counseling training programs ensure that each student in their program "understands curriculum design, lesson plan development, classroom management strategies, and differentiated instructional strategies for teaching counseling and guidance-related material" (2009, School Counseling Program Standard K.3.). Differentiated instructional strategies and classroom management are explored in Chapters 7 and 8; the remainder of this chapter discusses how to design a core curriculum and how to develop lesson plans.

When developing a school counseling core curriculum, school counselors should work closely with their school administrators and teachers to design a curriculum that is most appropriate for their school and students. In some states, this school counseling core curriculum is already designed at the state level and mandated for all school counseling programs to follow. In other schools, district-level student support services committees design the curriculum for all district school counselors to use. If not mandated from a state or district, school counselors should develop curricula locally by forming committees with various stakeholders such as parents, guardians, administrators, community members, and teachers. School counselors should also consider using their advisory council to help design the school counseling core curriculum.

Once it is clear which individuals will be directly involved in designing a state, district, or individual school's school counseling curricula, five steps are involved in creating the curriculum. First, student needs are evaluated in order to determine how school counselors can help students best in their academic, career, and social/ emotional development. Second, standards are selected to make up the core curriculum. These standards should be based on previously identified student needs

Figure 6.1 Example Action Plan

JOHN SMITH HIGH SCHOOL   **ACADEMIC YEAR: (2015-2016)**

SCHOOL COUNSELING CORE CURRICULUM ACTION PLAN

GOAL: This curriculum will enhance the emotional, social, and physical well being of the student by empowering knowledge to enhance their future through informed decisions.

Lessons and Activities Related to Goal:

Grade Level	Lesson Topic	Lesson will Be Presented in Which Class/Subject	ASCA Domain, Standard and Competency	Curriculum and Materials	Projected Start/End	Process Data (Projected number of students affected)	Perception Data (Type of surveys/ assessments to be used)	Outcome Data (Achieve merit, attendance and/or behavioral data to be collected)	Contact Person
11-12	Planning and Developing Careers	Career Connections	Career Planning and Exploration	Computer room w/ internet access (optional) and "Education/ Training Worksheet" student worksheet, and "Career Requirements" worksheet	Sept./Oct.	355	Pre- and Post-Test	Can identify required skills and required training for given job descriptions	Mrs Smith

123

as well as student development in the academic, career, and social/emotional domains. Counselors can write their own standards, if they choose, or they may choose to use the ASCA Mindsets & Behaviors for Student Success (ASCA, 2014) or state standards, if available. Third, standards are organized into comprehensive units around similar topics. Fourth, units are delineated into lessons, and objectives are written for each lesson. These objectives should clearly state expected behaviors for students to display and how these behaviors will be measured. Fifth, each lesson is designed to include developmentally appropriate learning activities. Each of these steps is detailed below, beginning with the all-important needs assessment process.

NEEDS ASSESSMENTS

Before a school counseling core curriculum can be created, the needs of students must be known. Needs assessments are critical tools school counselors can use to determine these needs (Erford, 2007). It is important to recognize that unlike other forms of accountability in the ASCA National Model, such as school counseling program assessments and goal analyses (ASCA, 2012), which evaluate what presently exists in a school counseling program, needs assessments assess what the present condition of a school counseling program is compared to identified goals and objectives (Wiles & Bondi, 1984). Needs assessments serve two primary purposes:

1. Needs assessments help school counselors understand the needs of students according to stakeholders in their school community. These stakeholders include students, guardians, faculty, staff, and community members. Needs assessments are particularly beneficial in assessing the needs of underserved populations, such as students experiencing achievement gaps or differential access to resources (Erford, 2007).

2. Needs assessments assist school counselors in establishing the priorities and improvements that guide their comprehensive school counseling programs.

Both of these purposes demonstrate the value of needs assessments when designing school counseling core curricula. Several CACREP core curricular standards and school counseling program standards also acknowledge the need for school counselors to be familiar with creating needs assessments and evaluating the resulting data. For example, core curricular standard G.8.C. states that students should understand "statistical methods used in conducting research and program evaluation" and G.8.D. requires knowledge of "principles, models, and applications of needs assessment, program evaluation, and the use of findings to effect program modifications" (CACREP, 2009, p. 13). The CACREP school counseling program standards also specifically acknowledge the importance of needs assessments and program evaluation. Standard C.2. states in part that school counseling students must know how to "evaluate programs to enhance the academic, career, and personal/social development of students" (CACREP, 2009, p. 38) whereas G.3 requires students to be able to identify "various forms of needs assessments for academic, career, and personal/social development" (CACREP, 2009, p. 42). Exercise 6.1 invites you to consider a scenario in which a school counseling department does not have a school counseling core curriculum or recent needs assessment data.

EXERCISE 6.1

IMAGINING A SCHOOL COUNSELING DEPARTMENT WITH NO CORE CURRICULUM OR RECENT NEEDS ASSESSMENT

You are in your first year as a school counselor and are working at a middle school alongside two veteran school counselors who have worked at that particular school for more than 10 years each. After working at the school for several months, you learn that a needs assessment for the counseling program has not been conducted in nearly 15 years, and no core curriculum exists for the school counseling program. When you mention this to your fellow counselors, they dismiss the idea of having a curriculum and conducting a needs assessment.

Discussion Questions

1. What can you say or do to convince your fellow counselors of the importance of conducting regular needs assessments?

2. What can you say or do to convince your fellow counselors of the need for a school counseling core curriculum?

3. Once your fellow counselors agree that a needs assessment is warranted, what are your first steps in creating a school counseling core curriculum?

There are two types of common needs assessments: data-driven needs assessments and perception-based needs assessments (Erford, 2007). Both types can be used to inform school counseling core curricula.

Data-Driven Needs Assessments

Data-driven needs assessments are focused on assessing real needs rather than perceived ones (Erford, 2007). The types of information that can inform data-driven needs assessments should be listed in what ASCA calls *the school data profile*. This profile is a summary of a school's record over a period of time and includes data about attendance, behavior, safety, and achievement (ASCA, 2012). When conducting a data-driven needs assessment, school counselors can begin by examining this profile and drawing conclusions about school needs. The ASCA National Model includes eight questions to ask when analyzing the data:

1. What strengths do the data suggest about your school?

2. What concerns do the data indicate at your school?

3. What achievement gaps exist in your school?

4. Are there any patterns of change in attendance rates?

5. What do the safety data tell you about your school?

6. How, if at all, is your school counseling program addressing gaps shown by the data?

7. How can your school counseling program help close gaps or address other concerns posed by the data?

8. What additional data are needed to fully understand the needs of your school? (ASCA, 2012)

By examining school data, school counselors can "present a picture of the current situation of student needs and issues and examine the practices that can lead to higher levels of success" (Dahir & Stone, 2003, para. 18). School counselors should examine both aggregated data, which combine students' results together to show schoolwide or gradewide results, and disaggregated data, which divide student data by subpopulations in order to analyze performance differences between and among groups. School counselors can use aggregated data to assess how the average student performs in a given class, grade, or school. Disaggregated data can be used to identify evidence of gaps in student performance and provide direction for interventions needed to close such gaps (Dahir & Stone, 2003; Erford, 2007).

At a minimum, when exploring data, school counselors should examine measures of central tendency and frequency (Oberman, 2010). When examining standardized test scores, for instance, school counselors should consider a data set's mean (average), median (middle score), and mode (most frequently occurring score) across grades and subpopulations. When examining attendance data, school counselors should investigate the frequency with which certain individuals or groups of students did not attend school. Beyond frequency and central tendency, school counselors may conduct more sophisticated analyses such as correlations, means tests, and regression analyses in order to further understand relationships and differences among student data (Oberman, 2010).

Three specific types of data may prove useful for school counselors conducting data-driven needs assessments: achievement data, behavior data, and school counseling data. These categories are further explained below.

Achievement Data

Achievement data are comprised of information regarding student academic performance. These data may include student course grades, benchmark test scores, end-of-course standardized test scores, promotion and retention rates, and graduation rates. Each of these measures is designed to measure how students are performing in the classroom in order to learn and successfully progress through the education system. School counselors benefit from examining achievement data in order to assess which needs they ought to address in the academic domain of student development. Achievement data may demonstrate gaps between different classrooms, different subpopulations of students, or between course grades and standardized test scores. Such gaps could suggest a variety of needs for school counselors to attempt to address when designing a school counseling core curriculum.

Behavior Data

Student infractions, suspensions, and expulsions traditionally make up behavior data. These kinds of information can help school counselors understand which types of behavior problems are most common among their students as well as which students are most commonly receiving behavior infractions. School counselors can examine behavior data for patterns indicating specific needs in the social/emotional domain of student development. In addition, behavior data can shed light on any patterns among faculty, staff, or administration who are involved in writing behavior infractions. Any of these patterns could serve as needs that school counselors should address through their comprehensive school counseling programs and, likely, their school counseling core curriculum. For example, potential needs that could emerge from behavior data include training in social skills, self-control, sexual harassment, and anger management.

School Counseling Data

School counseling data can also provide useful information to reference in a data-driven needs assessment. Such data can include pre- and posttest data from implementing previous classroom guidance lessons with students. These data may indicate whether specific needs are present among students or whether previous lessons adequately addressed these needs and do not need to be conducted with specific classes in the future. In addition, any data that school counselors have recorded about student visits to their office or counseling referrals can also be reviewed in data-driven needs assessments. This information may shed light on patterns of present problems that indicate student needs.

Ethical Considerations

Is examining school data an ethical obligation?

Employing data-driven needs assessments is not only best practice, it is an ethical obligation. ASCA Ethical Standard A.3.b requires that professional school counselors use "data to help close achievement gaps and opportunity gaps" in order to "ensure equitable academic, career, postsecondary access, and personal/social opportunities for all students" (ASCA, 2010, p. 2). Such an assertion suggests that to ignore school data indicating achievement gaps among students is an ethical violation.

Perception-Based Needs Assessments

Perception-based needs assessments are focused on the perceptions of school stakeholders (i.e., parents, administrators, teachers, community members) regarding primary student needs. School counselors should choose which stakeholders are best to survey based on which populations are most likely to be informed of school issues or needs, which groups are most accessible, and which groups will be most likely to complete and return the needs assessments. Regardless of which specific populations are selected, however, triangulation of needs should be attempted, if possible (Erford, 2007). By obtaining the perspectives of several populations, school counselors can likely conclude that needs suggested by multiple groups are those of highest priority.

Needs Assessment Content

In order to obtain perception-based needs assessment data to inform and guide school counseling core curricula, school counselors must be thoughtful and intentional in the design of needs assessment content and format. When selecting assessment content, school counselors may benefit from considering the following questions:

- What kind of information would be most helpful to learn from this needs assessment?
- Do I have a specific concern I want to ask stakeholders about or do I want more global feedback from this needs assessment?
- What type of data from this needs assessment would be most beneficial for planning my school counseling core curriculum and future classroom guidance lessons?
- Am I more interested in the *frequency* of needs or *priority* of needs, as perceived by stakeholders?
- Would it be more beneficial to assess student needs through a series of related questions or by directly asking which needs they perceive as most important?

In addition to using these questions to guide the needs assessment content, school counselors should be sure to use topical content rather than service-related content (Erford, 2007). For example, a needs assessment surveying student opinions about substance use, bullying, social skills, and graduation requirements would be more valuable than one assessing group counseling, classroom guidance, or consultation techniques. Content should also be related to a school counseling program's vision, mission, and goals so data can be easily translated into classroom guidance standards and goals (Erford, 2007).

In addition, school counselors should decide in advance whether their needs assessment will be anonymous. On one hand, by creating an anonymous needs assessment and allowing respondents to provide information without having to disclose their name or other identifying information, respondents may provide more honest, valuable information about needs at their school. On the other hand, asking respondents for their names, particularly when implementing student needs assessments, can serve as a convenient way to learn about particular student needs to address. For example, if a student is suicidal or knows of a classmate who is, such information can be disclosed on a needs assessment. Additionally, if a particular class or group of friends is experiencing an issue, it is beneficial to know which students are involved in order to help address the issue. Although other students' names can be collected anonymously from concerned stakeholders, this kind of information is typically more reliable if the respondent's identity is disclosed as well.

Needs Assessment Format

After school counselors determine the ideal content for their perception-based needs assessments, they should decide which format is most appropriate for the content they intend to use. Four example formats are described below.

Questionnaires. Questionnaires consist of formal or informal surveys and are the most commonly used format for perception-based needs assessment (Erford, 2007; Schmidt, 2003). Common questionnaire questions include those about students' attitudes, behaviors, or concerns. These questions should be based on standards that school counselors are considering for their school counseling core curriculum. For example, if a school counselor is focused on incorporating more standards from the career domain into its core curriculum, then needs assessment questions should address student knowledge, skills, and attitudes toward career counseling.

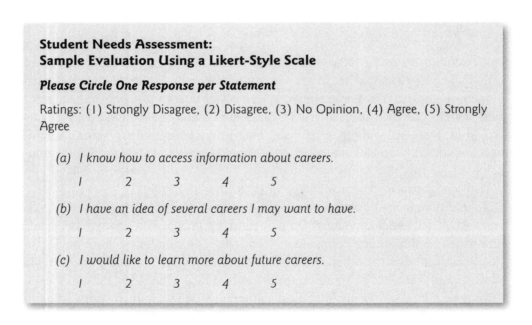

Student Needs Assessment:
Sample Evaluation Using a Likert-Style Scale

Please Circle One Response per Statement

Ratings: (1) Strongly Disagree, (2) Disagree, (3) No Opinion, (4) Agree, (5) Strongly Agree

(a) *I know how to access information about careers.*

   1   2   3   4   5

(b) *I have an idea of several careers I may want to have.*

   1   2   3   4   5

(c) *I would like to learn more about future careers.*

   1   2   3   4   5

Inventories. Unlike questionnaires, inventories collect frequency data instead of opinion data. Inventories can be used to determine the number of times a student engages in a certain behavior as reported by a student, parent, or teacher. Inventories can also be used to directly ask school stakeholders about the needs they perceive present at the school. For example, an inventory can provide a list of potential needs, such as bullying prevention, graduation requirements, college entrance requirements, study skills development, and so on. Respondents can also indicate which of the listed needs they perceive as the most important. This tool enables the school counseling department to effectively prioritize interventions to meet the most highly perceived needs of school stakeholders.

Open-Ended Surveys. Open-ended surveys are typically easier to design and allow respondents to contribute broader, more diverse data. However, these assessments are generally more challenging to interpret because of their larger range of data. In addition, it can often be difficult to translate open-ended survey responses into goals and objectives for school counseling programs, including for the school counseling core curriculum (Erford, 2007).

Example Open-Ended Survey
Questions for Parent/Guardian Needs Assessment

Please Respond to the Following Questions

(a) *What concerns do you have about your child as he or she enters middle school?*

(b) *How can the school counseling department at this school best help you and your child in the coming school year?*

Focus Groups and Interviews. Rather than distributing a questionnaire or inventory, school counselors may opt to conduct focus groups or interviews with school stakeholders in order to gain a sufficient understanding of school and student needs. A focus group requires interviewing multiple individuals together in a group setting. Focus group participants answer the same series of questions posed by a moderator while dialoging with one another about responses. Interviews entail meeting one-on-one with individual stakeholders and asking a series of questions. When used as a needs assessment, both focus groups and interviews can help school counselors gain an in-depth understanding of the needs that one stakeholder or a group of stakeholders believes is important to address. If multiple focus groups or interviews are conducted, school counselors can record and transcribe the answers shared and then review all transcripts for common themes about needs to address.

Data Collection

When collecting data using a questionnaire, inventory, or open-ended survey, school counselors must decide how they will distribute their assessment to respondents. Whether collecting data electronically or using paper and pencil, each method has its advantages and disadvantages.

Electronic Needs Assessments. Creating an electronic needs assessment is becoming an increasingly simple task. Online survey software such as Survey Monkey (http://www.surveymonkey.com) or Qualtrics (http://www.qualtrics.com) allow users to create online surveys with a variety of question types. These surveys can be distributed to respondents via web links and completed online. In many school districts, such survey software has been previously purchased and is already available for use by the district. Electronic needs assessments then can be designed by collaborating with school or district information technology personnel who are familiar with this software.

Arguably the greatest benefit of electronic needs assessments is their ease in calculating results; after collecting data, the survey software automatically collates and tabulates data for each question. In addition, electronic surveys can be easily distributed to school stakeholders by e-mailing the survey webpage address to parents/guardians and school staff. Students can also complete electronic surveys by logging onto school computers and clicking on a bookmarked link to the survey. Unfortunately, electronic access can also be a disadvantage when striving to collect data from a representative population of school stakeholders. Not all parents/guardians have Internet access or e-mail addresses, and this distribution method may exclude the voices of respondents with valuable information to share. Similarly, the electronic distribution of a needs assessment to students can be challenging. In some schools, not every classroom is equipped with computer access for every student, and in these cases, paper-and-pencil needs assessments proved to be more convenient. More and more, schools are aiming to provide every student use of a technological device to help close this gap.

Paper-and-Pencil Needs Assessments. As a result of the disadvantages described above, school counselors may choose to distribute paper-and-pencil needs assessments rather than using electronic methods. Such needs assessments can be easily designed in a word processor and printed so that hard copies can be distributed to school stakeholders. This printed version can usually be easily distributed to students and school staff to complete and return to the school counselor. Unfortunately, paper-and-pencil needs assessments may be more difficult to distribute to guardians. Some counselors found moderate success getting paper-and-pencil needs assessments to guardians by distributing them at teacher/guardian conferences and informational parent nights. Other disadvantages of paper-and-pencil needs assessments include the cost of printing the needs assessments and the time required for data input and analysis. Unlike an electronic needs assessment, data from paper-and-pencil needs assessments must be entered and tabulated by hand.

Regardless of the format used, it is prudent to design a needs assessment that is only approximately one page in length. Longer needs assessments may deter respondents from completing the assessment, thus decreasing the amount of valuable data obtained (Erford, 2007).

Frequency of Conducting Needs Assessments

Given the frequency of standardized testing in K–12 schools currently, school counselors would benefit from conducting data-driven needs assessments on a yearly basis. Doing so will allow school counselors and fellow staff members to recognize any concerning patterns in data before they become extensive trends in student achievement. However, school counselors may benefit from conducting perception-based needs assessments less frequently. This is in part because designing and implementing such needs assessments can be massive administrative undertakings that could monopolize a school counselor's time if conducted yearly (Erford, 2007). Perception-based needs assessment data are most valuable when they are used in a continuous cycle of evaluation. If assessments are conducted too frequently, school counselors may be assessing perceived needs before new initiatives have been fully implemented. By conducting perception-based needs assessments every few years rather than yearly, school counselors allow ample time for program development and evaluation to occur (Erford, 2007). Though there is no designated formula for specifically how often perception-based needs assessments should occur, Gysbers and Henderson (2000) recommend doing so every three years, and Erford (2007) recommends every six years for programs in need of large overhauls.

Translating Data into Classroom Guidance Programming

After collecting information from data-based and perception-based needs assessments, school counselors can begin translating the findings into their school counseling core curriculum. This process is made easier if needs assessments are designed correctly and rooted in standards such as the ASCA Mindsets & Behaviors for Student Success (ASCA, 2014; Erford, 2007). To begin using needs assessment data to create core curriculum, needs must first be prioritized. If an inventory was used as a perception-based needs assessment and respondents were asked to prioritize needs themselves, school counselors may agree with and use this order of priorities. However, information from data-based needs assessments can also be used to inform perception-based needs assessment prioritization and a new list of prioritized needs can be created based on both data sources. If questionnaires without prioritization are used to collect data, school counselors can tally the needs that respondents indicate as important and interpret the needs with the most tallies as those of highest priority. Triangulation should also be used to compare data from different groups of stakeholders, such as students, guardians, and faculty/staff (Erford, 2007). Exercise 6.2 asks you to consider how you might prioritize different needs as perceived by different groups of school stakeholders.

EXERCISE 6.2

PRIORITIZING DIFFERENT NEEDS AS PERCEIVED BY DIFFERENT GROUPS OF SCHOOL STAKEHOLDERS

You are in your fifth year working as a high school counselor. After organizing a schoolwide needs assessment, you and your counseling colleagues analyze the data obtained in the needs assessment. It is as follows:

- Students indicated that they believe their three most important needs are learning more about graduation requirements, receiving more career counseling, and reducing bullying.
- Teachers indicated that they believe the three most important needs of students are addressing substance abuse, increasing diversity awareness, and improving test-taking skills.
- Parents indicated that they believe the three most important needs of students are managing stress, learning anger-management skills, and improving self-esteem.

Discussion Questions

1. How would you make sense of these conflicting results?

2. Is there one group of stakeholders whose responses you would prioritize over the others? Why or why not?

3. Of the suggested needs, select three topics and design a classroom guidance lesson for each topic that could help address the need. Justify how your classroom guidance lesson would address this topic as well as how your lesson plan would address the ASCA Mindsets & Behaviors for Student Success.

IDENTIFYING STANDARDS

The second step in creating a school counseling core curriculum involves identifying standards and competencies. This process requires a comparison of student needs to the mission and vision of the school counseling program and deciding what outcomes are appropriate for students in that school. Detailed standards can either be selected from the ASCA Mindsets & Behaviors for Student Success (ASCA, 2014) or another school or district's counseling standards, or they may be drafted from scratch if standards are not already written that meet the needs of a school. Even if standards are drafted new, however, the ASCA National Model (ASCA, 2012) and the ASCA Mindsets & Behaviors for Student Success (ASCA, 2014) should be considered in the process. Though school counselors or curriculum committees may not choose to integrate all of the student standards into their own curriculum, these standards should not be ignored entirely, as they provide a valuable, agreed-upon framework of competencies for students in areas of academic, career, and social/emotional development.

DEVELOPING A UNIT

Once standards have been selected for a school counseling core curriculum, the standards can be grouped into logically formed units around similar themes. For example, the ASCA Mindsets & Behaviors for Student Success contains standards grouped into three domains: academic, career, and social/emotional development (ASCA, 2014). Though these same units can also be adopted for a school counseling core curriculum, school counselors may want to develop their own units. For instance, standards relating to social/emotional content can be broken down further into a unit containing standards about interpersonal relations among students, a unit with standards about self-esteem, and a unit with standards about respecting school staff.

When designing units, both vertical and horizontal considerations should be kept in mind. *Vertical articulation* refers to efforts to build a curriculum that sequentially contributes to students' skills and competencies. This means that units for one grade level build on those taught in previous grade levels and prepare students for the standards they will learn in future grades. Vertical articulation ensures that the standards students are learning are grouped into units so that no single lesson is isolated from the curriculum nor redundant of others taught. *Horizontal articulation* means creating connections between counseling curriculum and content in other subject areas, such as social studies, reading, math, and science. By integrating themes from other curricular areas into units in school counseling core curricula, school counselors can create a more enhanced learning experience for students.

WRITING OBJECTIVES

After student standards have been grouped into units, school counselors can begin organizing classroom guidance lessons to account for these standards and units.

Whether one lesson covers all standards in a unit or a separate lesson is used to teach students each standard independently, a school counseling core curriculum should ensure that all standards will be accounted for across lessons. Before classroom guidance lessons are drafted, however, objectives for each lesson must first be established. The importance of defining lesson objectives prior to identifying learning activities is illustrated by Wiggins and McTighe's (1998) backward design model. This model indicates that planning is most effective when desired results are identified before determining specific learning tasks. Identifying and listing specific learning objectives will assist school counselors in designing meaningful lessons that are tied to the standards in the school counseling core curriculum.

Quality learning objectives are based on the outcomes that school counselors want to achieve when students participate in each lesson (Goodnough, Pérusse, & Erford, 2007). Suitable learning objectives also each contain four components: the intended audience, expected behavior, conditions, and expected performance (Erford & McKechnie, 2004).

1. *Intended audience*—Learning objectives should be written specifically for the audience for whom they are intended. For most lessons, the audience will be each student individually participating in the lesson, but sometimes the audience is the entire class participating in the lesson.

2. *Expected behavior*—The behavior(s) that school counselors wish to see as a result of students' participation in a classroom guidance lesson should be listed clearly and specifically. Such behaviors include the cognitive, affective, or physical outcomes that may result because of the lesson.

3. *Conditions*—The conditions of a learning objective refer to the context in which the expected behavior will occur and be observed. The conditions also include how the learning objective will be measured.

4. *Expected performance*—Lastly, a learning objective should have an expected or ideal performance related to a student's behavior. This may include the frequency or duration of a desired behavior in order for the objective to be considered met.

Using the components above, school counselors can design objectives that clearly outline what is expected of students and how these behaviors will be measured. For example, Table 6.3 outlines a sample learning objective, which demonstrates how learning objectives can be written for a particular standard in each of the three school counseling domains (academic, career, and social/emotional development). Each learning objective includes all four recommended components.

Table 6.3 Sample Learning Objectives

Component		**Sample Learning Objective (Academic Development)** **(ASCA Mindsets & Behaviors for Student Success, Learning Strategy #4)**
	Intended Audience	All students in Mrs. Smith's 5th-period study skills class . . .
	Expected Behavior	will apply time-management and task-management skills . . .
	Conditions of Learning	by recording all school assignments and activities in their school planner and sharing completed daily entries with Mrs. Smith . . .
	Expected Performance	on a weekly basis for the duration of the semester.
Component		**Sample Learning Objective (Career Development)** **(ASCA Mindsets & Behaviors for Student Success, Learning Strategy #7)**
	Intended Audience	All students in Mr. Tucker's eleventh-grade chemistry classes . . .
	Expected Behavior	will be able to identify long- and short-term career goals . . .
	Conditions of Learning	by completing a career workbook plan of study . . .
	Expected Performance	by the end of the fall semester.
Component		**Sample Learning Objective (Social/emotional Development)** **(ASCA Mindsets & Behaviors for Student Success, Self-Management Skill #5)**
	Intended Audience	All ninth-grade students in the Carl Francis High School freshman academy . . .
	Expected Behavior	will demonstrate perseverance to achieve goals . . .
	Conditions of Learning	by identifying a desired goal, working toward the goal, and evaluating it . . .
	Expected Performance	on a semiannual basis while revisiting and adjusting prior goals as necessary.

DEVELOPING CLASSROOM GUIDANCE LESSONS

Following the establishment of learning objectives, classroom guidance lessons should be designed to provide assessment and learning activities that will ensure that objectives are delivered in an engaging, developmentally appropriate way. During the process of drafting lessons, school counselors should select the assessment tools they will use to evaluate whether students have mastered the standards and written objectives of the lesson. This task comprises the second stage of Wiggins and McTighe's (1998) three-step backward-design model, in which educators determine acceptable evidence to identify whether the learner has achieved the stated objectives and learning goals of a lesson. Assessments may vary from formal to informal measures, but it is important that a variety of forms be used to target students' depth of understanding.

Once assessments are selected, the remainder of a classroom guidance lesson plan can be conceptualized into three distinct parts: introduction, developmental activities, and conclusion. When a lesson is well-designed in each of these three parts, it is more likely to engage and interest students, thus allowing them to become invested and learn more (Goodnough et al., 2007).

The opening of a lesson sets the tone for what is to follow. When introducing a lesson, it is recommended that school counselors communicate an overview to students about what they will be learning (Goodnough et al., 2007). By emphasizing to students the purpose of a lesson and how it will benefit them, students may be more likely to recognize the lesson's relevance to their life and participate because they believe the lesson is a valuable one. In addition, developmental classroom guidance lessons build on students' previous knowledge and developmental stages. This process, known as *scaffolding*, supports students in moving beyond rote knowledge to develop an improved depth of understanding of content (Childre, Sands, & Pope, 2009). Furthermore, it can be helpful to explain to students that they already hold some knowledge related to the current lesson, as this can help build student interest and efficacy. As Goodnough et al. (2007) explained, "Activating previous knowledge helps students orient themselves to the lesson. It shows them that they already know some important information and . . . it also motivates students and provides a continued rationale for their efforts" (p. 159). In order to ensure that introductory activities are effective and engaging, school counselors should open lessons with essential questions, key vocabulary, problems to solve, and current issues. These activities not only engage students in the beginning of the lesson, but they also make learning more meaningful to students (Wiggins & McTighe, 1998). Other stimulus activities may include movement and props, depending on the setting and type of lesson. Regardless of the type of stimulus activity that is enlisted, it is the school counselor's responsibility to ensure that it will facilitate a connection between students' prior knowledge and the new information being presented (Skowron, 2006).

Next is the developmental activities portion of a lesson, which is also step three in the backward-design model (Wiggins & McTighe, 1998). These activities should be designed to facilitate students' mastery of the lesson's learning objectives and should be appropriate for students' cognitive and developmental strengths and weaknesses. Historically, school counselors have been encouraged to design learning activities that appeal to a range of student learning styles and Gardner's (1999) multiple intelligences (Goodnough et al., 2007). Recent research, however, suggests that learning styles may be nothing more than learning preferences and that student performance is equivalent regardless of the style in which one learns (Riener & Willingham, 2010). Irrespective of the outcome of this research debate, school counselors benefit from incorporating a range of different activities into their lessons. Such a variety can keep students engaged and appeal to different students' preferences. Examples of diverse learning activities include having students create a project, journal, role-play, create art, or do partner work or group work (Goodnough et al., 2007). Didactic presentations can also be beneficial as learning activities in some classroom guidance lessons in order to transmit key information to students. Lecturing should not be used all the time, however, and when used, it should be sensitive to the developmental needs of students (such as their attention spans).

Lastly, a classroom guidance lesson should end with a conclusion. The conclusion should include a summary of the overall learning objective for the lesson as well as a few important points students should keep in mind (Goodnough et al., 2007). For example, some counselors end every classroom guidance lesson with a "Big Takeaway" that consists of the most important main points students will remember from the lesson. If students forget some of the smaller details and information provided to them in the lesson, it may be comforting to know that many remember the "Big Takeaways" for years to come. Closing summaries are also helpful to highlight to students how the learning activities they participated in relate to their learning objectives for the lesson and how those objectives can be translated into their experiences outside of the classroom. When concluding a lesson, school counselors should conduct an assessment and distribute an evaluation that will assist in measuring student outcomes and improving the lesson for future audiences. Classroom guidance assessment is further detailed in Chapter 7.

By designing each classroom guidance lesson with these three components in mind, school counselors can ensure that lessons are appropriately tied to learning objectives, that students are engaging in the lessons being presented to them, and that student learning outcomes are measured. Though classroom guidance lessons range in type and activity, the three components detailed here ought to be present in most lessons. Exercise 6.3 asks you to apply a backward-design model to create a sample classroom guidance lesson.

EXERCISE 6.3

APPLY A BACKWARD-DESIGN MODEL TO CREATE A SAMPLE CLASSROOM GUIDANCE LESSON

You are an experienced elementary school counselor with a positive working relationship with your administrators. One day, your principal meets with you to discuss a growing concern about fourth- and fifth-grade students bullying one another, particularly via social media. She asks you to implement a series of classroom guidance lessons to address this concern.

1. How could you use backward design to design these lessons?

2. How could you use backward design to design this unit of lessons?

3. What are three objectives that you could draft for this unit of lessons?

4. Select one lesson for this unit and design it.

5. How will you account for developmental considerations, multicultural considerations, and students with special needs when designing this lesson?

In addition to these components, when designing classroom guidance lessons, school counselors should be cognizant of the developmental considerations, multicultural considerations, and special needs of their students. Both CACREP core curricular standards (G.3.E., G.3.F.) and school counseling program standards (A.6., E.4., F.1., L.3.) emphasize the need for school counselors to understand typical and atypical student development, recognize multicultural counseling issues, and differentiate interventions when designing classroom guidance lessons. These important elements of lesson design are explained next.

Developmental Guidance

School counselors adhere to various counseling theories and corresponding techniques to effectively work with students in their schools. However, theory extends beyond individual interactions with students and plays a key role in the design of effective classroom guidance lessons as well. Developmental counseling theories appear to be the most appropriate for classroom guidance (Goodnough et al., 2007). Developmental counseling theories include those by Piaget, Erikson, Loevinger, Kohlberg, Gilligan, and Selman (see Table 6.4 for descriptions of each). Because developmental stages form the basis for school counseling programs, considering these stages while designing and implementing classroom guidance is essential (Goodnough et al., 2007).

Common across all of the developmental theories mentioned is the idea that developmental changes occur during one's lifespan and that successfully moving into a new developmental stage is contingent on the successful completion of tasks in earlier stages. School counselors can use developmental theories when conducting classroom guidance programming to ensure that students' developmental changes are addressed in a sequential manner in their school counseling core curriculum. By using a developmental theory to frame classroom guidance efforts, school counselors can make sure that their services help students build on

Table 6.4 Descriptions of Developmental Theories

Theorist	Description
Jean Piaget	Four Stages of Development: **[1] Sensorimotor** (Birth–age 2) world perception via five senses and egocentricity; **[2] Preoperational** (ages 2–7) two substages: symbolic function and intuitive thought, egocentricity persists; **[3] Concrete Operational** (ages 7–11) logical thinking and understanding of reversibility; and **[4] Formal Operational** (age 11+) development of abstract reasoning
Erik Erikson	Eight Stages of Psychosocial Development: (Birth–18 mo.) trust vs. mistrust, (2–3) autonomy vs. shame and doubt, (3–5) initiative vs. guilt, (6–11) industry vs. inferiority, (12–18) identity vs. role confusion, (19–40) intimacy vs. isolation, (40–65) generativity vs. stagnation, (65+) ego integrity vs. despair
Jane Loevinger	Ten Stages of Ego Development: Based on Erikson's psychosocial model and the works of Harry Stack Sullivan. The ego is viewed as a lens or frame of reference one uses to construct and interpret the world.
Lawrence Kohlberg	Six Stages of Moral Development: Kohlberg's theory posits that moral reasoning, the basis for ethical behavior, has six identifiable developmental stages, each more adequate at responding to moral dilemmas than its predecessor.
Carol Gilligan	Three Stages of Moral Development: An adaptation of Lawrence Kohlberg's (1973) theory of moral development with same stages of preconventional, conventional, and postconventional. Emphasis of theory is on moral development of women.
Robert Selman	Five Stages of Perspective Taking: Focuses on the development of role taking (the ability to perceive issues from another person's perspective). The theory purports that role taking is essential in order to understand another person's feelings, thoughts, or motives (Siegler, DeLoache, & Eisenberg, 2011).

previous efforts and build toward new developmental milestones. This strategy is preferable to that of implementing unrelated, isolated units and lessons (Goodnough et al., 2007).

Bloom's taxonomy describes a classification system for a particular area of development, *cognitive complexity* (Bloom, Engelhart, Furst, Hill, & Krathwohl, 1956). The taxonomy includes six hierarchical levels that are cumulative, meaning they build on the skills learned in previous levels and range from low cognitive complexity to high cognitive complexity. The levels are knowledge, comprehension, application, analysis, synthesis, and evaluation (Bloom et al., 1956; Haag Granello, 2000). School counselors can use Bloom's taxonomy as a guide when designing classroom guidance lesson plans. The framework can be used to ensure that lesson plans developmentally meet the learning needs of students as well as occasionally challenge students' developmental levels by encouraging skills at higher levels of cognitive complexity.

Note that developmental counseling theories serve as guiding paradigms for understanding human development, but these differ from counseling theories, which focus on techniques and approaches that bring about change in counseling. School counselors can use counseling theories to guide their work in individual and group counseling and developmental counseling theories to understand student development. Exercise 6.4 invites you to consider how you might alter the same lesson to be developmentally appropriate for students in different grades.

EXERCISE 6.4

ALTER THE SAME LESSON TO BE DEVELOPMENTALLY APPROPRIATE FOR STUDENTS IN DIFFERENT GRADES

You are in your second year as an elementary school counselor, and you have just completed a unit of classroom guidance lessons with third-grade students. This unit focused on improving students' diversity awareness by exploring their own cultures, the cultures of their classmates, and character traits such as compassion and empathy. After completing the final lesson with the third-grade students, a kindergarten teacher approaches you about presenting the unit to his class. He mentions that he has heard positive things about the lessons and wants his students to increase their diversity awareness as well. The teacher's classroom is a collaborative learning classroom in which students with and without disabilities learn alongside one another, with both gifted education students and regular education students.

Discussion Questions

1. What might happen if you gave the same lessons that you gave to the third-grade students to these kindergarten students? Could positive outcomes result? Could negative outcomes result?

2. How might you adapt this classroom guidance unit and lessons to meet the developmental needs of kindergarten students?

3. How can you address the needs of all students in a collaborating learning classroom?

Multicultural Considerations

Though development frameworks are useful tools to conceptualize student development, not all students develop in the same fashion. Differences vary greatly among students, and these differences impact the ways students develop, perceive the world, and learn. If school counselors want to ensure that they are helping all students, as the ASCA National Model expects (ASCA, 2012), then multicultural differences among students cannot be overlooked when designing classroom guidance lesson plans. Acknowledging student differences when designing classroom guidance lessons also acknowledges numerous calls to value, respect, and respond to the cultural influences of students in ASCA position statements, ASCA Ethical Standards for School Counselors, and professional literature (Grothaus, 2012).

Defining Multiculturalism

Gone are the days when the term *multicultural* referred only to race or ethnicity. As the United States has increased in racial and ethnic diversity since the 1980s, cultural, religious, and linguistic diversity has increased as well and become accepted aspects of multiculturalism. Additional characteristics such as gender, sexual orientation, socioeconomic status, and ability level have also come to be seen as part of one's culture and multiculturalism in the U.S. (Sleeter & Grant, 2009). Given this all-encompassing definition of multiculturalism, it is easy to recognize that all counseling is multicultural counseling (Pedersen, 1991). For school counselors, multicultural counseling does not stop at the office door. Classroom guidance lessons also must be conducted using multicultural competence, and designing these lessons with multicultural considerations in mind is the first step to doing so.

Designing Multiculturally Competent Lessons

When designing classroom guidance lessons, it can be helpful to incorporate equity pedagogy into lesson plans. *Equity pedagogy* refers to techniques that have been proven to facilitate the achievement of students from diverse groups (Banks, 2004). Cooperative learning, for example, is a technique in which students are required to work together to successfully complete a task. In cooperative learning, students must share leadership responsibilities and responsibility for each other's achievement. When students succeed in cooperative learning, their efforts are rewarded for cooperating and sharing their learning with their classmates. This equity pedagogy technique assists students in developing conflict management skills, listening skills, and other group process skills (Sleeter & Grant, 2009). In addition to these benefits, cooperative learning is advantageous to use with students for two additional reasons. First, research has shown that cooperative learning may align better with the collaborative mindset emphasized in African American, Mexican American, and Hawaiian cultures rather than the competitive mindset emphasized in U.S. culture (Banks, 1993; Herring & White, 1995). An emphasis on the collective good rather than independent well-being is reflected in cooperative learning and may assist in diverse students' learning because of its familiarity. Second, research indicates that cooperative learning helps all students in reducing stereotypes and social rejection because of race, disability, or gender (Sleeter & Grant, 2009).

In addition to cooperative learning, school counselors can design art and music activities for classroom guidance lessons in order to appeal to a range of cultures and abilities. Art activities allow students to feel a sense of control over their own expression and to use personally relevant popular media or images in their art (Bruneau & Protivnak, 2012). Music activities can also allow students to express their cultural backgrounds in meaningful ways. Rap therapy, for instance, is a five-stage process for creating meaning through rap music. It has been documented as a useful activity with adolescents because it allows them to express their language and culture in a familiar way (Elligan, 2000). One key consideration when designing lessons with art or music activities is that a lesson's emphasis should be on the process of creating art rather than the final product students create (Bruneau & Protivnak, 2012). Overall, designing classroom guidance lessons with art and music activities provides an opportunity for students to express their unique cultural backgrounds without school counselors imposing their own cultural perspectives.

Lastly, school counselors can design culturally inclusive classroom lessons by directly integrating content relevant to students' lives (Grothaus, 2012). This content may take the form of books featuring culturally diverse characters, movie clips in languages other than English, or case studies of students who identify as LGBTQ or who have disabilities. Even when designing lessons for standards that do not traditionally have a multicultural focus (e.g., study skills, career exploration), school counselors can create culturally relevant lessons by integrating content and examples featuring a variety of cultures. This content integration can be particularly powerful when considering the expansive definition of multiculturalism (including race, ethnicity, language, socioeconomic status, gender, sexual orientation, religion, and ability level) and regularly incorporating diverse content addressing each of these characteristics in lessons.

Working with Students with Special Needs

Though ability level is often included when referring to multiculturalism (Sleeter & Grant, 2009), designing lessons for students with special needs can involve additional considerations, therefore we have outlined separate recommendations for designing lessons for this population. In any given public school classroom, there are usually some students with special needs, whether these needs have been formally diagnosed and addressed through an Individualized Education Program (IEP) or have been informally noticed and addressed by classroom teachers. In order to work with all students as the ASCA National Model charges (ASCA, 2012), school counselors must design classroom guidance lessons that are sensitive to the needs of students with disabilities and beneficial for all students. We have outlined four recommended steps below to integrate the needs of students with disabilities when designing classroom guidance lessons.

Step 1: When designing a classroom guidance lesson for a specific class of students, school counselors should have access to a list of students in that class who have current IEPs. A list of these students can be generated from a school database such as SASI. Prior to designing a lesson, it is critical to review students' IEPs in order to learn of their disability and the documentation related to their disability, what accommodations they are required to have in the classroom, and what strategies teachers and guardians have used with the student in the past. These previously used strategies can highlight which techniques have worked well with a student as well as which strategies have not been successful. By reviewing students' IEPs, school counselors can begin to understand how they should design a lesson plan in order to meet the needs of certain students.

Step 2: Although reviewing IEPs can provide school counselors with a lot of information about certain students, it is almost always beneficial to also consult with the classroom teacher of the class that a lesson plan is being designed for. For example, though IEPs provide invaluable data at times, these plans are typically only updated once or twice a year. Teachers, however, can provide recent updates and information about a student's current performance in class, what needs are apparent, and which strategies work well to address these needs. Moreover, consulting with teachers allows school counselors to learn about students who have needs that may not be formally addressed by IEPs. These students' needs must also be considered when designing a successful classroom guidance unit.

Ethical Considerations

What ethical considerations should you keep in mind when consulting with teachers about students? Does such consultation constitute a breach of student confidentiality?

When working with a student with special needs, it can be invaluable to consult with teachers in order to learn about successful teaching strategies for working with that student. As service providers, school counselors are permitted to consult with other educators in order to improve services for students. Such consultation would not constitute a breach of confidentiality if it involved discussing only the minimal amount of information needed to improve services. ASCA Ethical Standard C.2.E. highlights this behavior. It states that professional school counselors

"recognize the powerful role of ally that faculty and administrators who function high in personal/social developmental skills can play in supporting students in stress, and carefully filter confidential student information to give these allies what they 'need to know' in order to advantage the student. . . . The primary focus and obligation is always on the student when it comes to sharing confidential information." (ASCA, 2010, p. 4)

Step 3: After learning about specific students and their needs in a class, school counselors can begin examining how a new or existing lesson can be redesigned in order to meet student needs. Two approaches can be used to do so: differentiated instruction or universal design for learning (UDL). Akos, Cockman, and Strickland define differentiation as "an instructional philosophy aimed at equitably meeting the learning needs of all students in the classroom" (2007, para. 1). By altering learning activities slightly or greatly, school counselors can accommodate the learning needs of all students. See Table 6.5 for an example of how a learning activity design can be differentiated for multiple levels of ability. It demonstrates how a sample classroom guidance lesson for fifth-grade students about using Internet resources to explore careers can be differentiated for students with a variety of needs. Note that these suggestions are just examples, and lessons should be specifically differentiated for actual students based on their specific needs rather than mere diagnosis.

Table 6.5 Differentiated Learning Activity Design

Example Student Needs	*Differentiated Lesson Suggestions*
Reading disability	Ensure that the student has access to an audio recording of the material to listen to with headphones during the lesson.
Visual impairment	Ensure that the student has access to a screen reader in order to access the Internet resources alongside classmates.
Attention deficit/hyperactivity disorder	Include student helper tasks in the lesson plan and assign the student to some of these tasks, such as distributing handouts, writing on the board, or collecting papers.

UDL is an approach that employs technology-rich curricula to provide students with a range of options to meet their learning needs (Rose & Strangman, 2007). UDL curricula is designed so that the widest possible range of learners can be successful by emphasizing flexible methods of presentation, methods of engagement, and methods of expression (Wilson, 2012). One way that UDL curricula is more flexible for learners is that it often incorporates digital media rather than texts. Digital media allows for content to be customized in accessible ways for students, such as enlarging text, using visual images, or recording speech. Digital media can also allow students to use assistive technologies when needed, provide immediate feedback to student work, and be designed to test student knowledge after content is presented (Rose & Strangman, 2007).

Both differentiated instruction and UDL hold that curriculum should be adjusted in order to help all students succeed in the classroom. They differ in their approaches to doing so, however. Table 6.6 demonstrates the major differences between both approaches (Kristin, 2013; Wilson, 2012).

Table 6.6 Overall Differences between Differentiated Instruction and UDL Approaches

Differentiated Instruction	*UDL*
Relies on students' formative assessments to indicate learning obstacles, then modifies curricula in response to these challenges	Incorporates modifications to curricula from the outset in anticipation of students encountering challenges
Uses technology as often as other resources to meet students' needs	Emphasizes the use of technology frequently to meet students' needs
Emphasizes providing multiple learning opportunities to students	Emphasizes providing flexible learning opportunities that teach students how to make appropriate choices for their learning

Step 4: Lastly, after designing a classroom guidance lesson plan using differentiated instruction or UDL, school counselors benefit from evaluating the lesson during and after its implementation. School counselors should note how students with special needs participate in the lesson and later document any changes they would recommend when working with those students in the future or when implementing that lesson with other students in other classes. A continual cycle of designing, implementing, and evaluating will help to improve classroom guidance lessons in general and the differentiation within those lessons in particular.

PREPARATION AND ORGANIZATION

When school counselors design developmentally and multiculturally appropriate classroom guidance units based on a school counseling core curriculum, they are well-positioned to improve students' academic, career, and social/emotional development. For beginning school counselors, however, conducting even the most well-designed classroom guidance lessons can be unsettling and intimidating. But with sufficient preparation and planning, such intimidation can fade. Preparation for classroom guidance lessons can boost a school counselor's confidence by ensuring that a lesson goes as smoothly as possible. Such preparation can be organized into three key tasks: reviewing written lesson plans, communicating with teachers, and prepping materials.

In order to implement a well-designed classroom guidance lesson, a written lesson plan must exist for that lesson. Although school counselors may be tempted to present a lesson off-the-cuff, an unplanned lesson may lack the foundation of a school counseling core curriculum, its standards, and learning objectives. Leading a classroom guidance lesson without a written plan may create an ineffective learning experience for students that is isolated from other lessons, units, and goals of a school counseling program. To prepare for a classroom guidance lesson, then, school counselors should ensure that they have written a thoughtful lesson plan that includes meaningful learning objectives based on their school counseling core curriculum and outcomes related to student performance standards. In the week prior to the scheduled lesson, this lesson plan should be reread and reviewed. If the lesson has been previously implemented, it may be adjusted based on what went well and what did not in its previous implementation. If the lesson has been previously taught to students in a different grade than the one a school counselor is preparing for, developmental considerations should be accounted for, and the lesson should be adjusted accordingly. Even when using the most familiar lesson plans, counselors have found it useful to reread a classroom guidance lesson plan at least one week before, one day before, and one hour before a scheduled lesson takes place. Such repetition helps ensure that a school counselor is familiar with the lesson design and content, and it allows for adequate time if a lesson needs to be adapted and/or materials must be prepared.

Communicating with teachers is also of paramount importance when preparing for a classroom guidance lesson. It is essential that teachers know what day a lesson is scheduled, what time it will begin and end, and what the lesson topic will be. By informing teachers of the lesson's learning objectives, a school counselor increases the likelihood that a teacher may integrate themes related to the lesson topic into their own lessons and projects before or after the scheduled lesson. In addition to communicating with teachers about scheduling and lesson topics, it is equally important to communicate with them about the students in their classes. School counselors should know ahead of time about the student population of a class, and each class's respective teacher likely knows this information better than any other staff member. As previously mentioned, school counselors should prepare for students who need accommodations as well as those who may be sensitive to particular topics. For instance, if a school counselor is conducting a classroom guidance lesson about self-harm, it will be important to know if any students have had family or personal experiences with self-harm or self-injurious behaviors. These students may benefit from advanced notice about the topic or may even prefer to be excused from the lesson. These plans can be made in advance as long as the school counselor and teacher have been in communication.

Lastly, to increase the likelihood for a successful classroom guidance lesson, school counselors should organize all necessary materials well in advance of the scheduled lesson. This task may include photocopying handouts, designing electronic presentations, or organizing manipulatives for learning activities. While prepping these materials, it is also a good time to prepare an additional learning activity or two to conduct should there be extra time remaining in the scheduled time. Some school counselors believe it is more effective and less unnerving to have too many activities for a lesson than too few. If time is running short, school counselors can always cut an activity or two out and move onto their conclusion before wrapping up. All materials, including those for planned activities and extra activities, should be organized in the days leading up to a classroom guidance session.

With lesson plans reviewed, communication with teachers in place, and materials prepped, school counselors should feel confident and equipped to conduct developmentally appropriate classroom guidance lessons with students. By leading classroom guidance lessons rooted in a school counseling core curriculum based on needs assessment data, school counselors can assist students in developing the knowledge, skills, and awareness they need to be successful in their academic, career, and social/emotional development.

CONCLUSION

Designing a school counseling core curriculum is no simple task. It requires implementing needs assessments, evaluating needs assessment data, organizing units, aligning learning objectives with standards, and creating developmentally and multiculturally appropriate lesson plans. But the benefit of having a well-designed school counseling core curriculum far outweighs its labor. Once a state, district, or school counseling department has established a comprehensive school counseling core curriculum, the curriculum can easily be adapted over time to meet the changing needs of student populations. Having the foundation of such a curriculum to build from is an invaluable tool that deserves careful thought and implementation.

SUMMARY

A school counseling core curriculum serves as a blueprint from which school counselors can build comprehensive guidance programs. Ideally, this curriculum is based on both data-based and perception-based needs assessments that explore the opinions of multiple groups of school stakeholders. School counseling core curricula should also include organized units, learning objectives, and lesson plans for classroom guidance lessons. When designing these lessons, school counselors should be cognizant of the developmental, multicultural, and special needs of their students. Exercises 6.5a and 6.5b require you to synthesize your knowledge of school counseling core curriculum to complete an activity and consider a final case scenario.

EXERCISE 6.5A

SYNTHESIZING YOUR KNOWLEDGE OF SCHOOL COUNSELING CORE CURRICULUM

1. Interview an elementary school, middle school, and high school counselor about their school counseling core curricula. Ask questions about what this curriculum looks like, who designed the curriculum, how it is used, and how often it is updated.

2. Ask each school counselor you interview if you can view several of their classroom guidance lesson plans. Examine each lesson plan in depth. What developmental and multicultural considerations are made in each lesson plan? How do the lessons differ in style?

3. Design your own classroom guidance lesson based on what you have learned from the samples you have examined. Select one topic to teach to a class in a grade of your choice. Be sure to include appropriate learning objectives for the lesson and indicate several ASCA Mindsets & Behaviors for Student Success that the lesson could address as well as any related ethical codes.

4. Form small groups with two or three classmates and compare your classroom guidance lesson with others. Note any differences among your proposed plans, and consider adding components to your lesson plan that others have included in theirs.

EXERCISE 6.5B

SYNTHESIZING YOUR KNOWLEDGE OF SCHOOL COUNSELING CORE CURRICULUM

You are a middle school counselor at a school where you have worked for seven years. A new principal has been assigned to your school this year, and she recently began suggesting changes to your counseling program. Most recently, she called you in for a meeting and explained that she no longer wants you conducting regular classroom guidance lessons. Instead, she would prefer that you spend most of your time in your office, conducting individual and group counseling, and conduct a classroom guidance lesson only if a crisis warrants one.

1. How would you react to such feedback from a principal?

2. How might you show your classroom guidance lesson plans to your principal to demonstrate the value of conducting them? Where will you find relevant research on classroom guidance programming and how will you present the value of classroom guidance programming to your principal?

3. How might you use the ASCA Mindsets & Behaviors for Student Success to demonstrate to your principal the value of classroom guidance lessons?

KEYSTONES

- A school counseling core curriculum is the foundation of a school counselor's classroom guidance lesson units and lesson plans. It includes developmental lesson plans based on learning objectives and organized into units.

- School counseling core curricula should be based on data obtained from data-based and perception-based needs assessments. Perception-based needs assessments may take the form of questionnaires, inventories, or open-ended surveys and may be electronic or paper and pencil. Ideally, perception-based needs assessments are administered to several groups of school stakeholders in order to obtain a range of perspectives about student needs.

- After needs assessment data are obtained, school counselors should use these data to identify standards for their curriculum, outline units, and draft learning objectives for each classroom guidance lesson.

- The backward-design model is a three-step lesson planning model consisting of the following steps: (a) identify intended outcomes or objectives, (b) determine methods of evaluating student learning and understanding in relation to lesson objectives, and (c) create and identify developmentally appropriate learning activities that will facilitate student learning around the stated objectives for the lesson.

- Classroom guidance lesson plans should include an introduction, developmental activity, and a conclusion.

- When designing classroom guidance lessons, school counselors must take into consideration their students' developmental levels, multicultural backgrounds, and special needs.

School counselors can best prepare for classroom guidance lessons by ensuring that they review written lesson plans, communicate with teachers, and prep all materials needed for the lesson in advance.

REFERENCES

Akos, P., Cockman, C. R., & Strickland, C. A. (2007). Differentiating classroom guidance. *Professional School Counseling, 10,* 455–463.

American School Counselor Association (ASCA). (2010). *Ethical standards for school counselors.* Alexandria, VA: Author.

American School Counselor Association (ASCA). (2012). *The ASCA national model: A framework for school counseling programs* (3rd ed.). Alexandria, VA: Author.

American School Counselor Association (ASCA). (2014). *ASCA mindsets & behaviors for student success: K–12 college- and career-readiness standards for every student.* Alexandria, VA: Author.

Banks, J. A. (1993). Multicultural education: Development, dimensions, and challenges. *Phi Delta Kappan, 75,* 22–28.

Banks, J. A. (2004). Multicultural education: Historical development, dimensions, and practice. In J. A. Banks & C. M. Banks (Eds.), *Handbook of research on multicultural education* (pp. 3–29). San Francisco, CA: John Wiley & Sons.

Bloom, B. S., Engelhart, M. D., Furst, F. J., Hill, W. H., & Krathwohl, D. R. (1956). *Taxonomy of educational objectives: Cognitive domain.* New York, NY: McKay

Bruneau, L., & Protivnak, J. J. (2012). Adding to the toolbox: Using creative interventions with high school students. *Journal of School Counseling, 10,* 1–27.

Childre, A., Sands, J. R., & Pope, S. T. (2009). Backward design. *Teaching Exceptional Children, 41*(5), 6–14.

Council for Accreditation of Counseling & Related Educational Programs (CACREP). (2009). *2009 standards for accreditation.* Alexandria, VA: Author.

Dahir, C. A., & Stone, C. B. (2003). Accountability: A M.E.A.S.U.R.E. of the impact school counselors have on student achievement. *Professional School Counseling, 6,* 214–221.

Elligan, D. (2000). Rap therapy: A culturally sensitive approach to psychotherapy with young African American men. *Journal of African American Men, 5,* 27–36

Erford, B. T. (2007). Accountability. In B. T. Erford (Ed.), *Transforming the school counseling profession* (pp. 236–278). Upper Saddle River, NJ: Pearson Education.

Erford, B. T., & McKechnie, J. A. (2004). How to write learning objectives. In B. T. Erford (Ed.), *Professional school counseling: A handbook of theories, programs, and practices* (pp. 279–286). Austin, TX: PRO-ED.

Gardner, H. (1999). *The disciplined mind.* New York, NY: Simon & Schuster.

Goodnough, G. E., Pérusse, R., & Erford, B. T. (2007). Developmental classroom guidance. In B. T. Erford (Ed.), *Transforming the school counseling profession* (pp. 142–167). Upper Saddle River, NJ: Pearson Education.

Grothaus, T. (2012). Multiculturalism and the ASCA national model. In T. Grothaus (Ed.), *ASCA national model: A framework for school counseling programs* (3rd ed., pp. 37–39). Alexandria, VA: American School Counselor Association.

Gysbers, N. C., & Henderson, P. (2000). *Developing and managing your school counseling program* (3rd ed.). Alexandria, VA: American Counseling Association.

Haag Granello, D. (2000). Encouraging the cognitive development of supervisees: Using Bloom's taxonomy in supervision. *Counselor Education and Supervision, 40,* 31–47.

Herring, R. D., & White, L. M. (1995). School counselors, teachers, and the culturally compatible classroom: Partnerships in multicultural education. *Journal of Humanistic Education and Development, 34,* 52–64.

Kohlberg, L. (1973). The claim to moral adequacy of a highest stage of moral judgment. *Journal of Philosophy, 70,* 630–646.

Kristin. (2013, February 12). *Similarities and differences between universal design for learning and differentiated instruction* [web log post]. Retrieved March 30, 2015, from http://kristinspe322 .wordpress.com/2013/02/12/similarities-and-differences-between-universal-design-for-learning-and-differentiated-instruction/

Oberman, A. H. (2010). The accountability component and the school counselor-in-training. In J. Studer & J. Diambra (Eds.), *A guide to practicum and internship for school counselors-in-training* (pp. 133–145). New York, NY: Routledge.

Pedersen, P. B. (1991). Multiculturalism as a generic approach to counseling. *Journal of Counseling and Development, 70,* 6–12.

Riener, C., & Willingham, D. (2010). The myth of learning styles. *Change: The magazine of higher learning.* Retrieved March 31, 2015, from http://www.changemag.org/Archives/ Back+Issues/September-October+2010/the-myth-of-learning-full.html

Rose, D. H., & Strangman, N. (2007). Universal design for learning: Meeting the challenge of individual learning differences through a neurocognitive perspective. *Universal Access in the Information Society, 5,* 381–391.

Schmidt, J. J. (2003). *Counseling in schools: Essential services and comprehensive programs* (4th ed.). Boston, MA: Allyn & Bacon.

Siegler, R. S., DeLoache, J. S., & Eisenberg, N. (2011). *How children develop* (3rd ed.). New York, NY: Worth.

Skowron, J. (2006). *Powerful lesson planning: Every teacher's guide to effective instruction* (2nd ed.). Thousand Oaks, CA: Corwin.

Sleeter, C. E., & Grant, C. A. (2009). *Making choices for multicultural education: Five approaches to race, class, and gender.* Hoboken, NJ: John Wiley & Sons.

Wiggins, G. P., & McTighe, J. (1998). *Understanding by design.* Alexandria, VA: Association for Supervision and Curriculum Development.

Wiles, J., & Bondi, J. C. (1984). *Curriculum development: A guide to practice* (2nd ed.). Columbus, OH: Merrill.

Wilson, L. (2012). *Universal design for learning FAQ.* Retrieved March 30, 2015, from http://www.montgomeryschoolsmd.org/departments/hiat/FAQs/udl_faq.shtm

Chapter 7

Delivery, Evaluation, Analysis, and Reporting

Amy W. Upton
University of South Alabama

Julie is a middle school counselor who works with seventh-grade students. There are two additional counselors who work with sixth and eighth grades. Recently, a few of the seventh-grade teachers have spoken with Julie about the seventh-grade students being distracted by what appears to be more than normal conflicts. Although the students are trying to keep the teachers from seeing what is going on, the behaviors are affecting the teachers' instruction. After speaking with several of the seventh-grade teachers, Julie decides that she needs to find a way to address the problem and decides to conduct an informal needs assessment by giving the teachers a short survey regarding behaviors that they are observing. Additionally, Julie will look at class grades, class attendance, and behavioral referrals to try and determine whether certain classes appear to be having more problems than others. Once Julie has collected these data, she decides that a classroom guidance unit on conflict mediation and bullying should be developed. She designs a unit for three separate lessons and arranges a schedule with the seventh-grade teachers. At the beginning of the first lesson, Julie has the students conduct a pretest showing their preexisting knowledge about bullying and conflict resolution. After presenting the unit, she has the students complete a posttest assessing their knowledge gained of bullying and conflict resolution. She analyzes the results and finds that, indeed, the students' perceived knowledge did increase after the lesson. A few weeks after her lesson, she asks the teachers about their observations and looks again at the grades, attendance data, and behavior referrals to determine whether there has been a change. She finds that the teachers are reporting fewer distractions from the classes and instruction and the grades have minimally increased as potential outcomes of the classroom guidance unit.

What Julie has done is used data to drive the direction of her classroom guidance unit and lessons. Additionally, she used data to determine whether her lessons had any impact on student behavior and used multiple measures to link impact to the classroom guidance programming. Once all of the data are collected and analyzed, Julie will develop an informal report for her administrator and district supervisor to be included in her yearly program evaluation. Additionally, a summary of this report will be distributed to teachers and parents in the monthly counseling newsletter.

By the end of this chapter, you should be able to

- list steps as you prepare to implement classroom guidance programming,
- identify the individual and group needs that may require you to differentiate a classroom guidance lesson,
- name strategies for differentiating classroom guidance,
- explain why data collection is imperative when developing and implementing classroom guidance programming,
- list several types of data that you can collect in relation to classroom guidance programming and describe how these data might be used,
- identify the benefits of reporting the results of your data to your stakeholders, and
- describe how data evaluation and analysis of your comprehensive school counseling program and classroom guidance programming can impact your school counselors' performance assessments.

Classroom guidance programming is one of the American School Counselor Association's (ASCA) National Model delivery modalities and is considered a key component to a comprehensive school counseling program, as it facilitates providing services to all students in a school (ASCA, 2012). These lessons and units are clustered under the three domains of academic, career, and social/emotional student development. Although there are lessons that are often given to students each year based upon grade level, a school counselor should be conducting an annual program evaluation, which includes a needs assessment, in order to determine the following year's classroom guidance programming needs. Determining student and school community needs prior to developing a classroom guidance schedule is a strong first step in building accountability into your program. Choosing or developing an appropriate unit and lessons to address the specific identified needs would further enhance this accountability. Appropriate lessons can be found in a school district's guidance curriculum (if provided), outside resources such as ASCA's website for members, published articles and books, through discussions with colleagues, or by developing a learning or lesson plan yourself to meet the specific need. Classroom guidance lessons, objectives, goals, and outcome measures should be aligned with student needs. School counselors can link the outcomes to the specific knowledge, skills, and attitudes identified within the mindset standards and behavior standards of the ASCA Mindsets & Behaviors for Student Success (ASCA, 2014a)

Once the needs have been determined, the unit and lessons have been chosen or developed, and a classroom schedule for delivery has been created, the next step in ensuring accountability comes through the delivery of the content. School counselors make decisions as to how to deliver the content to specific grade levels while determining student individual and collective learning needs. Equity drives a school counseling program; you provide the services that each student needs.

PRESENTING CLASSROOM GUIDANCE PROGRAMMING

Multiple decisions are made about presenting a lesson before a school counselor walks into the classroom. Proper planning is essential to successful delivery of classroom guidance lessons, and decisions are made based upon the school, the setting, the needs of the school community, the resources that are available, and the school counselor's relationship with teachers and key stakeholders. Many school districts are site-based managed and, therefore, the setup for the school counselor may look very different. Counselor-to-student ratios can vary widely, with some being closer to ASCA's recommended ratios of 1:250 than others. Some schools have a guidance office where the school counselor's office is housed. In this configuration, the school counselor often travels to the various classrooms to deliver classroom guidance lessons. This counselor must travel with any resources or materials that they may need for the lesson and may be found pushing a cart from location to location. In other settings, school counselors may be given a classroom to work out of. In this configuration, the teachers will often bring their class to the counselor's classroom. When the counselor has a classroom and students are brought to that classroom, the classroom can be set with materials related to the guidance curriculum and the counselor will have all of the needed materials on hand. Decisions of how the space should be set up for classroom guidance lessons are made based upon the accessibility of materials and the stability of the setting. These decisions may be made yearly, quarterly, or for each lesson, depending on the space the school counselor is provided. The physical logistics of the classroom guidance environment are the first decisions that are made, but for each lesson, the school counselor has additional decisions to make.

Counselors must first determine the *who* of the lesson. Who will be involved in conducting the classroom guidance lesson? Who are the students and what are their individual learning needs? The *who* will often lead to decisions about classroom guidance lesson delivery. Student needs, class needs, and schoolwide needs should influence the delivery modality that a school counselor chooses. Second, counselors then must determine the *how* of the lesson. How should the lesson be delivered? How should counselors differentiate the instruction and activities so that all students are challenged and learning? How do counselors determine how much time to spend on certain portions of the lesson? Finally, how will counselors know that the lesson was successful?

The comprehensive school counseling program should be a schoolwide program that involves everyone in the school for its implementation. Classroom guidance programming provides a vehicle for delivery of a comprehensive guidance curriculum. School counselors can individually deliver this curriculum or they can co-teach this curriculum with a classroom teacher. Once the decision of who is involved in delivering the classroom guidance programming has been made, a school counselor needs to determine individual student needs and design methods for successfully differentiating the learning process for the students.

The initial decision of how a lesson should be delivered must be determined prior to entering the classroom. Whether the lesson is conducted as a counselor-led lecture, a whole-group discussion, or small-group activities, discussions and feedback are determined by the lesson content, the needs of the group, and the preference/philosophy of learning of the counselor and/or co-facilitator. It is important for a school counselor to prepare their lesson beforehand and to have all needed materials on hand before they enter a classroom. This is true even when the primary delivery method is small groups and class discussions. In anticipation of student discussions being less in-depth, a school counselor should have additional activities that can be used to stimulate further discussion. Each of these modalities has benefits and limitations however, utilizing a mixed approach driven by student/class/school needs that allows the counselor to differentiate the instructional modality to better meet the multiple learning styles and needs of the students he or she serves.

Differentiated Learning and Learning Styles

Differentiated instruction involves designing multimodal lessons that meet the learning styles, ability levels, and readiness to learn of all students in a classroom (Akos, Cockman, & Strickland, 2007). A school counselor ready to implement classroom guidance programming needs to determine the students' readiness to learn, value their individual differences, and design the instruction so that each student can learn.

Prior to going into the classroom, school counselors should be aware of any accommodations that students should be provided either through an Individual Education Plan (IEP) or Section 504 of the Individuals with Disabilities Act plan (504 plan). Just as teachers are held accountable for providing needed accommodations to their students with disabilities, so are school counselors when working with these students. The special education case managers for students with IEPs or 504 plans should provide an accommodations page for each student on their caseloads to all teachers and staff who will be required to provide these accommodations. A school counselor should still communicate with the classroom teacher to ensure that no student needs are overlooked. More often, school counselors will find a student's accommodations plan on the school database or electronically through a portal such as SASI.

All students, regardless of ability, learn differently (Akos et al., 2007). No two students are exactly alike, and attention needs to be paid to their individual differences. Also, students' learning styles can vary. It appears that, for some students, learning comes easier or they hold a preference for learning based upon how that information is obtained. Some students may prefer learning through seeing or *visual learning*. These students may have an easier time comprehending and retaining information that they read or see. Other students may have a preference for learning if they are able to hear the information presented. These *auditory learners* prefer to have information presented orally and may find it easier to comprehend and retain information this way. Lastly, some students may prefer to have a *physical* or *tactile interaction* with the information. They prefer to learn by doing or by connecting physical activity with the learning process. Keep in mind that many students have a combination of these learning style preferences. There is some disagreement within the literature regarding the existence or significance of learning styles (Reiner & Willingham, 2010); however, it appears to be supported within the educational literature (Reiner & Willingham, 2010; Threeton, Walter, & Evanowski, 2013). Within this literature, there are several learning style assessments that are aimed to identify the preference a person may have. Conducting a learning style assessment with students can provide a school counselor with some insight into a student's preferred way of learning. In order to differentiate a classroom guidance lesson, a school counselor can provide written and verbal instruction, create individual and group activities, and allow for active learning that allows the students to physically move around during lesson or activities. Understanding the preferred learning styles of your students and designing lessons that incorporate all learning style preferences should be common practice for school counselors. Further, students' learning preferences can be saved electronically or to a file so that all teachers and staff can access these profiles to be sure all needs are being met.

Learning needs as a result of a disability, individual learning differences, and preferred learning styles are all factors that influence instructional design. To fully design differentiated instruction that is equitable to all students, school counselors must also consider student culture and the influence that culture may play on the learning process. It is vital that school counselors continue to develop their multicultural awareness and social justice advocacy and be sensitive to the differences that may influence students' ways of learning and knowing.

Presenting effective classroom guidance programming requires appropriate planning and implementation. Decisions are made regarding what the needs of the students and school community are; what lesson or unit of lessons will best address those needs; who will participate in delivery of the lesson or unit of lessons; and how instruction and activities will be differentiated to meet the readiness, learning needs, learning styles, and cultural needs of the students in the classroom. Once all of these steps have been solidified, the school counselor will then follow in delivery of the classroom guidance programming while measuring and evaluating the effectiveness of the lessons and adjusting the delivery as needed.

DATA COLLECTION

Data collection should be an ongoing process within the comprehensive school counseling program and classroom guidance delivery. Supporting your program with data, both needs-driven and outcome-driven, helps a school counselor to demonstrate the accountability of the program. In the current era of educational accountability, demonstrating need and relevance of services, supporting instruction with outcome data and results, and being able to inform stakeholders of the success of your program is necessary for school counselors, teachers, and administrators alike.

Prior to planning a classroom guidance schedule, a needs assessment should be conducted. This may occur at the end of a school year for the upcoming year, at the beginning of a school year, or various points throughout the school year. This can be done by collecting qualitative data through individual and group interviews of the teachers, students, administrators, and parents. Additionally, a more formal survey may be distributed to the school community to further access the school's perceived needs. Schoolwide data on attendance and discipline also can assist a school counselor in both making choices about appropriate curriculum and lessons and in justifying the need for classroom guidance time in an era of high-stakes testing, where teachers often do not want to give up the instructional time.

Evaluation of a Lesson or Unit of Lessons

The initial evaluation of a lesson occurs when a counselor attempts to align the specific goals and objectives of a lesson to the needs and prior knowledge of the students. Outcomes of student performance standards should also be informative as these goals and objectives are identified. Before beginning a classroom guidance lesson, school counselors can assess the group of students' familiarity with the topic of the lesson. Conducting a needs assessment (the formal process of collecting perception data from students, teachers, parents, and/or administrators) is one method for ascertaining the needs of your specific student population (Dimmitt, Carey, & Hatch, 2007). Additionally, there are a number of less comprehensive or formal ways that counselors can gather this information, ranging from simply verbally asking what they already know about the topic to providing a pretest that indicates students' level of familiarity with various components of the topic. Once the level of awareness has been determined, school counselors can determine the amount and depth of information to focus on for the lesson. Once the lesson or unit of lessons have been delivered, evaluation of that lesson or unit allows counselors to further enhance their school counseling program with effective practices.

The ASCA National Model (2012) provides a School Counseling Core Curriculum Results Report template (Appendix 7.1), which can assist a school counselor in collecting multiple data sources for each lesson. Process data can be collected by asking the following questions: How many students did your lesson reach? What did students know or think they knew about a topic before the lesson? What did the students know or think they knew about that topic after the lesson? What are the thoughts, attitudes, and beliefs being held around a certain topic? These data can provide a record supporting your school counseling program, showing that it is designed to provide services to all students and demonstrating the impact of these lessons. Additional measures such as pretest/posttests and surveys can be administered for classroom guidance lessons as a means to collect perception data. Lastly, outcome data such as attendance rates, discipline referrals, grade point averages, and graduation rates can be reviewed by accessing additional schoolwide data, most likely through a data management system such as SASI (ASCA, 2012).

Pre- and Posttests

Pretests and posttests are instruments that are used to measure a group of participants' familiarity with a topic or competency. Pretests are administered prior to an intervention, such as a classroom guidance lesson, and posttests are administered following this intervention to measure the change in the group's awareness or familiarity with this same topic or competency as a result of the intervention (Creswell, 2008). Pretests can be used to access prior knowledge and to determine the depth and breadth of the lesson but can also be used as a data point for comparison of students' knowledge prior to a lesson and upon completion. Use of both a pretest and a posttest for a lesson or a unit of lessons can provide data that can be evaluated to access whether a lesson or unit of lessons was successful in meeting its objectives. Most frequently, a pretest that is administered at the onset of a lesson or a unit of lessons will ask the students to respond to questions by indicating whether or to what degree they are familiar with a topic or elements of a topic. Pretests and posttests can also be open-ended or fill-in-the-blank questions, where a student responds with what they perceive they know. Pretest results are gathered and compared to the results of the posttest to determine whether learning occurred or perceptions were altered (ASCA, 2012). Posttest questions are often identical to pretest questions to simplify analysis. Pre- and posttests can be designed in the form of true/false, multiple-choice, or yes/no questions (see Figure 7.1 for an example of a pre/posttest). More and more often, school counselors are administering pre- and posttests electronically to save time and resources such as paper. Tracking pretest and posttest data electronically is especially helpful for school counselors when they enter this information into data software for analysis. One example of software that can be used to analyze pre- and posttest data is E-Z Analyze.

Surveys

Surveys are one means of collecting data from various populations regarding various topics. They utilize a series of questions and answers that provide quantitative data that can later be evaluated and measured (Creswell, 2009; Dimmitt et al., 2007). These surveys can be created by the counselor or existing surveys can be used to measure the attitudes, opinions, knowledge, or perceptions identified by the school counselor. Surveys can be conducted with students, teachers, and parents to determine whether students are gaining knowledge and skills from the classroom guidance lessons that counselors facilitate. Additionally, surveys can provide both quantitative and qualitative data regarding stakeholders' knowledge and attitudes regarding a specific topic or competency. Surveys can also be used strictly to collect perception data regarding issues or challenges within the school. Perhaps the school counselor wishes to better understand the status of bullying within the school or to check on whether middle school students feel that they understand their academic choices for high school. Other possible perception data that a school counselor may use a survey to better understand could be regarding depression and coping skills. Surveys

Figure 7.1 Example of Pre/Posttest for a Bullying Prevention Lesson

Please read each statement and answer each statement with yes or no.

1. I know what bullying looks like.

   a. Yes   b. No

2. I know the difference between verbal, emotional, physical, and cyberbullying.

   a. Yes   b. No

3. I can name three things that I could do if someone were to bully me.

   a. Yes   b. No

4. I know what a bystander is.

   a. Yes   b. No

5. If someone tells me they hate me, this is bullying.

   a. Yes   b. No

6. If someone bullies me, I should ignore them.

   a. Yes   b. No

7. If someone bullies me, I should tell a teacher or adult.

   a. Yes   b. No

8. If someone repeatedly sends me mean texts, this is not bullying because it is not to my face.

   a. Yes   b. No

9. If I laugh along with the crowd while someone is being bullied, I am a bully, too.

   a. Yes   b. No

10. I know three ways to address a conflict.

    a. Yes   b. No

can assist a school counselor in understanding whether the elements of their comprehensive school counseling program are effective and meet the needs of the school community. Young, Hardy, Hamilton, Biernesser, Sun, and Neibergall (2009) published an article regarding a middle school counseling department's anti-bullying program, including the collection of data from surveys and pre- and posttesting over a three-year period. They were able to access the needs of their population (how many students were reporting that they had been bullied as well as the students' reported possession of strategies). They were also able to evaluate their interventions and adjust these accordingly. This article demonstrates the potential a school counseling program has to develop and improve on programs by utilizing ongoing data collection of students' beliefs, attitudes, and perceived knowledge in conjunction with achievement-related data such as referrals and attendance.

Surveys can be distributed at specific times of the year as part of a program evaluation conducted by the school counselor. This allows the school counselor to gain valuable feedback from multiple stakeholders regarding the perceived benefits, deficits, and needs of the school counseling program. This information can further enhance the evaluation of the classroom guidance curriculum. Survey results provide another piece of data that assist in the design and implementation of an effective school counseling program tailored to the needs of the school community.

There are various software and programs that can assist a school counselor in evaluating the data that are collected through surveys. Microsoft Excel is a program that can be used to evaluate the results of survey data. This program requires spreadsheet competency on the part of the school counselor because formatting the spreadsheet is necessary prior to analyzing data. Additionally, SPSS (developed by IBM) and Google have programs that can help with analysis of data. EZ Analyze is a fairly user-friendly program that allows the school counselor to enter the results and analyze the data that has been collecting with pre- and posttesting. An example of a student survey and a teacher survey can be found below in Figures 7.2, 7.3, and 7.4.

Formative and Qualitative Assessment

Ongoing assessments can provide valuable information to school counselors regarding the content and presentation of their curriculum. Entrance and exit tickets, thumbs-up, questioning, and 3–2–1s are examples of formative assessments. Entrance and exit tickets ask students to answer a couple of questions or complete a brief activity related to the lesson prior to leaving the classroom or to turn in at the onset of the next lesson in a unit. A student may be asked to list the different type of diplomas offered in a district as an entrance ticket to a lesson on academic four-year planning or a student may be asked to write three things they learned about applying to college that they had not known before as an exit ticket from a classroom guidance lesson on the college application process. Thumbs-up and questioning are ongoing assessments asking students to respond verbally to questions or to give a

Figure 7.2   Student Survey

Student Survey

1. I know my counselor.

    a. Strongly disagree   b. Disagree   c. Agree   d. Strongly agree

2. My counselor conducts classroom guidance lessons with my class regularly.

    a. Strongly disagree   b. Disagree   c. Agree   d. Strongly agree

3. I feel like I have someone to talk to if I have a problem.

    a. Strongly disagree   b. Disagree   c. Agree   d. Strongly agree

4. Conflicts within my class/grade are handled well by students.

    a. Strongly disagree   b. Disagree   c. Agree   d. Strongly agree

5. My counselor has spoken to my class and me about careers.

    a. Strongly disagree   b. Disagree   c. Agree   d. Strongly agree

6. I understand the connection between interests and career choice.

    a. Strongly disagree   b. Disagree   c. Agree   d. Strongly agree

7. My counselor has talked to my class and me about college.

    a. Strongly disagree   b. Disagree   c. Agree   d. Strongly agree

8. I understand the connection between schoolwork and college admissions.

    a. Strongly disagree   b. Disagree   c. Agree   d. Strongly agree

9. My counselor responds to my needs promptly.

    a. Strongly disagree   b. Disagree   c. Agree   d. Strongly agree

10. I feel like my counselor is there to help the students.

    a. Strongly disagree   b. Disagree   c. Agree   d. Strongly agree

---

thumbs-up to something they know or agree with, a thumbs-down if they do not understand or agree, and a sideways thumb if they are undecided. During a lesson on conflict mediation, a school counselor may ask the class to demonstrate that they understand the steps to take when working through a conflict by giving a thumbs-up if they understand what to do, a thumbs-down if they do not understand the steps, or

Figure 7.3 Teacher Survey

Teacher Survey

1. Our school counselor is accessible to students.

   a. Strongly disagree   b. Disagree   c. Agree   d. Strongly agree

2. Our school counselor is accessible to teachers.

   a. Strongly disagree   b. Disagree   c. Agree   d. Strongly agree

3. Our school counselor conducts regularly scheduled classroom guidance with my students.

   a. Strongly disagree   b. Disagree   c. Agree   d. Strongly agree

4. Our counselor is open to requests for lessons on specific topics related to my students' needs.

   a. Strongly disagree   b. Disagree   c. Agree   d. Strongly agree

5. Our school counselor collaborates with me and other teachers.

   a. Strongly disagree   b. Disagree   c. Agree   d. Strongly agree

6. I can refer students to the school counselor and he or she will respond.

   a. Strongly disagree   b. Disagree   c. Agree   d. Strongly agree

7. Our counselor provides lessons that are relevant to our students' needs.

   a. Strongly disagree   b. Disagree   c. Agree   d. Strongly agree

8. I understand the role of the school counselor.

   a. Strongly disagree   b. Disagree   c. Agree   d. Strongly agree

---

a thumbs sideways if they sort of understand but still have some questions. A counselor can simply initiate a question session where students are asked directly to respond to verbal prompts. Students can hold up individual white boards or paddles that indicate their awareness of or agreement with a certain topic. These boards can be decorated with symbols such as happy/sad faces or the words "Got It"/"Please Explain" to indicate their level of understanding as you teach the lesson. These assessment measures are utilized throughout a lesson to access whether the class is following and understanding the lesson; this allows the counselor to then focus on

Figure 7.4 Student Classroom Guidance Pretest/Posttest

Bullying Awareness Classroom Guidance Pretest/Posttest

1. Repeatedly calling a student mean names and saying mean statements to another student or students is considered _____.

   a. cyberbullying

   b. physical bullying

   c. relational bullying

   d. verbal bullying

2. Repeatedly and intentionally excluding someone from being part of a group is considered _____.

   a. cyberbullying

   b. physical bullying

   c. relational bullying

   d. verbal bullying

3. Repeatedly posting hurtful or cruel comments to a social media site is considered _____.

   a. cyberbullying

   b. physical bullying

   c. relational bullying

   d. verbal bullying

4. Unintentional or isolated events of being mean is considered bullying.

   a. True

   b. False

5. Quietly observing someone being bullied (or being a bystander) has no effect on bullying.

   a. True

   b. False

what the students need and not spend too little or too much time on certain parts of the lesson. Lastly, a 3–2–1 assessment (see Figure 7.5) asks students to briefly respond after a lesson with three things they learned, two things they disagree with or are unclear about, and one thing they would like to know more about, providing the counselor with information on what the students' needs are and how to further design classroom guidance.

Informal interviewing of teachers is another form of qualitative assessment. Ask individual teachers or groups of teachers what they think their students' needs are, whether they perceive that your lessons are having an impact, and in what ways. If students are having conflicts that are disrupting the learning in a certain class or classes, following up with teachers after a lesson or a unit of lessons on conflict resolution can provide valuable data to the school counselor about the effectiveness of a lesson or unit of lessons. This can be done in person or through e-mail.

Examining Additional Data

Collecting data from students and teachers offers beneficial information for enhancing the comprehensive school counseling programs. The counselor also has

Figure 7.5   Sample 3–2–1 Formative Assessment

| Name_____ | Date _____ |

3

List three things in the lesson that struck you as interesting either because they were new information or because they impacted your point of view.

2

List two things in the lesson that you disagree with or find unclear.

1

Write down one thing from the lesson that you wish to know more about.

access to a variety of schoolwide data that can provide direction and support for the school counseling program. The three types of schoolwide data that can assist a school counselor in designing a needs-based guidance curriculum include attendance data, discipline data, and achievement or grade data. This information can be disaggregated by grade level, teacher, gender, disability, or by any individual demographic variable. By examining these data, the school counselor can identify trends or needs within grade levels, teams, or teacher's classrooms; by another variable such as gender, race, special services provided (e.g., special education, 504 plan, gifted), or military affiliation; or by another identified demographic or academic variable that would provide the desired information. Once these trends or needs are identified, school counselors can design appropriate classroom guidance programming. One example of utilizing these academic-related data to evaluate program effectiveness would be to compare bullying referrals before, during, and after specific lessons and schoolwide programming efforts to address bullying.

Teacher Report/Assessment

Teacher reports and assessments also provide insight into student needs. Teachers are in the classrooms with these students daily and are able to identify issues within or among the group quickly. Understanding the wealth of information that teachers can provide to counselors about student needs provides direction for school counselors for programming and curriculum planning. School counselors can collect teacher perception data qualitatively by speaking with the teachers or through surveys or e-mails.

Ideally, a teacher report form could be developed and distributed to all teachers to complete following all guidance lessons.

There are additional means for ongoing evaluation of individual lessons or of overall program delivery. High school counselors have access to course selections; teacher recommendations for advanced coursework; and PSAT, ACT PLAN, SAT, and ACT scores along with districtwide assessments, state assessments, and AP exam scores. The College Board offers tools such as AP potential, which gives schools rosters of students who have performed at a level on the PSAT that indicates potential success in AP classes. Reviewing all of this information as well as other district or school data can be beneficial for school counselors in evaluating their lessons and program, paying special attention to whether or not they are addressing the various mindset standards and behavior standards and the associated competencies within the ASCA Mindsets & Behaviors for Student Success (2014). This broad array of data also provides school counselors with tools to identify and justify student course placement and selection.

Date of lesson: _____

Teacher name: _____ Grade level/subject: _____

Number of classes: _____

Number of students: _____

Topic of today's classroom guidance lesson: _____

Has your class experienced problems in this area? _____

Frequency of incidents or problems: _____

Has there been a change in the need for redirection or referrals since the classroom guidance lesson? If so, how and how much?

_____

_____

_____

Has there been a change in attendance since the classroom guidance lesson? If so, how?

_____

_____

_____

Do you think the lesson was successful? _____

Do you want the counselor to provide additional lessons in this area?

_____

_____

_____

Data collection is an important component of comprehensive school counseling programs and is aimed at addressing the needs of the students and school community. Data drive program design as well as provide a means to demonstrate the effectiveness of the program. School counselors regularly collect perception data to show the students served; the knowledge that the students believe they have or have gained as a result of the classroom lesson; and students', teachers', and stakeholders' attitudes and beliefs around a certain topic as well as general thoughts held by these populations. The collection of perception data through pretests/posttests, surveys, needs assessments, and program evaluations identify perceived needs, program strengths and weaknesses, and student shifts in perception or knowing. Perception data can be considered in relation to outcome data such as changes to attendance, discipline, or grades that can be attributed to the school counseling program. Additionally, perception data regarding school safety, sense of community, and student and teacher connectedness can be used to evaluate the school counseling program's efforts to improve school climate. Data collection, data evaluation, and data analysis also allow the school counselor to report the results of the program to the stakeholders, demonstrating how school counseling programs are tied to the mission of the school and to outcomes related to student performance standards (ASCA, 2012).

REPORTING TO STAKEHOLDERS

Collecting and analyzing data is integral to maintaining a data-driven comprehensive school counseling program. Classroom guidance lessons can be designed and presented to meet the identified needs of students and the school community. Effectiveness of lessons and additional needs can be determined through ongoing evaluation of individual lessons; stakeholder surveys; and schoolwide performance, attendance, and discipline data. School counselors use this ongoing evaluation process to improve their programs. These efforts can also serve to improve services for students.

Developing and running an effective school counseling program that impacts students and schools should drive the need to evaluate and analyze the classroom guidance programming component of the program. An additional benefit of the collection, evaluation, and analysis of classroom guidance data is that they provide an accountable format to share the results of the school counseling program with other stakeholders. Providing administrators and external stakeholders (such as community members and parents) with data that demonstrate to what extent the lessons impact student success can create a deeper understanding of what school counselors do and how their work is essential to the mission of the school (Stone & Dahir, 2011).

There are various ways to present the results of the school counseling program, including the classroom guidance curriculum. School counselors look at these documents and reports as both an effective public relationship tool to advocate for the school counseling program and the school counselor as well as an evidenced-based document to guide administrators and external stakeholders when they are conducting and evaluating the school counselor's performance and the comprehensive school counseling program. There are various formats available for presenting the data to stakeholders, and the school counselor will determine which format best represents his or her results. Gilchrist (2006) developed a model titled SOARING, and Stone and Dahir (2011) provide a guide for presenting school counseling program data titled MEASURE. (An overview of these two models is provided in Appendix 7.2 and Appendix 7.3, respectively.) These are but two of many data-driven accountability models that can guide school counselors in sharing their program results (Dollarhide & Saginak, 2012). There are also other program performance reports that a school counselor can use to track and report their data. GRIP (goals, results, impact statements, program implications) is one framework within the literature that is utilized to evaluate the components of a school counseling program (Brott, 2008). Most recently, Kaffenberger and Young (2013) introduced DATA—design (Set your goal), ask (How will you achieve this goal?), track (How will you analyze the data?), and announce (How will you share the results?)—as a tool for organizing and reporting program data.

School counselors need to become comfortable sharing what they do and how their work impacts student learning and success. Hosting an annual presentation to the teachers, parents, and community about the purpose, activities, and results of the school counseling program provides an opportunity for understanding and supporting the program. Additionally, it validates a school counselor's possible need for additional resources.

COUNSELOR PERFORMANCE APPRAISAL

Jose is completing his third year as the school counselor at Central Elementary School and is up for summative evaluation. The principal calls Jose into his office to discuss the evaluation process and what he needs from Jose. Throughout the year, Jose has been incredibly busy with his student population: meeting with students, running groups, and conducting classroom guidance. Jose has been able to work the last year with little interruption from the administration, which he feels is good because he has been so busy addressing the issues that have arisen. When he sits down with his principal, the principal asks Jose to help him with the evaluation. The principal recognizes that the evaluation instrument used by the district does not seem to really fit the job that Jose does; however, the principal does not really understand what exactly Jose is doing every day and would like Jose to translate what he does into each of the items on the evaluation instrument. Jose struggles to figure out how to best make his job fit into the evaluation instrument and to inform the principal of what he did all year. As a result, Jose's evaluation is okay but does not demonstrate the work that he does or how the students are different as a result of the school counseling program.

Data-driven comprehensive school counseling programs provide a less subjective evaluation of the program by stakeholders such as administrators. School counselor evaluations generally involve what the principal or supervising administrator understands about the work that a school counselor performs. Additionally, school counselors are often considered teachers or support staff within a school district's organizational plan and are therefore categorized for evaluations using the same criteria or rubrics as teachers or other support staff; sometimes a very generic counselor appraisal is used. In other cases, district supervisors complete the school counselor performance appraisal, which seems more appropriate. As a school counselor's job should be very different than that of a teacher, a librarian, or a nurse, it would be more appropriate for the evaluation criteria or rubric used to be more school-counseling specific. A data-driven school counseling program provides concrete and measurable criteria for evaluation. ASCA also provides a School Counselor Performance Appraisal template that can be shared with stakeholders or incorporated into a school district's evaluation rubric (ASCA, 2014b).

Reflection Questions

1. *In what ways does the district's appraisal instrument impact Jose's summative evaluation?*

2. *What could Jose have done differently to prepare the principal for Jose's evaluation?*

3. *How would the use of data in planning, implementing, and evaluating the school counseling program have impacted the evaluation process and outcome for Jose and for the principal?*

ASCA SCHOOL COUNSELOR PERFORMANCE APPRAISAL AS IT RELATES TO CLASSROOM GUIDANCE PROGRAMMING

The ASCA School Counselor Performance Appraisal is constructed with items related to the development, delivery, implementation, and assessment of a comprehensive school counseling program. As you can see, many of the items evaluate the school counselor on his or her ability to provide an overall comprehensive school counseling program, and this would include classroom guidance. Item 1.3 is used to evaluate how well a school counselor uses data to develop curriculum action plans, while Item 1.4 helps to evaluate whether the school counselor is spending an appropriate amount of time on delivery of direct services, including classroom guidance. Specific to classroom guidance, Item 2.2 is used to evaluate whether the school counselor is actually delivering curriculum through large group classroom guidance. The last section (3) on accountability has items that are used to evaluate how well the school counselor uses data to analyze the effectiveness of the program that is being implemented and the services that are being provided, including classroom guidance. Additionally, Item 3.7 is used to evaluate the school counselor's effectiveness at sharing the results with the relevant stakeholders (ASCA, 2012). All of the items in this performance appraisal represent the roles and duties a school counselor should be performing based upon the tenets of the ASCA National Model.

Reflection Question

In what ways would the use of the ASCA School Counselor Performance Appraisal have changed Jose's evaluation experience?

KEYSTONES

- According to the ASCA National Model (2012), school counseling programs are designed to provide services to *all* students. Classroom guidance curriculum and delivery is a major component of a comprehensive school counseling program in that they provide a vehicle to reach the large number of students on a school counselor's caseload.
- To be sure the needs of the school are understood, school counselors seek to design and implement a needs assessment to inform classroom guidance programming. Through the collection, evaluation, and analysis of process, perception, and outcome data, school counselors are able to design lessons that are relevant and meet school/community needs and to evaluate the effectiveness of the lessons they do provide.
- The results of this data analysis allow school counselors to improve their programs as well as to report to stakeholders how their programs are tied to the mission of the school and outcomes related to student performance standards. Informing and

educating the stakeholders can lead to enhanced support of the school counseling program, access to additional resources, and concrete evidence of the work that the school counselors do, which can ultimately impact their performance evaluation.

REFERENCES

Akos, P., Cockman, C., & Strickland, C. (2007). Differentiating classroom guidance. *Professional School Counseling, 10*(5), 445–463.

American School Counselor Association (ASCA). (2012). *The ASCA national model: A framework for school counseling* (3rd ed.). Alexandria, VA: Author.

American School Counselor Association (ASCA). (2014a). *ASCA mindsets & behaviors for student success: K–12 college- and career-readiness standards for every student.* Alexandria, VA: Author.

American School Counselor Association (ASCA). (2014b). *ASCA national model templates.* Retrieved April 8, 2015, from http://schoolcounselor.org/school-counselors-members/asca-national-model/asca-national-model-templates

Brott, P. E. (2008). *Get a GRIP.* In Virginia School Counselor Association (Ed.), *The Virginia professional school counseling manual* (pp. 86–93). Yorktown, VA: Virginia School Counselor Association.

Creswell, J. W. (2008). *Educational research: Planning, conducting, and evaluating quantitative and qualitative research* (3rd ed.). Upper Saddle, NJ: Pearson

Creswell, J. W. (2009). *Research design: Qualitative, quantitative, and mixed methods approaches* (3rd ed.). Thousand Oaks, CA: SAGE.

Dimmitt, C., Carey, J., & Hatch, T. (2007). *Evidence-based school counseling: Making a difference with data-driven practices.* Thousand Oaks, CA: Corwin.

Dollarhide, C. A., & Saginak, K. A. (2012). *Comprehensive school counseling programs: K–12 delivery systems in action.* Upper Saddle, NJ: Pearson.

Kaffenberger, C., & Young, A. (2013). *Making data work* (3rd ed.). Alexandria, VA: American School Counselor Association

Reiner, C., & Willingham, D. (2010). The myth of learning styles. *Change: The Magazine of Higher Learning, 42*(5), 32–35.

Stone, C. B., & Dahir, C. A. (2011). *School counselor accountability: A measure of student success* (3rd ed.). Boston, MA: Pearson.

Threeton, M. D., Walter, R. A., & Evanowski, D. C. (2013). Personality type and learning style: The tie that binds. *Career and Technical Education Research, 38*(1), 39–55.

Young, A., Hardy, V., Hamilton, C., Biernesser, K., Sun, L., & Neibergall, S. (2009). Empowering students: Using data to transform a bullying prevention and intervention program. *Professional School Counseling, 12*(6), 413–420.

APPENDIX 7.1

ASCA National Model (2012)
School Counselor Curriculum Results Report

Goal _____

Lessons and Activities Related to Goal:

Grade Level	Lesson Topic	Lesson Will Be Presented in Which Class/ Subject?	ASCA Domain, Standard, and Competency	Curriculum and Materials	Start /End	Process Data (Number of Students Affected)	Perception Data (Surveys or Assessments Used)	Outcome Data (Achievement, Attendance, and/ or Behavior Data)	Implications

APPENDIX 7.2

SOARING

S	Standards	What standard does the specific activity or intervention address?
O	Objectives	What are the objectives of the activity or intervention? Make sure the objectives are measureable, are aligned with the activity or intervention, and support the school's mission.
A	Assessment	Decide in what ways you will measure whether you were successful in meeting your objectives. Decide what data you need to collect. (This can be achievement data, achievement-related data, or survey or pre- and posttest data.)
R	Results	Once activities or interventions are complete and data have been collected, evaluate the results. Present these data in graphs or charts. Make the information very clear, giving percentages and change (both positive and negative).
I	Impact	Write an impact statement. Summarize what change occurred as a result of your activity or intervention.
N	Network	Get out and let the stakeholders know the results of your program's activities and interventions. Communicate and publicize how the students are different as a result of these activities and interventions. This can be done in flyers, reports, presentations, brochures, and so on. Share this information with all stakeholders (administrators, parents, teachers, community members, and school board members).
G	Guide	Review the results of your activities and interventions. Identify what issues you still need to address. Make plans for the next steps.

SOARING may be best suited for identified needs that the school counselor chooses to address through school counseling activities, classroom guidance lessons or units, small group counseling, or consultation and collaboration with teachers and parents. It provides a process and format to follow that demonstrates how the need was identified, sets the goal to address the need, evaluates activities and intervention, and summarizes and publicizes the results of the school counseling program's activities. An example may be that the school counselor receives several referrals from seventh-grade students and teachers that bullying appears to be occurring within the seventh grade. The counselor can pull attendance and discipline data as well as administer a pretest before developing a classroom guidance unit on bullying. Afterward, the counselor can administer a posttest and reexamine the attendance and discipline data. Graphs and charts can be developed to represent the data and an impact statement can be written, and this information can be shared with stakeholders. Once the intervention is complete and the data are analyzed, the counselor can identify continuing needs and plan for further activities or interventions as needed.

APPENDIX 7.3

MEASURE

M	Mission	Tie the program to the school's mission and goals. How does your program support the school mission? How does your program impact student achievement?
E	Elements	What are the key elements of the school improvement plan? Examine the school data: What are the grade, attendance, and behavior patterns within the school community?
A	Analyze	Analyze the identified data. Are there trends? Strengths? Weaknesses? Which of these elements fit within the school counseling program? Look closely at the data, including disaggregated data. Are there certain groups or subgroups that indicate needs (grade, gender, race, socioeconomic class, neighborhoods, etc.)? Identify the needs that can be addressed by the school counseling program.
S/U	Stakeholders Unite	Get the stakeholders onboard! Identify the people that can help facilitate change in these identified critical elements. Try to get them to agree to be part of the effort. This could include administrators, teachers, parents, and community members. Develop a plan to address the critical elements and specifically identify what each stakeholder will do.
R	Reanalyze, reflect on, and refine results	Once interventions have been put into place, examine the results of the efforts. Reexamine and reanalyze the results, and identify what has been achieved, what needs more-specific intervention, and how your team can address continuing concerns.
E	Educate	Publicize your results! Create a report card or flyer that reflects the mission, the goals, the interventions, and the results. Share this with administrators, the school board, parents, community members, and teachers. This is how you substantiate what you have done to address your school community's needs.

MEASURE offers counselors the opportunity to plan their program for the upcoming year. In doing so, the counselor must first tie the school counseling program's mission to the school mission and school improvement plan. By examining schoolwide data and school improvement plan goals, the school counselor can identify specific needs within the school community. In an effort to be more specific in identifying needs, the counselor can disaggregate the school data by variables such as race, gender, grade level, zip code, and socioeconomic class. Once specific needs are identified, the counselor can enlist stakeholders who are positioned to facilitate change and engage them in schoolwide efforts to address these needs. An example may be that females in the ninth grade are underperforming academically in math and science compared to males, primarily as a result of less-rigorous course selections. The counselor can work with the math teachers at the high school as well as the counselor and math teachers at the middle school to identify female students who have the potential, based on grades and standardized test scores, to be successful in more-rigorous math courses. Tutoring programs can be initiated, strategic course planning and parent communication can be undertaken, and classroom guidance lessons on careers with math backgrounds that are inclusive of females can be presented. Longitudinal data on course selections and grades can be collected to follow the females that have been identified to assess the impact of the multimodal interventions. Efforts and results can be shared with stakeholders such as principals, teachers, and parents to assist in these efforts and to gain support for the interventions. Additional areas of need can be identified by analyzing and reanalyzing the data as time passes. Lastly, the program and the results of the program should be shared with all stakeholders and publicized to educate the entire school community about the successes of the program.

Chapter 8

FACILITATION SKILLS AND CLASSROOM MANAGEMENT

NATOYA HILL HASKINS
University of Georgia

"I feel disconnected from my counseling identity. I really enjoy classroom guidance but I wish I could integrate counseling skills into my interactions with students. I am also concerned about my lack of preparation related to classroom management and using technology."

School counselors, like the one above, often struggle with maintaining their counselor identity while spending many hours in the role of teacher in the classroom guidance setting. This school counselor is also experiencing a lack of confidence and efficacy regarding classroom management and technology usage and implementation.

After reading this chapter about counseling strategies, classroom management, and technology applications, you will be able to

- identify and apply basic counseling and group counseling skills while delivering classroom guidance programming,
- integrate theoretical orientation into classroom guidance programming preparation and implementation,
- identify and address maladaptive behaviors observed in a classroom in a clinical manner,
- identify ways to integrate technology into classroom guidance programming to enhance content and experiential activities, and
- identify key ethical considerations in the areas of classroom delivery and technology.

Although classroom guidance programming has been a distinct delivery system for school counselors for several decades, counseling and behavior management skills for the classroom are overlooked in literature, research, and counselor preparation programs. Counseling and behavior management skills can assist counselors in enhancing their classroom guidance curriculum and promoting their professional identity as a counselor. Counseling and behavior management skills allow the school counselor to move the classroom guidance process into a more clinically based delivery system. Furthermore, these skills can assist school counselors with enhancing their clinical expertise, therapeutic orientation, and professional role. These skills can also enhance the relational connection between the counselor and client. Some scholars suggest that counselors are clinicians *and* educators by providing counseling in a school setting. Therefore, classroom guidance programming provides opportunities for counselors to reach more students by teaching and delivering lessons (Ziomek-Daigle, McMahon, & Paisley 2008).

GROUP COUNSELING SKILLS IN CLASSROOM GUIDANCE PROGRAMMING

While large-group guidance is not group counseling in the traditional sense, many basic group-counseling skills can be applied by school counselors in the classroom. Similar to psychoeducational groups, these classroom guidance sessions focus on K–12 student knowledge and skill acquisition (Association for Specialists in Group Work, 2000). Researchers indicate that group process and dynamics, group stages, group facilitative procedural skills, and group personal leadership style are important aspects that school counselors should consider using when conducting classroom guidance (Giltner, Cunningham, & Caldwell, 2011).

Group Process and Dynamics

It is important for school counselors who facilitate classroom guidance programming to understand that members in large-group guidance are engaged in the group process. Group process is based on the notion that the behavior of people in groups is largely determined by the interactions between the person and the environment (Lewin, 1951). In large-group guidance, this implies that the students in the classroom environment influence the behavior of all students. As a result, the classroom group environment can prompt change in students' attitudes, behaviors, and values (Adler, Kless, & Adler, 1992). The school counselor should be aware of the group's dynamics and determine whether the dynamics are aiding the group process or hindering the process.

Group coalitions are also important phenomena for school counselors to observe and identify prior to and during classroom guidance lessons. School counselors should observe these subsets of rules or norms that influence students' behavior. Kottler and Englar-Carlson identify several questions school counselors need to consider:

What roles are various individuals playing in the group? Who has the power in the group? Which coalitions have formed? Who is aligned with whom? Which members are in conflict with one another? Are the boundaries within a group open enough to allow new information to enter the group? How do members communicate with one another? Are the lines of communication clear and direct? Where do members direct their attention when they speak? Do group interactions tend to move in patterns that move toward keeping the system stable? What norms have developed in the group that regulate behavior? How is information exchanged among group members? How did people share what they know with one another? Who was excluded or ignored? Did change in a system occur via the use of positive and negative feedback? (2010, pp. 63–64)

Attending to these questions will allow school counselors to make intentional decisions in how they pair or group students for classroom guidance activities. It will also enable school counselors to determine their level of engagement with students. Let's apply group dynamics to Exercise 8.1 below.

EXERCISE 8.1

ADDRESSING GROUP DYNAMICS

Identify a classroom of students in which you would like to understand the group dynamics more fully. Using the information presented above, explore the communication and group structure of this class of students. Plot out the subsystems using a sociogram in the class of students. This drawing should include the coalitions, communication patterns, control and power issues, and boundaries currently in place. After completing your graphic depiction, answer the questions listed above to sort out the roles played by various students: Who has power? What are the norms in this group? What is your final assessment regarding the observed strengths and growing edges of this group of students? If you do not have access to a K–12 classroom for this exercise, use your current class or another class in the program as an example.

Discussion Questions

1. How will you use this information to adapt your classroom guidance lesson?

2. How will you use the students in this adaptation?

3. How will you handle difficult or dysfunctional coalitions during your guidance lesson?

Group Stages

All groups move through five group stages: forming, storming, norming, performing, and adjourning. Aspects of the forming, performing, and adjourning group stages are particularly useful in helping school counselors structure their classroom guidance curriculum and lessons (Tuckman, 1965). Aspects of the initial group counseling stage that school counselors should include in their preparation include the following (Gladding, 2008):

1. Create a justification for the classroom guidance curriculum or lesson based on the needs of the students.

2. Identify what activities and type of content are practical for the developmental level of the students.

3. Develop rules (described later in the chapter).

4. Decide on the structure of the lesson and communicate it to the students.

Typically, a classroom guidance unit includes between one and four classroom sessions. With that in mind, school counselors need to start the classroom guidance experience with the end of the curriculum and student outcomes in mind. Several aspects of the final stages of counseling and psychoeducational group are useful for school counselors to incorporate. Have students use writings or drawings to describe what they learned during the lesson and how they will use the new skills. This adds closure and something tangible to your time together. School counselors can also use an assessment of the lesson (i.e., Did you learn the identified skills?) to gain a better understanding of the student knowledge gained. At the end of the lesson, school counselors should make note of which students to follow up with. Additionally, school counselors should include a summarization of the lesson as part of the closure activity and provide homework if appropriate.

Group Facilitative Procedural Skills

Group facilitative skills that enhance the classroom guidance experience include linking, blocking, drawing out, and processing. *Linking* connects the experiences, feelings, and thoughts of group members by identifying similarities. School counselors can use this skill in classroom guidance to connect the students to one another as well as help normalize student experiences and create bonds between the students. For example, the school counselor can make a statement such as, "Craig and Joy, it seems like both of you had a positive experience role-playing conflict resolution skills."

Blocking or *cutting off* is required when students broach topics that are irrelevant to the current lesson or that may need to be discussed in the privacy of the school counselor's office. For example, if a student states that "I had something traumatic happen when I was younger that relates to this topic," the counselor may say, "It sounds like that's something you might like to talk about in more detail, but right now we are focusing on our lesson. Can we schedule time to talk later?"

Drawing out is another important skill for school counselors to use to ensure that all students engage in the classroom guidance lesson. Drawing out can help students feel connected and more invested in the lesson. The school counselor may say, "Allen, we haven't heard from you yet; what information would you like to add?" The counselor may also use less-pointed communication, such as a round to draw out students who are more silent. In a round, the school counselor asks a question and allows each student to share his or her answer.

The final facilitative procedural skill that will be discussed in this chapter is *processing* (Council for Accreditation of Counseling & Related Educational Programs standard II.G.6.a). By using processing as a skill, school counselors are able to explore the emotions, thoughts, and actions of the students participating in a classroom guidance lesson. It is also designed to help the students transfer the skills they learn during the lesson to their life after the lesson ends (Stockton, Morran, & Nitza, 2000). Some examples of process questions include the following: How can you apply these skills to your relationships? How will you continue to work on your personal and class goals? What can you do to improve your conflict resolution skills here at school? Now that you know how to address situations differently, how do you feel? Using these facilitative skills, let's address the case study below.

CASE STUDY

The school counselor is fifteen minutes into his or her classroom guidance lesson on diversity and differences when he or she begins to notice that a few students are monopolizing the discussion. In addition, the counselor is concerned that one student has broached several topics that are not related to the classroom guidance lesson. The counselor wants to address the concerns but does not want the students to feel targeted or uncomfortable nor stop participating.

1. What facilitative procedural skills might the counselor use?
2. How might the counselor employ these skills?
3. What issues or concerns might the counselor address?
4. How should the counselor deal with these concerns?

Group Personal Leadership Style

The three major styles of group leadership include authoritarian or autocratic, participative or democratic, and laissez-faire or free reign (Gladding, 2008). Although good leaders use all three styles (one of them is normally dominant), ineffective leaders tend to stick with only one style. Leadership styles serve to help maintain a safe therapeutic setting, explore resistance, and model behavior during groups. They can also be used to override group norms when dealing with challenging situations and student misbehavior. The school counselor's leadership style should unite the students as they work toward the lesson's goal. Furthermore, leadership styles can assist school counselors in keeping the students motivated, diffusing conflict, and ensuring the success of the lesson. Identifying the school counselor's leadership style can be useful in determining strengths and challenges when on the cusp of implementing classroom guidance programming. Take a moment to assess your leadership style based on Lewin and colleagues' leadership characteristics (see Exercise 8.2).

EXERCISE 8.2

LEADERSHIP STYLE QUIZ

Rate the following prompts: 5 = always, 4 = often, 3 = sometimes, 2 = rarely, 1 = never

1. ____ All policy and procedures are determined by the school counselor.
2. ____ The school counselor's lesson goal is developed with the class.

(Continued)

(Continued)

3. ____ There is complete freedom for the group to decide on all aspects of the lesson without the school counselor's input.

4. ____ The leader does not participate in the decisions or procedures.

5. ____ Techniques and lesson activities are designed by the school counselor.

6. ____ The school counselor suggests two or three alternatives from which the students may choose.

7. ____ The school counselor should assign the work tasks.

8. ____ The school counselor should share information but not take part in discussions.

9. ____ All policies and procedures are a matter of group discussion.

10. ____ The students select who they would like to work with.

11. ____ The school counselor gives comments very infrequently.

12. ____ The school counselor should select students for group work.

13. ____ The school counselor should praise and critique each group member.

14. ____ The division of tasks is left up to the whole group (school counselor and students).

15. ____ The school counselor does not attempt to participate.

16. ____ The school counselor should remain aloof from active group participation.

17. ____ The school counselor is objective in his or her praise or critique of each member.

18. ____ The school counselor does not interfere with what takes place in the classroom.

Compute your score:

Add 1, 5, 7, 12, 13, 16 ____ authoritarian

Add 2, 6, 9, 10, 14, 17 ____ democratic

Add 3, 4, 8, 11, 15, 18 ____ laissez-faire

Your highest score indicates the leadership style that you typically prefer. However, you may use elements of each style, depending on your interactions with the students during the classroom guidance lesson.

Reflect: When might you use each of these styles to deliver your classroom guidance lesson?

This exercise was developed based on content from Lewin, K., Lippitt, R., & White, R. K. (1939). Patterns of aggressive behavior in experimentally created "social climates." *Journal of Social Psychology, 10,* 271–299.

BASIC COUNSELING SKILLS IN CLASSROOM GUIDANCE

Basic counseling skills that can be utilized by school counselors in classroom guidance curriculum include nonverbal and verbal facilitative skills, reflecting skills, and assessment skills (Giltner et al., 2011). Table 8.1 briefly discusses these skills.

Table 8.1 Basic Counseling Skills

Skill	*Purpose in Classroom Guidance*
Nonverbal Facilitative Skills	
Eye contact	Increase connection Demonstrate listening
Facial expressions	Determine inconsistencies and positive/adverse responses
Gestures	Augment verbal meaning
Space	Suggest a relationship Indicate desire for a relationship
Touch	Increase connectedness
Vocal cues	Emphasize content Improve credibility
Clothing	Increase trustworthiness Enhance approachability
Verbal Facilitative Skills	
Encouragers	Convey empathy Demonstrate listening
Open questions	Gather information regarding experiences

(Continued)

Table 8.1   (Continued)

Skill	Purpose in Classroom Guidance
Closed questions	Gather concise data
Reflecting Skills	
Paraphrasing	Communicate empathy Express understanding of content
Summarizing	Ensure understanding of lesson Identify future plans
Reflection of feeling	Show understanding of emotion
Assessment Skills	
Goal setting	Identify the large group objectives and individual objectives for each student
Giving feedback	Provide information regarding learned content

Nonverbal Facilitative Skills

Two-thirds of communication among individuals is nonverbal (Mehrabian, 1968; Vedantam, 2006). Nonverbal communication refers to behaviors that are typically sent intentionally (Burgoon, Buller, & Woodall, 1996). Scholars identified the following as nonverbal communication useful to use or recognize by school counselors: eye contact, facial expressions, gestures, space, touch, vocal cues, and clothing (Ekman, 1993; Pearson, Nelson, Titsworth, & Harter, 2011).

Eye Contact

Good eye contact conveys that the school counselor is listening when a student is talking (Ridley & Asbury, 1988). School counselors conducting classroom guidance programming should make a concerted effort to make eye contact with every student in the classroom. The school counselor who rarely or never looks at their students may appear disinterested in them, and the students may feel ignored (Pearson et al., 2011). The school counselor should also keep in mind cultural communication patterns and maintain or break prolonged eye contact as appropriate.

Facial Expressions

There are over 5,000 cultural-specific facial expressions (Blum, 1998), all of which the school counselor may experience at some point in a classroom guidance lesson. As a result, the counselor should observe all students to discern facial expressions, which may convey affirmative (e.g., enjoyment, engagement) or adverse emotions (e.g., boredom, contempt, fear). In addition, the school counselor needs to be aware of his or her own facial expressions and what messages they may send to students. Negative interpretations may affect the students' engagement.

Gestures

Gestures are movements that are categorized as emblems (i.e., substitute movement for words), illustrators (i.e., reinforce verbal messages), affect displays (i.e., face and body movements used to display emotions), and regulators (i.e., control the pace of communication) (Ekman, 1993; Ekman & Friesen, 1969). A school counselor may use these when they are ending group work, transitioning, emphasizing meaning, and/or reinforcing content. It is very important that school counselors understand that these gestures may have different meanings across cultures.

Space

Fifty years ago, Hall (1966) defined four distances. In more recent literature, two of these distances are noted as useful for counselors in interactions with students or clients (Corey, Corey, & Corey, 2010; Gladding, 2008). School counselors in classroom guidance should use *personal distance* and *social distance*. Personal distance ranges from 18 inches to 4 feet; most individuals use this distance for conversation. Social distance ranges from 4 feet to 12 feet; this distance is used to carry out business in the workplace and in formal teaching interactions (Pearson et al., 2011). Personal distance and social distance convey a relationship; school counselors can use these in the classroom when students are working on individual or group activities. In addition, the proximity of the counselor to the student can provide a level of assurance and serve to keep students on task.

Touch

Typically, touch is viewed as positive, enjoyable, and supportive (Driscoll, Newman, & Seals, 1988). In classroom guidance, touch may be used to emphasize a point or convey caring and respect (Older, 1982). For example, a school counselor may shake the hand of students entering or exiting the classroom, high-five a student on occasion to reinforce positive behavior, and touch the shoulder of a student to show encouragement and engagement. Touch should be handled responsibly, as it may not be acceptable in some school settings.

Vocal Cues

In nonverbal communication, some sounds are included. These sounds include nonwords such as "mmm," and "mmhmm." Nonword sounds encompass, pitch, volume, rate, quality, articulation, and silence. In the classroom guidance setting, vocal cues can have a persuasive effect (Vaish & Striano, 2004) and help the school counselor establish credibility, especially with students with whom they have had little interaction. School counselors can use pitch, volume, and rate to add emphasis, make slight changes in meaning, or tell their students whether they are asking a question or making a statement. The use of silence in counseling has been used as a key facilitative skill. The school counselor can use silence to signify respect or empathy or to allow a student to gather their thoughts to provide a response. However, the school counselor in a classroom setting needs to be aware how various cultures may use silence. Students that feel marginalized due to sexism, racism, or sexual orientation may fall silent because of abuse, embarrassment, or shame. The school counselor should be observant of consistent silence and disengagement from students (Olson, 1997).

Clothing

What a school counselor wears during their interactions in the classroom can signify personality, approachability, and power. Clothing of the counselor can also become a distraction for students. As a result, the counselor should be intentional in what they choose to wear while in the classroom. Using your knowledge of facilitative skills, complete Exercise 8.3 below.

EXERCISE 8.3

NONVERBAL FACILITATIVE SKILLS

You are in a classroom with 20 students and want to effectively transition from the discussion part of the lesson to the experiential portion while also validating the students' experiences. What type of nonverbal facilitative skills might you use in this situation?

_____

_____

What types of nonverbal skills should you not use?

_____

_____

What are some cultural considerations you may need to consider in this interaction?

_____

_____

Verbal Facilitative Skills

The school counselor's role in the classroom is not only to teach content but also to provide encouragement and increase students' personal, social, and academic efficacy. In this regard, using verbal facilitative skills can encourage students to speak and/or participate in the classroom guidance programming. More specifically, verbal encouragers, open questions, and closed questions will be discussed below.

Verbal Encouragers

Scholars identified two types of verbal encouragers—semiverbal (or minimal) and short phrase (or door openers)—that are relevant to school counselors' classroom interaction with students (Bolton, 1979; Hill, 2004). Semiverbal encouragers may accompany nonverbal encouragers and include words that tell the students that you understand what they are saying, such as "Okay," "I see," or "Uh-huh" (Young, 2009). Semiverbal encouragers may also include repeating an important word or phrase used by one or several students. For example, the school counselor may say "Can you say a little more?", "Let's talk about it," or "What are you thinking?" These encouragers help students to expand the current discussion, go deeper, and participate more fully.

Closed Questions

Closed questions do not normally require complex thoughts or responses and are generally used to gather facts or concrete information (Pate, 2011). School counselors using these closed questions in classroom guidance are attempting to determine whether students are able to recall information and to assess the knowledge gained after the classroom guidance lesson.

Open Questions

Open questions allow for intentional, student-focused discussion (Grambo, 1997; Shaunessy, 2000). Open questions specifically help the counselor understand the students' experiences of the lesson as well as provide cues as to students' ongoing learning needs. Open questions may take the following forms: Identify one new nugget of knowledge you learned from today. What are your thoughts about the lesson? What are some important take-aways from the lesson? What are some things you'd like us to talk about in our lesson regarding (insert topic)? Apply these skills in Exercise 8.4 below.

EXERCISE 8.4

IDENTIFYING FACILITATIVE SKILLS

You are teaching a classroom guidance lesson on decision-making skills. You want to gather information and hear the students' experiences of the lesson. Identify closed questions and open questions that you may include in the lesson.

_____

_____

Reflecting Skills

Reflecting skills allow the students to see that you understand their story or the information they have provided related to the classroom guidance lesson. Using reflecting skills also encourages the students to disclose additional information and participate more fully in the experience. Reflecting also communicates empathy. For example, when a student seems apprehensive to share with the class, the school counselor can use reflecting skills such as "You said that you are not sure; it seems like you feel uncomfortable" or "Several of you have shared concerns about a bully and a couple of you feel uncomfortable saying more. Is that correct?" The following reflecting skills will be discussed below: paraphrasing, summarizing, and reflection of feeling.

Paraphrasing

School counselors can use paraphrasing after they have used verbal encouragers and open questions to facilitate communication during the classroom guidance lesson. Paraphrasing allows the students to feel understood and heard and reinforces content. Brammer and MacDonald (1999) outlined a three-step process for using a paraphrase: (1) listen for the basic content expressed; (2) restate this content in a brief way; and (3) note the student's nonverbal and verbal response to your restatement to determine the accuracy of your paraphrasing. Below is an example of how a school counselor can use paraphrasing while engaging in a classroom guidance lesson:

School Counselor:	Does anyone have an example of a time when they used a conflict resolution skill?
Student:	(raises his/her hand) I do.
School Counselor:	Would you like to share that with the class?
Student:	Sure; two of my friends were arguing about where we were going to sit for lunch and I wanted them to compromise. So that day we sat in section A, and the next day we sat in section B. Everyone was happy.
School Counselor:	(paraphrasing) So you used the conflict resolution skill of win-win, where both of your friends were able to sit where they wanted?
Student:	Exactly. I made sure they stayed friends. If I wasn't there, I'm not sure how it would have turned out.
School Counselor:	(paraphrasing) Being there and using conflict resolution made a difference in their friendship and in yours.

This paraphrase interaction can set the stage for school counselors to bring in other students and allow them to talk about their experiences. In addition, it can model for students and teachers how to express empathy and understanding when communicating in the classroom.

Summarizing

An effective summary should include four aspects: content, major feelings, themes, and future plans (Young, 2009). School counselors should use summarizing primarily at the conclusion of an activity, at the end an important segment of the lesson to provide a transition, and at the end of the lesson. Summarizing can also assist school counselors in the classroom with flow and can give direction to students regarding their current experience and future applications. At the end of the classroom guidance lesson, a school counselor may say:

"We've addressed several strategies related to career exploration today, such as discussing future goals, career decision-making skills, and connecting personal qualities with education and the world of work; many of you are excited and have expressed interest in receiving additional information about career and college readiness. Over the next several weeks, your counselors will meet with you to discuss career and college options. Until then, continue to identify coursework, college or post high school work or training, and career interests individually and then discuss these interests with your parents or guardian."

School counselors can use various methods to facilitate the summarization process within a classroom guidance lesson. Some additional ways to enhance the summarization process include developing class contracts or creating a new list of classroom rules based on what the students learned during the classroom guidance lesson.

Reflection of Feeling

Reflection of feeling encompasses observing the students' verbal and nonverbal responses and identifying the main feeling. School counselors may find this useful when dealing with what appear to be bored, confused, angry, or offended students. Additionally, school counselors may want to reinforce positive decision making or encourage students to take pride in their work when noticing happiness, excitement, and satisfaction. The example that follows describes how a counselor might use reflection of feeling to address students who seem to be confused: "Several of you have started to look around the room and several others have stopped participating. I'm wondering if you might be confused by the material. Is that the case?" Here, the school counselor would go on to talk to the students about these feelings. In response, he or she may choose to incorporate different content to meet the needs of the students.

Assessment Skills

Goal Setting

In individual counseling, goals may be more fluid and primarily client driven. In classroom guidance programming, the school counselor often comes into the classroom with overall goals for the students (e.g., increase critical-thinking skills, increase problem-solving skills, increase motivation). However, large-group and individual goal setting should still take place with students in classroom guidance.

EXERCISE 8.5

GOAL SETTING

Identify three strategies a school counselor might use to incorporate students in the development of the overall classroom goal during a lesson regarding anger management strategies.

_____

_____

_____

This will allow students to take ownership of the lesson, intentionally apply the content to their lives, and create a habit of setting and achieving goals. Exercise 8.5 will give you practice in helping students set goals.

The school counselor can discuss the overall goals at the beginning. In addition, school counselors can ask students to help develop and contribute to the goals of the classroom guidance lesson. School counselors will want to ask the students what goals they have in mind. (Please note: These may or may not be different from the school counselor's initial goal.) The school counselor should then make a list of goals and suggest a few related to the lesson that did not immediately surface. Students should then come to a consensus. After the class goals are solidified, the school counselor can then encourage students to identify their own personal goals. The counselor can use the personal classroom guidance goal sheet on the next page.

Feedback Skills

The school counselor should always incorporate opportunities to provide feedback when delivering classroom guidance programming to students. Informal feedback can be given to students throughout the classroom guidance process in the forms of support (i.e., "You all are doing very well completing the lesson on time!") and challenges ("I would encourage you to focus on the questions on the screen; let's try again"). Support and challenge are appropriate and effective ways to enhance the development level of students as well as increase their self-confidence and independence (Hunt, 1969; Stoltenberg, 1981). Exercise 8.6 will help you practice these skills.

Personal Classroom Guidance Goal Sheet

Student's Name_____   Classroom Guidance Lesson Topic_____

****

Class Goals _____

1. Identify a time when you had difficulty with (insert class topic).

_____

_____

_____

2. How did you handle it?

_____

_____

_____

3. Using the content and skills you learned today, how do you want to handle similar situations in the future?

_____

_____

_____

4. Identify two personal goals related to the above situation and class topic.

_____

_____

_____

5. Identify two ways you will know that you have accomplished your goals.

_____

_____

_____

EXERCISE 8.6

SUPPORTIVE AND CHALLENGING FEEDBACK

The school counselor realizes that the students understand three of the five conflict resolution strategies but are still having a difficult time understanding and practicing the last two.

Identify three supportive feedback statements.

Identify three challenging feedback statements.

_____   _____

_____   _____

_____   _____

RESPECT, GENUINENESS, EMPATHY, AND UNCONDITIONAL POSITIVE REGARD

Another skill set that school counselors can utilize in their interactions with students during classroom guidance are the four core counseling skills. The quality of the school counselor-student relationship is the foundation of effective classroom interactions (Marzano, 2003). Utilizing respect, genuineness, empathy, and unconditional positive regard allows counselors to enhance their classroom guidance interactions by infusing skills known to have a positive impact on the helper/client relationship. These basic skills assist counselors in maintaining and facilitating a strong relationship between school counselors and their students. By intentionally infusing basic counseling skills into classroom guidance programming, school counselors will create a classroom environment that facilitates communication, increases understanding, and creates community (Shapiro, 1968).

During classroom guidance sessions, school counselors can show respect for their students by valuing their well-being, perspectives, input, and different beliefs. School counselors can also demonstrate genuineness by being open and authentic (Rogers, 1961). If counselors are able to see the world through the student's eyes (i.e., empathize), they are able to be of more assistance during classroom guidance interactions (Rogers, 1957). Unconditional positive regard is evident when students believe that school counselors honestly care about them and think of them positively (Farber & Doolin, 2011). Respect, genuineness, empathy, and unconditional positive regard can all be conveyed through the use of basic counseling and inter-personal skills. In Exercise 8.7, you will have an opportunity to explore how a school counselor can apply genuineness.

EXERCISE 8.7

INTEGRATING THE CORE COUNSELING CONDITIONS

A school counselor is interacting with elementary school students in a classroom guid-ance session based on conflict resolution. This is the first time the school counselor has used this lesson plan, which is causing the school counselor some discomfort. In addition, this is the first time the counselor has conducted classroom guidance with this particular class. In this regard, several students have expressed that they do not know the counselor.

How should the counselor integrate genuineness? How would this integration affect the counselor's interactions with the students?

_____

_____

Identify what the counselor could do to infuse respect and unconditional positive regard.

_____

_____

Empathy is critical to connect with students. What might the counselor do to demon-strate empathy with these students?

_____

_____

INTEGRATING YOUR THEORETICAL ORIENTATION

As the school counselor integrates basic counseling and group counseling skills, it is imperative that they also incorporate their theoretical orientation. The school counselor's theoretical orientation reveals the persona of the individual and can enhance classroom guidance pedagogy. A school counselor's theoretical orientation may affect how they respond to students, how questions are acknowledged and addressed, and how decisions are made as a group (e.g., activities, discussion topics). Aspects of person-centered therapy have been addressed earlier in the chapter; however, other counseling approaches should be considered as the school counselor develops and implements classroom guidance lessons, as seen in Table 8.2.

School counselors that use individual psychology (i.e., Adlerian counselors) focus on how their students can learn from one another (Dreikurs, 1969). These school counselors also understand that students' individual goals are related to interpersonal goals (Gladding, 2008). School counselors that have a strong existential leaning may attend to increasing the self-awareness of the students and improving personal responsibility (May & Yalom, 2000). These counselors also focus on helping students search for meaning in their lives.

Reality-therapy-based school counselors emphasize current behaviors and choices. These school counselors also help students develop a plan to meet the needs related to the classroom guidance topic. In addition, they use WDEP (want, do, evaluate, and plan), a model developed by Wubbolding (2000) to enhance students' ability to make effective choices. Cognitive behavioral therapy oriented school counselors primarily focus on problem-solving skills, decision-making skills, and behavioral skills during classroom guidance. They may ask students to share concerns related to the class topic, then ask the other students to provide suggestions for addressing the issue. These school counselors may reinforce new behaviors through role-play. School counselors that use solution-focused therapy focus on solutions and exceptions and spend very little time on problem behaviors. Narrative school counselors ask students to identify a current problem related to the classroom guidance topic. These school counselors will have the students explore what influences this problem as well as identify times of success.

Reflection Questions

- What is your theoretical approach?
- How do you use your approach in your classroom guidance lessons?
- In what areas of your lesson could you intentionally integrate your theoretical orientation for your classroom guidance lessons?

Table 8.2 Theoretical Orientation Classroom Guidance

Theoretical Orientation	Philosophy or Focus	Reflection	Question	Classroom Techniques
Adlerian Therapy	Motivated by social interest and individual positive capacities, early experiences create self	"Those past challenges seem to be impacting you now." (early recollection)	"How are the past difficulties impacting you now?"	Early recollections, identifying personal priorities, offering encouragement
Existential Therapy	Awareness, freedom of choice, responsibility, anxiety, authenticity, living, dying	"It sounds like this career would really give your life purpose." (meaning)	"How would this career or job give your life meaning?"	Borrow techniques to address freedom, responsibility, meaning, and developing relationships
Person-Centered Therapy	Positive view of people, self-actualization, increased awareness, trust in self	"These qualities are important to who you are. We are all proud of you." (awareness)	"What about you is unique?"	Use the three core conditions, focusing on developing self-awareness through active listening
Behavior Therapy	Behavior comes from learning, classical/operant principles	"It seems like it's easiest to do homework when you are working with others." (behavior check-in)	"How might you use the same skills when working by yourself?"	Reinforcement, modeling, social skills, desensitization, mindfulness, rehearsal, coaching
Cognitive Behavior	Faulty thinking leads to emotional/behavioral concerns	"Your negative thoughts might have an impact on your actions." (confronting)	"Do those teachers really dislike you?"	Socratic dialogue, homework, coping skills, role-playing, change words, confronting faulty beliefs
Reality Therapy	Quality relationships are key; issues result from resisting control of others	"It sounds like you want to change how you make decisions." (WDEP)	"What are you willing to change?"	Determine willingness to change, develop a plan of action, and make a commitment, WDEP
Solution-Focused Therapy	Capable of effective behavior, positive focus, no problem is constant, future oriented	"Can you find times this hasn't occurred?" (exceptions)	"If the issue was solved overnight, how would you know?"	Exception, miracle, and scaling questions
Narrative Therapy	Reconstruct their life story, separate self from dominant stories, map the influence	"It sounds like your peers have influenced you." (map the influence)	"How has this problem impacted you?"	Externalization, document the evidence

200

Basic counseling and group counseling skills, empathy, and theoretical orientation are central to effectively conducting classroom guidance. The use of these skills allows school counselors to embrace their counselor identity while simultaneously using best practices from teaching. The following section will highlight the key teaching and classroom management strategies helpful for school counselors conducting classroom guidance.

THE BASICS OF TEACHING AND MANAGING

While school counselors infuse counseling practices into their classroom guidance application, they are also tasked with effectively using teaching and classroom-management strategies. Teaching and management skills allow school counselors to organize content and manage challenging situations. The following section will discuss effective teaching strategies, classroom management strategies, and strategies for handling misbehavior and misdirection.

Teaching Strategies

Cashin (1990) identified several recommendations for effective teaching, which school counselors can use to enhance their classroom guidance programming:

1. Design the lesson to the developmental level of your students.

2. Focus your topic: Remember, you cannot cover everything in one lecture.

3. Prepare an outline that includes 5–9 major points you want to cover in your lesson.

4. Organize your points for clarity.

5. Select appropriate examples, illustrations, and activities.

6. Repeat points when necessary (i.e., paraphrase and summarize).

7. Be aware of their students; notice their feedback (i.e., verbal and nonverbal).

8. Be enthusiastic; the students should know that you are excited about the topic.

As indicated above, the school counselor should consider these teaching elements prior to walking into the classroom. Understanding the developmental needs of the school level, class grades, and individual students are imperative to the success of classroom guidance programming. In addition, the school counselor should be prepared with alternative class activities in case students fail to engage in the initial content. This information would be revealed through evaluation measures.

The National Association for the Education of Young Children (2009) has specifically identified developmentally appropriate teaching strategies that school counselors can use when working with K–12 students when delivering classroom guidance programming. Acknowledge what the students say in class. School counselors can do this verbally or nonverbally (e.g., head nods, smiling). Encourage persistence and effort instead of only praising students who complete the task ("You're thinking of a lot of study habits; let's keep going"). This can also assist school counselors in addressing the learning differences and learning styles of students. Provide explicit feedback rather than general comments ("Kevin, thank you for sharing. You helped to enhance our understanding of this particular conflict resolution skill by providing that example").

Model behaviors, attitudes, and ways of making good decisions, showing children rather than just telling them ("Sandy said something earlier that we might want to try. Sandy, can you tell us again what your idea was?"). Challenge students to go a little beyond the task. For example, ask the students to identify the individuals they should contact if they or someone they know experience bullying, and then challenge them to go beyond the task by asking the students to explore how it would feel to have to talk to this individual about the bullying incident. In addition, the school counselor can ask questions that provoke the students to think deeper and more critically ("If you couldn't talk to your partner, how else could you let him know what to do?"). School counselors also need to be open to providing assistance. For example, if students are having difficulty coming up with ideas, the school counselor can provide some clues or suggestions to help them.

Classroom Management Strategies

One of the more significant conclusions from classroom management research is that early attention to facilitation, behavior, and climate at the beginning of the session is a critical ingredient to success (Emmer, Evertson, & Anderson, 1980; Sanford & Evertson, 1981). Additionally, good classroom managers and facilitators are school counselors who understand and use "withitness," (Kounin, 1970).

"Withitness" involves a keen awareness of disruptive behavior or potentially disruptive behavior and immediate attending to that behavior whether verbally (i.e., to stop the disruptive student) or by ignoring (i.e., for the attention-seeking student). "Withitness" involves the following dimensions:

1. *Rules and procedures*. First, identify specific rules and procedures for your time in the classroom. These rules should be posted and potentially consistent

with the classroom teacher's rules. Involve students in the design of the rules and procedures (Evertson, Emmer, & Worsham, 2003; Marzano, 2003).

2. *Disciplinary actions.* Cotton (1990) has estimated that only about half of all classroom time is used for instruction and that disciplinary problems occupy most of the other half. It is very important that school counselors understand how to address discipline concerns with their role as counselor and not as the disciplinarian. Misdirection and misbehavior will be discussed in detail in the next section.

3. *Establishing the counselor-student classroom relationship.* The counselor-student relationship in the classroom is one that can be a little tricky because the school counselor often has close relationships with many students in the school over the course of several years. As a result, students may attempt to have personal counseling conversations or seek additional assistance while the school counselor is conducting classroom guidance lessons. This can be addressed in a review of the rules and procedures. For example, the school counselor can let the students know that follow-up meetings can be scheduled outside the classroom.

4. *Taking on a classroom frame of mind.* School counselors should maintain or heighten their awareness, learn how to react quickly, and plan for challenges. These strategies can be achieved by observing more-experienced teachers and school counselors in the classroom.

5. *Allowing students to take part in managing themselves.* The school counselor should utilize classroom rules and procedures that allow students to take responsibility. For example, school counselors can have students create a written statement of beliefs that includes the expected behaviors of the classroom (Netolicky, 1998).

6. *Co-teaching.* Co-teaching can assist school counselors in developing classroom guidance lessons that not only integrate counseling skills but also state student performance standards. This collaboration can strengthen the counselor's delivery and allow them to develop more-inclusive lessons. For example, the school counselor could collaborate with the language arts or English teacher(s) to integrate writing performance standards into curriculum while also helping students to write about academic-, social-, or career-related topics.

7. *Friendliness and flexibility.* Being friendly and enthusiastic about the lesson can help school counselors pace the lesson and remain flexible should any

changes in the structure occur (Tileson, 2000). School counselors can use humor to manage the classroom behavior during a classroom guidance lesson (Huss, 2008). For example, the school counselor might use humor to help relax or deescalate a situation by telling a humorous story. Including humor can make classroom guidance more fun and help motivate students in a developmentally appropriate way (Geltner & Clark, 2005).

Using the teaching strategies in this section can assist school counselors in organizing and managing their classroom lesson. However, additional management strategies may be useful with dealing with students who display misbehavior. The following section will discuss how school counselors can address misbehavior during their classroom guidance lesson.

Strategies for Handling Misbehavior and Misdirection

One of the significant challenges school counselors face when conducting classroom guidance is dealing with students who display behaviors to gain attention, power, or revenge or to demonstrate inadequacy (Adler, 1958; Albert, 1996; Nelsen, 1987). Colvin (2010) identifies five types of misbehaviors typically displayed by elementary and secondary school students: off-task behavior, rule infractions, disrespectful behavior, agitation, and noncompliance. All of these can interfere with classroom guidance implementation. Below, the five types of misbehaviors are described (see Table 8.3).

Off-task behavior denotes any behavior in which the school counselor's directions are not followed or in which the student is engaged in activities unrelated to the assigned task. Rule infractions take place when a student

Table 8.3 Types of Misbehavior

Misbehavior	Identifiers	Counselor's Response
Off-task behavior	Not engaged in class activities	Redirect, token economy, guidance helper
Rule infractions	Behaves in contrast to class procedures	Clarify rule, token economy
Disrespectful behavior	Infringes on others negatively	Address calmly, token economy
Agitation	Displays distracting emotions	Identify the signs, use calming strategies, guidance helper
Noncompliance	Defiance, refusal to cooperate	Repeat in private, focus on choices, token economy

acts in a way that is in contrast to the identified rules and procedures of the classroom lesson. Disrespectful behavior involves the student displaying actions that infringe on the rights of others, including bullying, harassment, rudeness, or intimidation. Agitation includes emotional responses such as withdrawal, anxiety, anger, frustration, and worry. Noncompliance can be the most difficult to address in the classroom, as students often refuse to follow directions and demonstrate insubordination of authority.

General Strategies for Misbehavior Used by the Counselor

Scholars have identified several effective strategies to address misbehavior: leaving the ego at the door, empathy, admiring negative attitudes and behaviors, praising students for on-task behavior, calming strategies, follow-up, and positive behavior interventions and supports (Colvin, 2010; Rogers & Renard, 1999).

Leaving the Ego at the Door. The school counselor should guard against giving in to emotions such as anger, exasperation, or displeasure. When they fail to do so, their judgment and counseling role is impaired. This skill should be viewed as a prerequisite to all other skills outlined in this chapter (Beaty-O'Ferrall, Green, & Hanna, 2010). School counselors would benefit well from knowing that classroom management is similar to running a small group of 25+ individuals. People will have reactions to the content and to each other, and all arrive and leave with certain preexisting stresses. The lesson is important, but it is also important to keep in mind that on any given day, some students will be fully present and participatory and others may not.

Empathy. Empathy demonstrated by the school counselor allows the student to feel understood (Hanna, Hanna, & Keys, 1999). Empathetic relationships are significantly important for students experiencing behavioral challenges in the classroom (Beaty-O'Ferrall et al., 2010; Mordock, 1991). For example, if a student is experiencing agitation and anger, the school counselor can convey empathy by stating, "It makes sense that you would be angry; I probably would be upset, too." This can assist the student in connecting to the counselor and potentially changing their behavior.

Admiring Negative Attitudes and Behaviors. The student's negative behavior is a skill he or she has been practicing and refining for many years (Beaty-O'Ferrall et al., 2010; Seligman, 1999). In the case of an angry male teen, for example, being angry might have been the only or best way of getting his needs for attention met in his family. Consequently, it is expected that he would bring those same coping skills into his relational interactions at school. Instead of engaging in a discussion about the impact of the anger and focusing on the student changing his anger, the counselor will want to acknowledge the anger that has assisted the student in the past and then focus on redirecting it. Subsequently, the counselor should reframe the skill. The counselor may say, "I have observed that you have a lot of emotions and it's good that you are getting them out. What are some other ways that you might express those emotions?" This admiration and redirection can challenge the student to find a creative way of using the skill, which the counselor can help facilitate.

Praising Students for On-Task Behavior. Encouraging students who are exhibiting on-task and/or appropriate behavior is very useful, as it engages a positive atmosphere (Quarto, 2007). It can also help school counselors manage the classroom and promote on-task behavior for all students. School counselors can also intentionally observe students who are displaying some off-task behaviors and focus on the times they demonstrate on-task behavior or use students as guidance helpers. For example, when Jenny, who has had her head down all class, finally decides to participate, the school counselor may state, "Jenny, your group is really benefiting from your ideas. Keep up the good work."

Calming Strategies. Calming strategies include focusing the student, providing space, presenting options, providing assurances and additional time, and permitting preferred activities as well as movement activities; all of these are useful in deescalating student misbehavior (Ehrenreich & Fisak, 2005; Sprick & Garrison, 2008). The school counselor can assist by focusing the student, helping them organize materials, and redirecting them to the task at hand (Quarto, 2007). Providing space to the student may help a student who is experiencing agitation or misbehavior to gradually settle down and refocus. The school counselor can also present options to students that remain off-task, as this gives them a chance to focus, take some of their power back, and calm down. Providing assurance/additional time is another strategy school counselors can use to assist students whose behavior may worsen when certain tasks have to be met. For example, the school counselor may say, "You have a little more time, Kelly. Keep working." The school counselor may also choose to permit the student who is having difficulty to engage in activities that they prefer individually. For example, the school counselor may allow Chris, a fourth grader who has difficulty in group activities, to sit by himself and work until he feels more ready to take part in the group work. In addition, the school counselor can also utilize movement activities, which can decrease misdirected behavior and provide new energy and a time to refocus (Colvin, 2010).

Follow-Up. It is very important that school counselors follow up with the misdirected student after the lesson is complete. Following up can help decrease misdirection in the future with the student and allows the student to know that the counselor remains available unconditionally. The follow-up should include focusing on the student-counselor relationship, mapping the influence of the behavior, and determining what the student needs that can affect their behavior positively in the future.

Positive Behavior Intervention & Supports (PBIS). While school counselors can engage individually with students to address misbehavior, school counselors can also work with school behavior support teams, such as positive behavior interventions & supports (PBIS), to address students' misbehavior. PBIS is a multi-tiered approach to prevention that focuses on improving the behavioral expectations of all students and decreasing misbehavior collectively. In this type of team, the school counselor works with three to five other school personnel (e.g., administrators, teachers, parents, and support staff) to address identified behavioral expectations. School counselors, along with the other team members, use schoolwide and individualized interventions to improve school environment (OSEP Technical Assistance Center on Positive Behavior Interventions & Supports, 2009).

In Tier 1, the approach focuses on addressing schoolwide behavioral initiatives to address behavioral concerns (i.e., schoolwide/universal needs). Tier 2 is designed to target the students with behavioral needs; the team may work with the identified student to address an identified behavioral concern (i.e., targeted/selective). If change does not occur using the Tier 2 approach, the team then proceeds to Tier 3 with the targeted students. The students take part in a functional behavioral assessment, which allows the members to determine the focus of intervention and create an individualized support structure (i.e., individual/indicated). See Table 8.4 for more detail.

Table 8.4 Positive Behavior Interventions & Supports Tiers

Tier	Focus	Data	Outcomes
1	Create a positive setting	School benchmarks	Students demonstrating increases in appropriate behaviors
	Include social skill instruction	Incident reports/referrals	Implementation fidelity, student behavior
	Infuse a recognition system	Academic data	Decrease in crisis

(Continued)

Table 8.4 (Continued)

Tier	Focus	Data	Outcomes
	Apply a system for monitoring	Schoolwide evaluation tool (Sugai, Lewis-Palmer, Todd, & Horner, 2005)	Implement intervention and discipline system
2	Include an individualized goal for some students	Incident reports	Students demonstrating targeted behavior
	Provide frequent social skills instruction	Academic data for targeted students	Decrease targeted students
	Check in/check out for identified students	Individual evaluation tool (Anderson et al., 2011)	Decrease discipline referrals
	Move students along a continuum of supports	Monitoring Advanced Tiers Tool (Horner, Sampson, Anderson, Todd, & Eliason, 2012)	Intensify or fade supports based on target behavior
3	Create an individual behavior support plan based on a full behavioral assessment	Full behavioral assessment data	Student making progress toward behavior goals
	Use of positive/proactive intervention	Student plan	Decrease in student's problem behavior
	Teach replacement behaviors	Individual evaluation tool (Anderson et al., 2011)	Feedback from wraparound services (e.g., social work, psychologist)
	Use consequence strategies	Academic data	Increase in target behavior based on reinforcements

Adapted from Simonsen, B., & Sugai, G. (2013). PBIS in alternative education settings: Positive support for youth with high-risk behavior. *Education and Treatment of Children, 36,* 4–14.

CASE STUDY

The school counselor has just finished giving directions to the students for the next activity in the classroom guidance lesson and has asked the students to pay careful attention. Billy, who has had his head down, says loudly, "What do you want us to do?" Before the counselor can respond, Julie turns to Billy and says, "You are so stupid; no wonder you are in the seventh grade again." The counselor quickly realizes that he or she needs to respond.

First, identify the misbehaviors displayed in this case study:

_____

What should be the counselor's priority in addressing the misbehaviors?

_____

How does the school counselor respond to Billy, Julie, and the entire class?

_____

The teaching and managing skills discussed above can assist students that have challenges and ensure that school counselors are able to meet the needs of students that demonstrate challenging behaviors in the classroom. School counselors can utilize technological processes to enhance their management of the classroom and engage students who may have difficulties with attention concerns. The next section will identify technological strategies and competencies that school counselors can use to enrich their classroom guidance curriculum.

TECHNOLOGY IN THE CLASSROOM

Research indicates that the use of technology can enhance school counselor's effectiveness (Hayden, Poynton, & Sabella, 2008), improve students' academic success (Bain & Ross, 1999), improve students' creative and critical thinking (CEO Forum on Education and Technology, 2001), and increase students' self-confidence and scholastic motivation (Sivin-Kachala & Bialo, 2000). In this section, technological counseling competencies and key technological classroom-based practices will be described.

Technology Competencies

Fifteen years ago, initial technology competencies were developed for practicing school counselors (Hartman, 1999; Hines, 2002; Sabella, 2000). These competencies have been integrated into accrediting and counseling organizations. Council for Accreditation of Counseling & Related Educational Programs (2009), American Counseling Association (2014), and American School Counselor Association (2012) all suggest that school counselors have technological competence. These accrediting bodies and organizations suggest that school counselors should have knowledge in the following technological areas:

- Web-based career information and computer-based career information systems, such as PowerSchool, SASI, Skyward, and SIMS
- Technology-based career development applications and strategies, including computer-assisted career guidance and information systems and appropriate websites such as The Career Key (http://www.careerkey.org), O*Net Online (http://www.onetonline.org/), and My Next Move (http://www.mynextmove.org).
- Computer-managed and computer-assisted student assessment methods such as state computer-based assessment, district-level online assessment, PSAT, SAT, and ASVAB
- Technology and statistical methods used to conduct research and program evaluation, such as SPSS, Microsoft Excel, and EZ Analyze
- Current and emerging technology in education and school counseling to assist students, families, and educators in using resources that promote informed academic, career, and social/emotional choices using technology such as parent portals, blogs, and wikis
- The use of technology in the design, implementation, monitoring and evaluation of a comprehensive school counseling program, such as Hallways school counseling software and noteCounselor software

Specific technological techniques that school counselors can use to support students' learning during classroom guidance programming include learning management systems (LMS), Web 2.0 technologies, synchronous instruction technology, and productivity technology. (See Table 8.5.)

Table 8.5   Technology in Education

Types of Technology	Uses
Learning Management System	Moodle, Canvas, Drupal
Web 2.0 technologies	Blogs, wikis, social bookmarking tools, podcasts, educational games
Synchronous instruction technologies	Blackboard Collaborate, Skype, Panopto
Social networking technologies	Facebook, LinkedIn, Pinterest, Flickr, Twitter
Productivity technologies	Prezi, Google Docs, Mindmap, IHMC Cmap, VoiceThread
Other	Dropbox

Source: Czerkawski, B.C. (2013). Strategies for integrating emerging technologies: Case study of an educational technology master's program. *Contemporary Educational Technology, 4,* 309–321.

Learning Management System (LMS)

An LMS is a software platform designed to manage a coherent educational electronic system. Modular Object-Oriented Dynamic Learning Environment (Moodle), which has been useful in K–12 settings, is an LMS designed to share useful information and manage content such as classroom guidance curriculum content (Psycharis, Chalatzoglidis, & Kalogiannakis, 2013). Moodle can help school counselors enhance their classroom guidance lessons and provide additional content to students, teachers, and parents related to the classroom topic (Perkins & Pfaffman, 2006). Moodle can also be helpful for students who are absent during classroom guidance to access the content so that missed instruction can be accessed. (See http://www.moodle.org for more information.) Other LMS platforms include Blackboard, Canvas, and Drupal.

Web 2.0 Technologies

Web 2.0 denotes a concept that lets individuals collaborate with one another and contribute to the authorship of content, customize websites for their use, and rapidly publish their thoughts (Heafner & Friedman, 2008). Examples of Web 2.0 technologies that school counselors can use to enhance their school counseling guidance curriculum include blogs, wikis, and podcasts. Blogs can be used to allow students to view the progress of their thinking or for school counselors to share their thoughts regarding their classroom guidance curriculum (Ellison & Wu, 2008). For example, a school counselor may post important remainders or keystones from the lesson on their blog for parents and students, or school counselors might monitor an ongoing blog where students can post their experiences regarding the college application process.

In addition, school counselors can use Wikipedia or wikis during classroom guidance lessons. Wikis allow students to exchange ideas, share multiple perspectives, and clarify understandings related to classroom guidance topics (Coutinho & Bottentuit Junior, 2007). For example, students can create wikis related to information they learned during the classroom guidance lesson (e.g., anti-bullying practices, anger management strategies, career exploration tools).

Podcasts are an alternative learning form for students that may be integrated into the classroom guidance lesson or suggested for follow-up learning (Crane, 2012). Using podcasts, school counselors can enhance students' social skills by allowing students to collaborate with one another on the selected podcasts. In addition, school counselors can use the podcasts they have developed to enhance their classroom guidance lessons, reuse their classroom guidance lessons, collaborate with teachers to meet student performance standards, and follow up with students who may have missed instruction.

Synchronous Instruction Technologies

Virtual collaboration is when two or more people work together to accomplish a task without the use of face-to-face interaction (Czerkawski, 2013). One such technology that school counselors can use to enhance their classroom guidance lessons is Skype. Skype is a free communication software that allows individuals to make calls, instant message, and video conference online. School counselors can invite guest speakers to virtually discuss elements of the classroom guidance lesson. This is certainly applicable when facilitating classroom guidance lessons involving career and college content. Other synchronous instruction technologies include Blackboard Collaborate and Panopto.

Social Networking Technologies

Social networking technologies are websites on the Internet that allow people to come together in one location to communicate about ideas, interests, and activities as well as allow individuals to make new friends across political perspectives, economic backgrounds, and geographic regions (Crane, 2012). Social networks include Twitter, Facebook, Edmodo, My Space, and SchoolTube, to name a few. School counselors can use these modes of technology to communicate with students and parents about important dates and information. For instance, school counselors may develop a Facebook or Schooltube group for their seniors where the school counselor posts information about graduation, scholarships, college application due dates, and so on. This type of social networking technology can allow students to comment and ask questions to the school counselor as well as communicate with other seniors in the group.

Productivity Technologies

Productivity technologies that can be used to enhance the classroom guidance lesson include Prezi, Google Docs, and Mindmap. Prezi is an online Adobe Flash-based nonlinear presentation program (Settle, Abrams, & Baker, 2011). Prezi can specifically be utilized by school counselors in classroom guidance content presentations. Prezi can also be used by students to enhance socialization and decision-making skills. For example, students can collaboratively work on short presentations in small groups related to the classroom guidance lesson. In addition, school counselors can use Prezi to present content that students, parents, and teachers can view during and after the lesson from anywhere by using the online link. School counselors can also use Prezi to co-teach content related to student performance standards (Settle et al., 2011). School counselors can also use

Mindmap to enhance students' note-taking ability, recall, creativity, and problem solving. All of these are needed skills school counselors can address during classroom guidance lessons. Mindmap technology applications allow school counselors to help students brainstorm new ideas and help them enhance organization skills. Google Docs are also productivity technologies that school counselors can use to promote collaboration. For example, school counselors can develop Google Doc brainstorming sessions based on classroom guidance curriculum topics to help enhance students' teamwork and creativity.

Dropbox

Dropbox is a tool that helps individuals store and organize information wherever they are. This technology application allows students to synchronize information across all of their devices as well as see their revision history and share files with others. For instance, school counselors can utilize Dropbox when conducting a classroom guidance lesson on organization. In addition, school counselors can also create a sharing folder for each grade level and classroom guidance curriculum to make information available to your students and parents (e.g., PowerPoints, handouts, reading assignments, etc.).

In the twenty-first century, technology is a central component in education and an important tool for school counselors to utilize in their classroom guidance curricula. Adding tools from LMS, Web 2.0 technologies, synchronous instruction technologies, and productivity technologies will allow school counselors to enhance their practice while also integrating technological structures that students need to understand and use. Although these implements are useful, school counselors need to consider potential ethical concerns related to technology and classroom guidance instruction. See the following case study for an example of technology use in the classroom.

CASE STUDY

Allen, a school counselor who has typically used PowerPoint and smartboard technology in his classroom guidance lessons, wants to enhance his lesson by adding Prezi, podcasts, and Skype. He is currently working on a Prezi presentation for his "Exploring College and Career Opportunities" lesson.

(Continued)

(Continued)

When and how can Allen integrate podcasts to enhance the Prezi lesson?

_____

How might Allen use Skype to enhance the Prezi lesson?

_____

ETHICS IN CLASSROOM GUIDANCE

Considering ethics when conducting classroom guidance is something that may be overlooked, as ethics is often discussed primarily when conducting individual and group counseling. However, ethical considerations should apply to all school counseling activities, including classroom guidance. Here, classroom and technology ethical consideration will be discussed and strategies will be provided to help school counselors conduct ethical classroom guidance.

Classroom Considerations

School counselors should consider the following when conducting classroom guidance: confidentiality, informed consent, cultural sensitivity, clinical limits of delivery method, and effectiveness of classroom guidance. School counselors should disclose the limits of confidentiality in a developmentally appropriate manner. In classroom guidance, as in other small counseling-based groups, confidentiality is not guaranteed; as a result, the school counselor should select the classroom guidance topics carefully.

Consent to participate should be sent at the beginning of the year. However, school counselors should also send information to parents and teachers prior to the lesson regarding when lessons will be conducted and the lesson topic. School counselors should also note that at any time, parents could choose to opt out of guidance services, including the classroom guidance curriculum. School counselors should have a plan in place for students who cannot participate in the lesson. For example, the student might go to another classroom, serve as an office helper, or help the teacher outside of the class (e.g., develop a bulletin board).

Cultural competence and sensitivity are also ethical considerations that school counselors should attend to. When developing curriculum, school counselors should explore the role of privilege and oppression on its development and identify how the curriculum might marginalize underserved populations and advantage others. In addition, school counselors should examine personal belief systems to ensure that their beliefs and values are not imposed on their students when conducting classroom guidance.

School counselors should acknowledge that there are clinical limits to this delivery method. Prior to starting the lesson, the school counselor should discuss this with the students, informing them that this lesson might bring up emotions and thoughts that they might want to discuss in private or when they can provide more confidentiality. In addition, the school counselor can discuss follow-up procedures with the students to ensure that they understand that the school counselor is open to talking with them in the future.

Another ethical consideration is in the use of effective curriculum. School counselors should use classroom guidance curriculum that is supported by literature and shows an effectiveness in enhancing academic, career, and social/emotional skills. In addition, school counselors should use assessments that show improvement. This information should be shared consistently with stakeholders.

Use of Technology

While technology is vast and consistently used in schools to enhance instruction, ethical challenges abound. The American School Counselor Association and the American Counseling Association ethics codes describe the ethical constraints of using technology when working with students (or clients). The main issues school counselors should be aware of include the limitations of technological applications, equal access for all students, and cyberbullying.

School counselors need to ensure that their classroom guidance lessons address the developmental, academic, career, and social/emotional needs of all students. In addition, school counselors need to make certain that students know how to use the applications. Furthermore, follow-up sessions with the students can also help to confirm that students are using the technology and answer questions, if necessary. Anther ethical concern is related to equal access to technology for all students. When school counselors ask students to work on an application, such as O*Net Online, they need to provide options for students who may not have computer access at home. For example, they might schedule library time for parents and students in the evening or provide computer time during the school day (i.e., during study hall or lunch). The last major technological ethical concern is cyberbullying. Cyberbullying has become a significant issue in schools, and school counselors should try to guard against this when they use or engage students in using technology when conducting classroom guidance. When school counselors do ask students to use technology, the school counselor should engage in a discussion regarding cyberbullying. For example, discussing what cyberbullying is, the impact of cyberbullying, and law regarding cyberbullying can help students understand why it is important to not use technology in that manner.

These classroom and technological ethical considerations are a critical aspect of implementing classroom guidance. School counselors should endeavor to attend to them consistently and seek out support and supervision whenever necessary.

SUMMARY

This chapter highlighted some of the basic competencies that school counselors should consider as they merge aspects of counseling and education in classroom guidance programming. Integrating basic counseling skills and theoretical orientation can enhance the classroom guidance application and help school counselors clarify their counselor identity as they provide academic, career, and social/emotional development in the classroom. This chapter also illuminated the importance of attending to teaching and classroom management strategies. The identified strategies can assist school counselors in addressing challenging students as well as enhancing the structure of their school counselor's classroom guidance lesson. This chapter presents key technological applications, which school counselors can use to improve their curriculum and connect with stakeholders. Lastly, this chapter explores potential classroom and technological ethical considerations for school counselors in classroom settings.

KEYSTONES

- Counseling and behavior management skills allow the school counselor to move the classroom guidance process into a more clinically based delivery system.
- Group process and dynamics, group stages, group facilitative procedural skills, and personal leadership styles are important group aspects that school counselors should consider using when conducting classroom guidance (Giltner et al., 2011).
- Basic counseling skills that can be utilized by school counselors in classroom guidance curriculum include nonverbal and verbal encouragers, reflecting skills, and assessment skills (Giltner et al., 2011).
- A school counselor's theoretical orientation may affect how students are responded to, how questions are acknowledged and addressed, and how decisions are made as a group.
- School counselors can utilize several effective strategies to address misbehavior: leaving the ego at the door, empathy, admiring negative attitudes and behaviors, praising students for on-task behavior, calming strategies, redirecting, and follow-up (Colvin, 2010; Rogers & Renard, 1999).

- Specific technological techniques that school counselors can use to support students' learning during classroom guidance programming include LMS, Web 2.0 technologies, synchronous instruction technologies, and productivity technologies.

REFERENCES

Adler, A. (1958). *What life should mean to you.* New York, NY: Capricorn.

Adler, P. A., Kless, S. J., & Adler, P. (1992). Socialization to gender roles: Popularity among elementary school boys and girls. *Sociology of Education, 65,* 169–187.

Albert, L. (1996). *Cooperative discipline.* Circle Pines, MN: American Guidance Service.

American Counseling Association. (2014). *ACA code of ethics.* Alexandria, VA: Author.

American School Counselor Association. (2012). *The ASCA national model: A framework for school counseling programs* (3rd ed.). Alexandria, VA: Author.

Anderson, C. M., Lewis-Palmer, T., Todd, A. W., Horner, R. H., Sugai, G., & Sampson, N. K. (2011). *Individual student systems evaluation tool, version 2.8.* Eugene: University of Oregon.

Association for Specialists in Group Work. (2000). *ASGW professional standards for group counseling.* Alexandria, VA: Author.

Bain, A., & Ross, K. (1999). School reengineering and SAT-1 performance: A case study. *International Journal of Education Reform, 9*(2), 148–153.

Beaty-O'Ferrall, M., Green, A., & Hanna, F. (2010). Classroom management strategies for difficult students: Promoting change through relationships. *Middle School Journal, 41,* 4–11.

Blum, D. (1998). Face it! *Psychology Today, 31*(5), 32–39.

Bolton, R. (1979). *People skills: How to assert yourself, listen to others, and resolve conflicts.* Upper Saddle River, NJ: Prentice Hall.

Brammer, L. M., & MacDonald, G. (1999). *The helping relationship: Process and skills* (4th ed.). Needham Heights, MA: Allyn & Bacon.

Burgoon, J. K., Buller, D. B., & Woodall, W. G. (1996). *Nonverbal communication: The unspoken dialogue* (2nd ed.). New York, NY: McGraw-Hill.

Cashin, W. E. (1990). Students do rate different academic fields differently. In M. Theall & J. Franklin (Eds.), *Student ratings of instruction: Issues for improving practice* (no. 43, pp. 113–121). San Francisco, CA: Jossey-Bass.

CEO Forum on Education and Technology. (2001). *Education technology must be included in comprehensive education legislation.* Washington, DC: CEO Forum on Education and Technology.

Colvin, G. (2010). *Defusing disruptive behavior in the classroom.* Thousand Oaks, CA: Corwin.

Corey, M. S., Corey, G., & Corey, C. (2010). *Groups: Process and practice* (8th ed.). Pacific Grove, CA: Brooks/Cole.

Cotton, K. (1990). Schoolwide and classroom discipline. *School improvement research series, close-up #9.* Portland, OR: Northwest Regional Educational Laboratory.

Council for Accreditation of Counseling & Related Educational Programs (CACREP). (2009). *CACREP accreditation and procedures manual.* Alexandria, VA: Author.

Coutinho, C. P., & Bottentuit Junior, J. B. (2007). Collaborative learning using wiki: A pilot student with master students in educational technology in Portugal. *Proceedings of World Conference on Educational Multimedia,* 1786–1791.

Crane, B. E. (2012). *Using Web 2.0 and social networking tools in the K–12 classroom.* Chicago, IL: Neal-Schuman Publishers.

Czerkawski, B. C. (2013). Strategies for integrating emerging technologies: Case study of an online educational technology master's program. *Contemporary Educational Technology, 4,* 309–321.

Dreikurs, R. (1969). Social interest: The basis of normality. *Counseling Psychologist, 1*(2), 45–48.

Driscoll, M. S., Newman, D. L., & Seals, J. M. (1988). The effect of touch on perception of counselors. *Counselor Education and Supervision, 27,* 344–354.

Ehrenreich, J., & Fisak, B. (2005). Anxiety management. In M. Hersen, J. Rosqvist, A. Gross, R. Drabman, G. Sugai, & R. Horner (Eds.), *Encyclopedia of behavior modification and cognitive behavior therapy* (Vol. 2, pp. 663–667). Thousand Oaks, CA: SAGE.

Ekman, P. (1993). Facial expression and emotion. *American Psychologist, 48,* 384–392.

Ekman, P., & Friesen, W. V. (1969). The repertoire or nonverbal behavior: Categories, origins, usage, and coding. *Semiotica, 1,* 49–98.

Ellison, N., & Wu, Y. (2008). Blogging in the classroom: A preliminary exploration of student attitudes and impact on comprehension. *Journal of Educational Multimedia and Hypermedia, 17*(1), 99–122.

Emmer, E. T., Evertson, C. M., & Anderson, L. M. (1980). Effective classroom management at the beginning of the school year. *The Elementary School Journal, 80*(5), 219–231.

Evertson, C. M., Emmer, E. T., & Worsham, M. E. (2003). *Classroom management for elementary teachers* (6th ed.). Boston, MA: Allyn and Bacon.

Farber, B. A., & Doolin, E. M. (2011). Positive regard. *Psychotherapy, 48,* 58–64.

Geltner, J. A., & Clark, M. A. (2005). Engaging students in classroom guidance: Management strategies for middle school counselors. *Professional School Counseling, 9*(2), 164–166.

Giltner, J. A., Cunningham, T. J., & Caldwell, C. D. (2011). Identifying curriculum components for classroom management training for school counselors: A Delphi study. *Journal of Counselor Preparation & Supervision, 3*(2). Retrieved April 4, 2015, from http://repository.wcsu .edu/jcps/vol3/iss2/2

Gladding, S. T. (2008). *Groups: A counseling specialty* (5th ed.). Upper Saddle River, NJ: Pearson Education.

Grambo, G. (1997). Questions in your classroom. *Gifted Child Today, 20*(3), 42–43.

Hall, E. (1966). *The hidden dimension: Man's use of space in public and private.* London, England: The Bodley Head Ltd.

Hanna, F. J., Hanna, C. A., & Keys, S. G. (1999). Fifty shades for counseling defiant, aggressive adolescents: Reaching, accepting, and relating. *Journal of Counseling & Development, 77*(4), 395–404.

Hartman, K. E. (1999). Technology and the school counselor. *Education Week.* Retrieved December 20, 2002, from http://edweek.com/ew/1998/09hart.h18.

Hayden, L., Poynton, T. A., & Sabella, R. A. (2008). School counselor's use of technology within the ASCA national model's delivery system. *Journal of Technology in Counseling, 5*(1).

Heafner, T., & Friedman, A. (2008). Wikis and constructivism in secondary social studies: Fostering a deeper understanding. *Computers in the Schools, 25*(3/4), 288–302.

Hill, C. E. (2004). *Helping skills: Facilitating exploration, insight, and action* (2nd ed.). Washington, DC: American Psychological Association.

Hines, P. L. (2002). Student technology competencies for school counseling programs. *Journal of Technology in Counseling, 2*(2).

Horner, R. H., Sampson, N. K., Anderson, C. M., Todd, A. W., & Eliason, B. M. (2012). *Monitoring advanced tiers tool, beta version.* Eugene, OR: University of Oregon, Education and Community Supports.

Hunt, J. M. (1969). The epigenesis of intrinsic motivation and the fostering of early cognitive development. In J. M. Hunt (Ed.), *The challenge of incompetence and poverty* (pp. 94–111). Urbana: University of Illinois Press.

Huss, J. A. (2008). Getting serious about humor: Attitudes of secondary teachers toward the use of humor as a teaching strategy. *Journal of Ethnographic & Qualitative Research, 3,* 28–36.

Kottler, J. A., & Englar-Carlson, M. (2010). *Learning group leadership: An experiential approach.* Thousand Oaks, CA: SAGE.

Kounin, J. S. (1970). *Discipline and group management in classrooms.* New York, NY: Holt, Rinehart & Winston.

Lewin, K. (1951). *Field theory in social science.* New York, NY: Harper.

Marzano, R. J. (2003). *What works in schools.* Alexandria, VA: ASCD.

May, R., & Yalom, I. (2000). Existential psychotherapy. In R. J. Corsini & D. Wedding (Eds.), *Current psychotherapies* (6th ed., pp. 273–302). Itasca, IL: Peacock.

Mehrabian, A. (1968). Inference of attitudes from the posture, orientation, and distance of a communicator. *Journal of Consulting and Clinical Psychology, 32,* 296–308.

Mordock, J. B. (1991). *Counseling the defiant child.* New York, NY: Crossroad Publishing.

National Association for the Education of Young Children. (2009). *10 effective DAP teaching strategies.* Washington, DC: Author.

Nelsen, J. (1987). *Positive discipline.* New York, NY: Ballantine Books.

Netolicky, C. (1998). *Strike four: An educational paradigm servicing troublesome behavior students.* Perth, Australia: Edith Cowan University.

Older, J. (1982). *Touching is healing.* New York, NY: Stein & Day.

Olson, L. C. (1997). On the margins of rhetoric: Audre Lorde transforming silence into language and action. *The Quarterly Journal of Speech, 83,* 49–70.

OSEP Technical Assistance Center on Positive Behavioral Interventions & Supports. (2009). *School-wide PBS: SWPBIS for Beginners.* Retrieved April 10, 2015, from https://www.pbis .org/school/swpbis-for-beginners

Pate, R. S. (2011). Open versus closed questions: What constitutes a good question? *CEDER Yearbook,* 28–39.

Pearson, J. C., Nelson, P. E., Titsworth, S., & Harter, L. (2011). *Human communication* (4th ed.). New York, NY: McGraw Hill.

Perkins, M., & Pfaffman, J. (2006). Using a course management system to improve classroom communication. *The Science Teacher, 73*(7), 33–37.

Psycharis, S., Chalatzoglidis, G., & Kalogiannakis, M. (2013). Moodle as a learning environment in promoting conceptual understanding for secondary school students. *Eurasia Journal of Mathematics, Science & Technology Education, 9*(1), 11–21.

Quarto, C. J. (2007). Managing student behavior during large group guidance: What works best? *Journal of School Counseling, 5*(7). Retrieved April 5, 2015, from http://files.eric.ed.gov/ fulltext/EJ901168.pdf

Ridley, N., & Asbury, F. (1988, March). Does counselor body posture make a difference? *The School Counselor, 35*(4), 253–258.

Rogers, C. R. (1957). The necessary and sufficient conditions of therapeutic personality change. *Journal of Consulting Psychology, 22,* 95–103.

Rogers, C. R. (1961). *On becoming a person.* Boston, MA: Houghton Mifflin.

Rogers, S., & Renard, L. (1999). Relationship-drive teaching. *Educational Leadership, 57,* 34–37.

Sabella, R. (2000). School counseling and technology. *Managing your school counseling program: K–12 strategies,* 337–357. Minneapolis, MN: Educational Media Corporation.

Sanford, J. P., & Evertson, C. M. (1981). Classroom management in a low SES junior high: Three case studies. *Journal of Teacher Education, 32*(1), 34–38.

Seligman, M. E. (1999). The president's address. *American Psychologist, 54,* 559–562.

Settle, Q., Abrams, K. M., & Baker, L. M. (2011). Using Prezi in the classroom. *NACTA Journal, 55,* 105–106.

Shapiro, J. (1968). Relationships between visual and auditory cues of therapeutic effectiveness. *Journal of Clinical Psychology, 24,* 236–239.

Shaunessy, E. (2000). Questioning techniques in the gifted classroom. *Gifted Child Today, 23*(5), 14–21.

Sivin-Kachala, J., & Bialo, E. (2000). *2000 research report on the effectiveness of technology in schools* (7th ed.). Washington, DC: Software and Information Industry Association.

Sprick, R. S., & Garrison, M. (2008). *Interventions: Evidence-based behavior strategies for individual students* (2nd ed.). Eugene, OR: Pacific Northwest.

Stockton, R., Morran, D. K., & Nitza, A. G. (2000). Processing group events: A conceptual map for leaders. *Journal for Specialists in Group Work, 25,* 343–355.

Stoltenberg, C. D. (1981). Approaching supervision from a developmental perspective: The counselor complexity model. *Journal of Counseling Psychology, 28*(1), 59–65.

Sugai, G., Lewis-Palmer, T., Todd, A. W., & Horner, R. H. (2005). *School-wide evaluation tool, version 2.1.* Eugene: University of Oregon.

Tileson, D. W. (2000). *Ten best teaching practices.* Thousand Oaks, CA: Corwin.

Tuckman, B. (1965). Developmental sequence in small groups. *Psychological Bulletin, 63,* 384–399.

Vaish, A., & Striano, T. (2004). Is visual reference necessary? Contributions of facial versus vocal cues in 12-month-olds' social referencing behavior. *Developmental Science, 7,* 261–269.

Vedantam, S. (2006, October 2–8). A mirror on reality: Research shows that neurons in the brain help us understand social cues. *The Washington Post National Weekly Edition, 23*(50), 35.

Wubbolding, R. E. (2000). *Reality therapy for the 21st century.* Philadelphia, PA: Brunner-Routledge.

Young, M. E. (2009). *Learning the art of helping: Building blocks and techniques* (4th ed.). Upper Saddler River, NJ: Pearson.

Ziomek-Daigle, J., McMahon, G. H., & Paisley, P. O. (2008). Adlerian-based interventions for professional school counselors- Serving as both counselors and educational leaders. *Journal of Individual Psychology, 64*(4), 450–467.

PART IV

OTHER CONSIDERATIONS IN CLASSROOM GUIDANCE

Chapter 9

School Counselor as Active Collaborator

CHRISTOPHER JANSON
University of North Florida

SOPHIE MAXIS
University of North Florida

School counselors must practice as leaders in order to engage in active collaboration with other school staff, students, and community members so that they can develop, implement, and facilitate high-impact classroom guidance curriculum. At the end of this chapter, you will be able to

- identify the context for students in schools and communities that require school counselors to collaborate with others in order to develop and deliver effective classroom guidance programming;
- describe various ways that school counselors can consult with administrators, teachers, parents, and community members in order to best meet the needs of students through effective classroom guidance programming;
- identify ways that school counselors can synthesize other sources of community and educational wisdom with traditional sources of the classroom guidance curriculum;
- recognize ways that classroom guidance can be integrated into the larger academic curriculum as well as the common core curriculum; and
- critically examine scenarios involving school counseling classroom guidance as well as thought-provoking questions.

Professional school counselors are collaborators by training, by philosophy, and by the position they occupy in schools and communities. School counselors are well positioned to lead in the collaborative efforts that are needed to improve the educational outcomes of students and strengthen communities (Bryan & Holcomb-McCoy, 2007; Clark & Breman, 2009). Classroom guidance programming provides school counselors with powerful opportunities to collaborate within the school and community and extend their influence while doing so (American School Counselor Association [ASCA], 2005; Myrick, 2003). Through collaboration with teachers, administrators, families, community members, and students themselves, school counselors can reframe and reimagine classroom guidance programming so it is not only tied more closely to the academic mission and purpose of education but can also serve to better support student and community development. Exercise 9.1 will provide you with opportunities to meet with and ask pointed questions of school counselors in your community.

EXERCISE 9.1

COLLECTING AND EXAMINING SCHOOL COUNSELOR COLLABORATION NARRATIVES

The construction of knowledge is a process that is both intrapersonal and social. The best learning is rooted in relationships through which we share and exchange experiences, knowledge, and insights. We make the most meaning from these conversations, and when we engage in them with purpose, the learning is even deeper. We encourage you to make the opportunity to learn through a relationship with a practicing school counselor. Identify a school counselor in your local community and schedule time to have a conversation with him or her by phone or in person. In order to help facilitate this process, we suggest that your conversation include the following questions/topics:

1. Invite him to discuss and explore how he uses classroom guidance as a vehicle to build helpful, developmental relationships. Encourage him to comment about how these relationships can both inform the content and improve the quality of classroom guidance programming and how his collaborative partners can grow through their partnerships around classroom guidance.

2. How does she identify potential productive partners with whom to collaborate? Does she consider disposition? Does she consider their philosophy regarding youth and education? Their position within the school? Does she have other considerations?

3. Explore his perspective on how he establishes and nurtures relationships with other professionals in the school. Ask him what strategies he uses to help him do so.

(Continued)

(Continued)

4. Ask her to share stories about the importance of collaborations with community allies and partners in her own work and practices. What does she see as her roles, responsibilities, and opportunities when working with community members?

5. How can relationships with parents, family members, and caregivers shift from those of client-service provider to partners?

6. How does he believe that his collaborations with students can be used to empower youth voice? Why does he believe it is important to include youth in collaborative efforts toward building school culture and improving school practices and processes?

Just as the landscape of public education and the roles of school counselors within it have continued to evolve, the learning objectives and goals of classroom guidance programming should also continue to shift and change. In order for classroom guidance and the collaborations that support it to be optimally effective in supporting the development of youth in schools, they must be framed by objectives and pedagogical goals that are rooted in various curricular sources. The development of classroom guidance learning objectives and goals should reflect the intent of school counseling being conceptualized and enacted as a program rather than a position. School counseling needs to shift in design from being a position individuals hold to a comprehensive program in order to meet the democratic imperative of public education to effectively reach and serve all students. Likewise, classroom guidance programming should be reimagined in order to meet the developmental needs of all students and the schools and communities in which they learn and live.

As described in a previous chapter (Chapter 6), the objectives and goals and the subsequent guidance curriculum have historically been developed from the ASCA Mindsets & Behaviors for Student Success (ASCA, 2014a) as well as individual school and community data emerging from needs assessments. However, given the strained and stressed landscape of public education due to the demands of the accountability movement (Militello, Gajda, & Bowers, 2009), the reality is that there may be little opportunity for the guidance curriculum to be delivered to students when classroom teachers continue to feel such intense pressures in keeping up with the furious pedagogical pace the current public school environment demands. In most places and in most cases in public schools, counselors need to work collaboratively with school staff to infuse their curriculum within the broader school content curricula (see Figure 9.1). Otherwise, the guidance curriculum will be in danger of falling into disuse for being perceived as being ancillary to the school focus—a perception that has historically hindered school counseling practices and professionals.

As we continue to better understand the social and cultural complexity of schooling, we should acknowledge that the guidance curriculum might be best developed from other sources as well. The ASCA National Model (ASCA, 2005) and the standards and competencies that accompany it (ASCA, 2014) may be strong templates for classroom guidance programming, but they cannot inform curriculum on the levels of community and culture. This is a dynamic curriculum source that is best developed from people and the stories they tell and the lives they lead. In order to tap into this deep and valuable source of curriculum, school counselors must once again embrace new roles. If school counselors are to develop and deliver classroom guidance programming that will best support students and communities, then they must be consultants within and beyond the school walls, leaders who champion and steward classroom guidance programming, and facilitators of school learning communities that recognize and use the wisdom and abundance of school staff, students, and community members. Each of these new roles bring with them opportunities and challenges, but those opportunities will be enhanced and those challenges will be met through school counselors' positioning, training, and commitment to one powerful practice: collaboration.

Figure 9.1   Sources of Classroom Guidance Curriculum

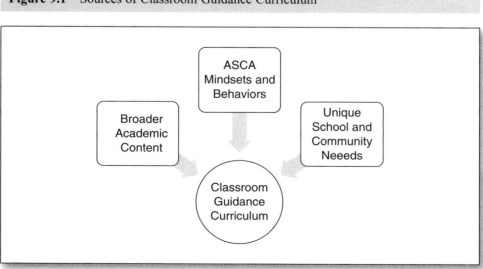

COUNSELOR AS CONSULTANT

Professional school counselors are trained to intervene on behalf of the academic, career, and social/emotional needs of students through the use of responsive services, including individual counseling, small-group intervention, large-group guidance, classroom guidance, advocacy, strategic assessment, collaboration, and consultation (ASCA, 2005; Myrick, 2003). Although responsive services may have some impact on student outcomes, there remains a need for more holistic integration of comprehensive school guidance programs rather than the reactive model of counseling that is often reported. By nature of most school counselors' training in implementing school counseling programs, school counselors can be an invaluable resource when positioning themselves as consultants within the school for collaborating with and educating students, parents, teachers, administrators, and communities about how to foster optimal school environments and cultures for success. Thus, the role of school counselor as consultant is a key ingredient in the development of advocacy, school climate, and school-community relationships that correlate to the educational outcomes of students (Bemak & Chung, 2005; Lapan, Gysbers, & Sun, 1997; Whiston & Quinby, 2009).

School-based consultation is recognized as a critical component of the delivery of the school guidance curriculum. Within this section, consultation will be discussed as the medium of engagement with key partners related to the successful delivery of the guidance curriculum, specifically, administrators, teachers, parents, and the community. Among the key roles that school counselors have within the school system, the counselor as consultant presents with opportunities to explore and challenge the ways in which school counselors engage with administrators, teachers, parents, and the community to support the educational success of students. Given the systemic nature and interrelated dimensions of school communities, school counselors are well positioned to lead as school-based consultants. School counselors potentially have access to the various partners related to the school community as well as opportunities to develop relationships among these partners through their roles as consultants.

Consultation, when approached as a multidirectional process, potentially yields shared benefits among consultants and consultees. The traditional connotation of the counselor as consultant is that of imparting of counselor expertise to consultees. However, in collaborating to develop effective guidance curriculum, school counselors are also beneficiaries of the insight, wisdom, and assets that are offered from administrators, teachers, parents, and the community. Assuming such a learning disposition as a consultant would be especially helpful upon entering a new school community or when seeking to demonstrate the value of school counseling in the climate of mandates and accountability.

Consultation with Administrators

The quality of the relationship and the level of support provided to the school counselor by administrators are critical in how effectively the school counselor can expand their services to all students (Rafoth & Foriska, 2006). Administrators are a source of support and provide a unique perspective for the programmatic implementation of counselors' schoolwide efforts. The degree to which change can occur within schools has been shown to depend significantly on the support that is offered by school administrators (Bryan & Griffin, 2010). Thus, it is helpful for the school counselor to consider ways in which they can develop strong relationships with administrators and position themselves as consultants with administrators for programmatic issues that are present within the school community. A consideration in consulting with administrators is their multiple roles and tasks, which may present as a limiting factor to collaborating with school counselors. However, school counselors will need to communicate and demonstrate effectively the ways in which consultation and collaboration will advance the overall goals and objectives of the schools' mission.

Consultation with Teachers

Professional school counselors, like teachers, are accountable for the academic success of students (ASCA, 2005). School counselors, in collaboration with teachers, can foster the high academic expectations, school climate, and caring relationships that are found to correlate to student achievement (ASCA, 2005; Bemak & Chung, 2005). As part of the services provided within a structured school guidance curriculum, consulting with teachers can impact instructional quality and affect the experiences of students within the classroom environment as well as improve the counselor's development of classroom guidance delivery skills. Furthermore, consultation with teachers is a critical relationship for integrating guidance services into the larger academic curriculum.

Consultation with Parents and Families

Attempts to improve parental and family engagement in schools are an added challenge to the general decline of involvement from parents of all income and ethnic backgrounds as students matriculate from primary to secondary education. Parents and caregivers that remain engaged in their students' education will more likely realize success with their students' schooling experiences (Amatea & West-Olatunji, 2007). However, school-related factors, more than personal characteristics, may limit family engagement in schools (Darling-Hammond & Friedlaender, 2008). Issues such as school climate, the quality of communication between school and home, and beliefs demonstrated by school representatives about the value of family contributions to the school influence how fully parents engage with schools. These school-related factors are within the capacity of school counselors to impact in consultation and collaboration with parents.

Parent education and training are common interventions when consulting with parents and can yield positive outcomes related to how parents further develop skills to engage with their children. The popular use of the ecologically based Conjoint Behavioral Consultation (CBC) approach (Sheridan & Kratochwill, 2007) for collaborating with parents represents a shift away from direct instructional interactions to a more egalitarian consultation relationship. Although there is a place for such interventions within a school counseling program, it is recommended that school counselors supplement the traditional models with more culturally responsive and collectivist approaches when consulting with parents, caregivers, and family members.

Conjoint Behavioral Consultation (CBC): A Closer Look

The popular use of the ecologically based Conjoint Behavioral Consultation (CBC) (Sheridan, Kratochwill, & Bergan, 1996) approach for collaborating with parents represents a shift away from direct instructional interactions to a more egalitarian consultation relationship (Garbacz et al., 2008; Sheridan, Eagle, & Doll, 2006). The CBC approach utilizes a partnership model of consultation and collaboration, including a distinguishing purpose to support the development of all parties within the consultation process. The goals of CBC are "to address students' needs through evidence-based intervention procedures, to promote parent engagement and involvement in learning, and to build relationships and facilitate partnerships across families and schools" (Garbacz et al., 2008, p. 34). Specifically, CBC is collaboratively delivered, with consideration to the identified mutual needs of all parties, through four stages via structured interviews:

1. Needs identification

2. Needs analysis

3. Plan development

4. Plan evaluation

Although there is a place for such interventions within a school counseling program, it is recommended that school counselors supplement the traditional models with more culturally responsive and collectivist approaches when consulting with parents, caregivers, and family members.

Suggested readings regarding CBC:

Sheridan, S. M., Eagle, J. W., & Doll, B. (2006). An examination of the efficacy of conjoint behavioral consultation with diverse clients. *School Psychology Quarterly, 21*, 396–417.

Sheridan, S. M., Kratochwill, T. R., & Bergan, J. R. (1996). *Conjoint behavioral consultation: A procedural manual.* New York, NY: Plenum Press.

Garbacz, S. A., Woods, K. E., Swanger-Gagné, M. S., Taylor, A. M., Black, K. A., & Sheridan, S. M. (2008). Conjoint behavioral consultation: The effectiveness of a partnership-centered approach. *School Psychology Quarterly, 23*, 313–327.

In addition to helping parents and caregivers develop skills and assume more responsibilities in collaboration, partnering with parents can be a means to position them as active leaders in family-school engagement. As school-based consultants, school counselors have opportunities to integrate the positive contributions that are made from the home, offer additional ways to encourage parents to collaborate, position parents to teach and learn from each other about shared schooling experiences, and take more leadership with educating their children.

Examples of activities utilizing parent education and training models typically include outside, expert-led experiences such as workshops, information sessions, skills-training sessions, and problem-focused discussions based on parent-generated topics. The shift to a more culturally responsive and collectivist approach of parent consultation can be demonstrated by moving beyond parent-generated topics to parent-led engagement in the efforts that are self-identified as relevant for the schooling of their children. In this model of parent consultation, parents' and families' personal narratives and shared experiences related to the schooling of their children generate the motive for engaging and seeking changes with the issues that are present at school.

The distinctions between traditional parent/caregiver education/training approaches and more culturally responsive, family-centered models are illustrated below in Table 9.1 and Exercise 9.2.

Table 9.1 Shift from a Traditional to Family-Centered Approach

Traditional Parent-Education Approach		Family-Centered Education Approach	
Strategy	*Example*	*Strategy*	*Example*
Outside expert-led workshop	University admissions personnel leading financial aid workshop	**Parent-led peer-learning**	Parent-facilitated financial aid registration session
Information session	School counseling department presentation on paying for college	**Learning exchange model of engagement**	Structured learning exchange around paying for college, including students, parents, and family members and high school alumni who have graduated from or are attending college
Expert-led skills training	Local college writing instructor providing college admissions essay tips	**Expert-initiated session, then skills practice session**	Local college writing instructor providing college admissions essay tips *followed by* student essay, peer feedback, and revision teams
Problem-focused discussion	Administration and school counselor lead conversations on attendance	**Family-led solution-focused conversation**	Cross-family conversations strategize ways to support student attendance

EXERCISE 9.2

REFLECTIVE DISCOURSE: SHIFTING TOWARD A FAMILY-CENTERED APPROACH

The construction of knowledge is a process that is both intrapersonal and social. When we have opportunities to share and exchange around a topic, then together, we can make even more meaning. Working in pairs, please explore the following questions:

1. How might family-centered approaches to collaborations with students' parents, caregivers, or other family members impact the relationships with them? How might it impact the relationships with students?

2. What are the implications when we shift from *advocating for* individuals or groups to *advocating with* them?

3. Why are family-centered approaches, as represented by the qualities listed above, engaged in less frequently in our schools?

4. Describe and discuss the different knowledge, skills, and dispositions that are required when school counselors shift to a family-centered approach from a traditional parent-education approach when working with parents, caregivers, or families? Which of the described and discussed knowledge, skills, or dispositions do you each believe you would have to acquire in order to more fully work from a family-centered approach?

Consultation with the Community

Consulting and collaborating with the community provides opportunities to integrate the contributions of non-school partners in the delivery of the comprehensive school counseling program. Thus, school counselors' knowledge about systems, culturally appropriate practices related to families, and communication skills become more critical when engaging with the community.

INTEGRATION INTO BROADER ACADEMIC CURRICULUM

The demands on teachers to optimize instructional time within their classes have never been more intense (McDonnell, 2004). Teachers are tasked with completing their instruction around increasingly proscriptive and standardized curricula that their students will be held accountable for throughout the year and often across many levels, including district, state, and federal (Ravitch, 2010). The high-stakes nature of these tests extends far beyond the lives of students. The performance of teachers, principals, schools, and entire districts are now closely linked to student testing outcomes. This linkage has real-world implications. As a result of teacher merit pay, administrator job security, and district decisions to maintain or close neighborhood schools being linked to student performance on standardized tests, school staff members understandably protect each minute of class time for instruction.

So what are school counselors to do? According to the template represented by the ASCA National Model, school counselors should be spending anywhere from 15%–45% of their time on the delivery of the guidance curriculum (ASCA, 2005). More important still than any model emerging from a professional organization are the personal and social development needs of students in schools. Given the challenging ratios of school counselors to students, the delivery of classroom guidance programming provides the most efficient and effective way to provide services to all students in schools. And those services are crucial. Classroom guidance programming provides opportunities to not only deliver psychoeducational and socioeducational curriculum to every student (in areas such as recognizing and appreciating cultural differences to building skills for coping with peer pressure) but also to support their academic growth and performance by building their knowledge, skills, and dispositions (ASCA, 2014a). So how can school counselors and schools attempt to support student development in holistic ways that honor and nurture the personal, social, academic, and career development of our youth?

One solution lies in the possibilities that emerge when classroom guidance programming is conceived of and planned not as something else that schools need to squeeze in within the small cracks of time found between the instruction of core content areas. Instead, classroom guidance programming can be integrated with the broader academic curricula of the school rather than being ancillary to it. This approach to classroom guidance programming necessitates much deeper levels of collaboration beyond classroom teachers and schools making time within their classes and school days for counselors. Instead, counselors, teachers, and administrators must work collectively while planning, delivering, and assessing this synthesized curriculum. Through this collective approach, leadership around classroom guidance programming is distributed across multiple school leaders rather than being the sole responsibility of the counselor. For many counselors and schools, this collective leadership approach represents a paradigm shift, but it is not one without precedent for school counselors. To the contrary, this approach is highly congruent with the foundational philosophy that school counseling is best considered a program shared across stakeholders rather than a position held by individuals. Exercise 9.3 presents an example of a counselor sharing responsibility and leadership across stakeholders.

EXERCISE 9.3

INTEGRATING CLASSROOM GUIDANCE INTO BROADER ACADEMIC CURRICULUM

Over the course of two weeks, there have been a handful of documented incidents of bullying and harassment at Nosam High School. Even more alarming, some of these incidents involved the use of racial/cultural slurs. Notably, each one of the incidents occurred among ninth-grade students. The administrative team has handled each individual incident effectively from the standpoint of the school code of conduct, but they and the other school staff members recognize that a pattern may be emerging and call a ninth-grade team meeting in order to determine how best to respond.

As per the culture at Nosam High School, each ninth-grade academic-content teacher (language arts, science, math, social studies), the assistant principal, and the ninth-grade school counselor attended the meeting. The assistant principal and the school counselor facilitated the meeting, and after the team summarized and discussed the specific incidents and the students involved, the conversation turned in focus to opportunities and options for an intervention that would involve all ninth-grade students. After discussing possibilities ranging from bringing in a topical assembly speaker to principal-lead conversations in each classroom, group consensus began to coalesce around classroom guidance lessons that could begin to open up spaces for conversations that might build students' capacities for understanding the points of views of others, particularly those "others" who are particularly vulnerable for various reasons within communities.

Although all of the academic content teachers recognized the potential value of these classroom guidance lessons, they each also expressed concerns over how much such classroom guidance would cut into their instructional time. The school counselor listened closely and, thinking about the power of intentional and purposeful questions, then asked each of the teachers to share briefly about their current curricular unit. The math teachers talked about being in the midst of a unit on fractions and percentages. The science teachers shared that they were teaching about cell division. In social studies, they were studying the geography of poverty. And the language arts teachers were in the middle of a unit built around Arthur Miller's play about the Salem witch trials, *The Crucible*.

While listening intently, the school counselor thought to herself about how gifted the ninth-grade language arts teachers were at talking to students about sensitive and vulnerable topics. She explored with them a bit further about the types of projects students were completing in order to understand the themes and elements of *The Crucible* more deeply. She heard the teachers talk about emphasizing students' exploration of themes of intolerance and the dynamic of power and the roles they play in relationships and communities. Not long into that sharing and conversation, the school counselor realized, along with the others, that there was tremendous opportunity to integrate classroom guidance lessons on the value of understanding others' points of view, particularly the points of view of people who, because of the differences from the majority, are often more vulnerable to derision and bullying.

Following the lead of the school counselor and language arts teachers, the team began mapping out ways in which the lessons developed for *The Crucible* could be infused with the identified guidance curricular goals. To begin this process, the school counselor distributed copies of the ASCA National Standards and the team began to identify the handful of standards that best addressed the complex issues at Nosam High School. The team focused on standards in the domain of "Social/emotional Development." Within this domain, they selected five standards that seemed best suited for integration within the ninth-grade language arts unit on *The Crucible* in order to facilitate powerful learning experiences around the bullying, harassment, and racial/ethnic slurs:

(Continued)

(Continued)

- PS:A2.1   Recognize that everyone has rights and responsibilities.
- PS:A2.4   Recognize, accept, and appreciate ethnic and cultural diversity.
- PS:B1.7   Demonstrate a respect and appreciation for individual and cultural differences.
- PS:C1.5   Differentiate between situations requiring peer support and situations requiring adult professional help.

Over the next few weeks, the school counselor organized collective instructional efforts designed in part to address the ASCA National Standards (ASCA, 2005). Out of recognition of the importance of first helping the students understand the importance of what had occurred among them, all of the team members co-facilitated conversations with students in each class around the responsibilities all students and staff in the school share in creating a safe environment for everyone (PS:A2.1) as well as when situations or incidents require intervention by adults in the school or community (PS:C1.5). Following these initial conversations, when learning activities needed to be framed within the context of the ASCA standards and involved ideas and sharing that were more sensitive, they were co-facilitated by the language arts teachers along with the school counselor and sometimes the assistant principal.

Discussion Questions

- Based on the scenario described at Nosam High School, are there other ASCA National Standards for Students that you believe were overlooked by the team?
- What other school counseling practices do you believe should be enacted in order to properly intervene in the scenario at Nosam High School?
- The team in this scenario developed curriculum from two sources: the ninth-grade language arts curricular unit on *The Crucible* and the ASCA National Standards (ASCA, 2005). What are other possible sources that would strengthen this composite classroom guidance curriculum?

An essential part of this process involved assessing student growth around an understanding of the four standards. There are many different ways to assess student growth, ranging from indirect forms (e.g., student self-reporting through responses on pretest/posttest surveys) to more direct forms (e.g., student assignments, written reflections, etc.). Given the complex set of social and cultural issues being addressed and the interpersonal and intrapersonal challenges of addressing them, the team chose to use a direct form of assessment. In order to do so, the team structured periodic student written reflections in response to prompts constructed around the standards. Over the duration of the unit, the team members tracked the student reflections and were able to document that many of the students did indeed appear to increase their understanding of the ideas behind the standards as well as their value. As is most often the case in schools and communities, solutions to deep social problems are not solved easily or quickly, and this was no exception. However, as a result of the collective efforts of the team, students grew in their recognition of, appreciation of, and respect for differences while also having opportunities to see adults in their school sharing in responsibility for social issues and addressing them together.

Test Bank Items and Responses

Multiple Choice

1. Among the many practices that school counselors engage in, which one is suggested as critical to accomplishing the goals and objectives of a comprehensive guidance curriculum?

   a. facilitate small groups

   b. collaboration

   c. academic advising

   d. coordinate standardized testing

Answer: B

2. In what ways are school counselors well positioned as school-based consultants?

   a. School counselors have access to various partners of the school community.

   b. School counselors can facilitate relationships with administrators for programmatic issues.

   c. Consultation with teachers can impact instructional quality.

   d. all of the above

Answer: D

3. Which is *not* an approach that school counselors can use to consult and collaborate with parents for the schooling of their children?

   a. coordinate parent education and training

   b. engage in CBC

   c. advocate the school as the primary expert for parenting

   d. use family-centered approaches

(Continued)

(Continued)

Answer: C

4. When planning classroom guidance programming, it is important to

   a. collaborate with teachers and leaders to integrate it into the broader academic curricula.
   b. deliver lessons in between the instruction of core content areas.
   c. remember that programming is best planned alone.
   d. make sure to deliver on psychoeducational and socioeducational topics.

Answer: A

5. The Multi-Tiered Systems of Support (MTSS) is an opportunity for school counselors to

   a. demonstrate their roles as partners only in the nonacademic development of students.
   b. intervene on behalf of students who struggle academically and behaviorally.
   c. tutor students for standardized test-taking.
   d. both A and C

Answer B

Essay

1. Given the social and cultural complexity of schooling, why would it benefit school counselors to embrace the role of school-based consultants within the school community?

2. Discuss the importance of integrating classroom guidance into the larger academic curriculum. Within the discussion, provide an example of such integration.

SCHOOL COUNSELORS AND MULTI-TIERED SYSTEMS OF SUPPORT (MTSS)

The Multi-Tiered Systems of Support (MTSS) presents school counselors with rich opportunities to demonstrate their roles as critical partners in the academic outcomes and behavioral development of all students. The ASCA National Model and MTSS process are inherently aligned in their shared emphasis of data-driven interventions, particularly for students that experience the most difficulty academically and behaviorally (ASCA, 2014b). Given that interpretations and applications of MTSS vary across states, several models exist, of which the more widely known is Response to Intervention (RTI). Overall, the MTSS approach includes three tiers of academic intervention, targeting all students (Tier 1), students at some risk (Tier 2), and students at high risk (Tier 3) (ASCA, 2014b). As an integral member of school-based MTSS teams, the ways in which counselors can support content area educators through MTSS instructional interventions and school administrators with school improvement goals are limited only by the creativity of the RTI team collaboration. Within each tier of intervention, the ways that school counselors can contribute include the following:

- Advise on the use of data to assess patterns and gaps in school-level student outcomes, designing and planning guidance curriculum that enhance academic development.
- Collaborate on MTSS design and implementation.
- Advocate for research-based and culturally responsive interventions.
- Consult and evaluating behavioral interventions.
- Integrate standards-based guidance curriculum with MTSS intervention plans.
- Provide responsive services (both individual and small-group) with target issues identified by school data.

COMMON CORE CURRICULUM

Any discussion of how school counselors can integrate classroom guidance programming within the broader academic curricula in schools would be incomplete without mention of the Common Core State Standards (National Governors Association Center for Best Practices & Council of Chief State School Officers, 2010). The Common Core State Standards (CCSS) were developed from the underlying belief that all students are capable of graduating from high school and that in doing so, they should be college and career ready (Porter, McMaken, Hwang, & Yang, 2011). From this emphasis on college and career readiness and the concern that too many students were not ready in those ways, the CCSS emerged as a national movement. More recently, the CCSS have been the subject of intense political and pedagogical controversy and conversation, and this controversy has now led to policy changes regarding the standards within a number of states. Initially, 45 states adopted the CCSS, but at the time of this writing, a number of states had since repealed, defunded, or delayed their adoption and/or implementation.

The CCSS were initially developed to set high academic expectations in English/language arts and mathematics. By design, each standard was developed with the goal of helping schools and students stay on track so that students can succeed in college and be career ready. The standards both define and describe the skills and knowledge each student should be able to employ and know following the completion of each grade. In keeping with our era of accountability, by 2014, schools in participating states must use assessments aligned with the standards.

The CCSS is distinct from previous state standards in two aspects: an adoption of unified curriculum nationally for all students and the expressed emphasis of moving beyond skill mastery to becoming college and career ready upon completion of high school. The emphasis on college and career readiness is highly congruent with school counselors' preparation and practices as demonstrated with the ASCA National Model's charge to intervene on behalf of students' academic, career, and social/emotional needs.

However, in order to intervene effectively, school counselors will need a comprehensive understanding of how the CCSS will impact the delivery of guidance services. The CCSS push for college and career readiness for all high school graduates positions school counselors as ideal collaborators for integrating the school counseling program into the larger academic curriculum throughout all grade levels. Furthermore, a comprehensive school counseling program is well suited to complement the implementation of CCSS at all grade levels, given the counselor's knowledge about the developmental and psychological aspects of student learning.

COUNSELOR IN LEADERSHIP ROLES

School counselors must practice as leaders in order to engage in active collaboration with other school staff, students, and community members so that they can develop, implement, and facilitate high-impact classroom guidance curriculum. This imperative to lead is eased by how well positioned school counselors are for leadership due to their position, training, and skills (Borders & Shoffner, 2003; Dollarhide, 2003; Gysbers & Henderson, 2001). Importantly, the foundation of school counselor leadership is collective or collaborative in nature, better characterized by the distribution of leadership tasks than unilateral actions (Janson, Stone, & Clark, 2009).

The development, implementation, and facilitation of classroom guidance programming are complex tasks that simply require that leadership be stretched across many different school staff members. Although the ideas and concepts of collective and distributed leadership are much more prevalent today in principal preparation programs (Militello & Janson, 2007), they are by no means ubiquitous. That being the case, in many schools, the counselor might have to take on the responsibility of educating the principal about leadership approaches that are based on shared, collective, or distributed models.

The relationship between school counselors and principals, particularly in situations in which the principals are practicing a more traditional and solitary leadership approach, must be intentionally developed to be more effective. School principals may not know much about school counselor skills, preparation, practices, or comprehensive counseling programs. However, when school counselors view their role as including educating their principal about the nature of their training and practices, their working relationships are perceived to be stronger (Janson, Militello, & Kosine, 2008). In addition to educating the principal using the eight elements of effective school counselor-principal relationships (Janson & Militello, 2009), school counselors and principals might work with the intent to construct stronger and more effective relationships by working from places of strength that currently exist in their relationship.

For instance, in one middle school, a new principal was tasked with addressing the lack of female students enrolling in STEM-related elective courses (science, technology, engineering, and mathematics). The principal, valuing the career development knowledge and skills of her school counselors (mutual value, awareness of the other's repertoire), enlisted them to work with her in order to increase the awareness of women working in STEM fields (purposeful and focused collaboration). Together, the principal and two school counselors reflected upon the issue and discussed possibilities and strategies for intervening (open and reflective communication). Ultimately, they decided to co-plan and facilitate a daylong "Fem-STEM-Fest" in which local women working in STEM occupations would discuss their educations and work (collective enterprise) and, more importantly, engage participating female students in activities designed to show them how thinking like a scientist is relative to their lives now. While preparing for Fem-STEM-Fest, the school counselors and principal recruited women in STEM professions. The principal secured donations of prizes and food while the school counselors helped the volunteering professional women design engaging and powerful learning activities (stretched leadership).

**Eight Elements of Effective
School Counselor-Principal Relationships**

1. **Mutual value**. The principal and the school counselor value each other's job responsibilities, tasks, and contributions to the school and its educational mission.

2. **Open and reflective communication**. The principal and school counselor are accessible and available to each other in order to discuss issues related to their individual or shared roles in the school as well as issues relevant to the educational mission of the school.

3. **Shared belief in interdependency**. The principal and school counselor believe that many aspects of their individual roles cannot be accomplished without contributions from the other.

4. **Trust**. The principal and school counselor trust one another to support their own individual practices as well as their individual contributions to the shared educational mission of the school.

5. **Collective enterprise**. The principal and school counselor share in facilitating the development of the common educational mission of the school.

6. **Awareness of the other's repertoire**. The principal and school counselor understand each other's scope of training and professional expectations and standards.

7. **Purposeful and focused collaboration**. The principal and school counselor collaborate with intention around specific goals and strategies related to the common educational mission of the school.

8. **Stretched leadership**. The principal and school counselor share in leadership tasks and practices related to meeting the educational mission of the school. (Janson & Militello, 2009)

PROFESSIONAL LEARNING COMMUNITIES

Nothing contributes more to student academic achievement than learning from effective teachers (Sanders & Rivers, 1996). In fact, not only do effective teachers most positively impact student academic achievement *while* they are teaching them, but the effects of that teaching stretch for years to come. Conversely, the impact of ineffective teaching and teachers is also pronounced and those negative impacts on student performance may linger for years to come (Marzano, Pickering, & Pollock, 2001). Thus, the single best way that school leaders can improve student learning and achievement is to improve the effectiveness of their teachers.

So how can school counselors in their roles as school leaders help contribute to the improvement of teacher effectiveness in their schools? One way is to help support and lead the development of professional learning communities (PLCs). The purpose of a PLC is to provide collaborative space in which teachers and other school staff can engage in reflection, examine impacts, and make changes to improve school practices—instructional practices in particular (McLaughlin & Talbert, 2006). By engaging in shared leadership toward the establishment and facilitation of a PLC, school counselors put into action an important element that frames their work: being a systemic change agent.

The idea that school counselors should be systemic change agents spun originally from the movement to recast school counseling as a lever for movement toward more equitable and just schools (House & Hayes, 2002; Paisley & McMahon, 2001). Notably, this new emphasis on school counselors being systemic change agents necessarily involved school counselors performing as leaders in schools (McMahon, Mason, & Paisley, 2009). Later, this connection between leadership and systemic change was further captured within both Council for Accreditation of Counseling & Related Educational Programs (CACREP) ("Understands the important role of the school counselor as a system change agent," Standard O.4.) and ASCA School Counselor Competencies ("Applies the school counseling themes of leadership, advocacy, collaboration and systemic change, which are critical to a successful school counseling program," Competency I-B-1c.).

School counselors can play very important roles within PLC. Their training as facilitators makes them ideal for facilitating conversations and activities that involve reflection, exploration of data sets, and the change processes teachers will invariably have to engage in if they are to shift their practices toward greater effectiveness. By doing so, school counselors have a compelling opportunity to apply their basic counseling and group skills to the larger processes of staff development and school improvement (see Table 9.2).

Although leadership within school PLCs may seem novel or divergent to some, it falls squarely within the knowledge and skills of school counselors. It also is in alignment with CACREP school counselor preparation standards. Please see Table 9.3 for a list of CACREP standards for school counseling programs that could apply to school counselors' leadership within professional learning communities:

HOMEROOM ADVISORY PROGRAMS

Homeroom advisory programs provide school counselors with yet one more valuable opportunity to collaborate with other school staff. Such collaborations need not involve classroom guidance curriculum, but they might, depending on

Table 9.2 Examples of Professional Learning Community Topics, Practices, and School Counselor Roles

Examples of Professional Learning Community Topics, Practices, and School Counselor Roles			
School Level	*Topic*	*PLC Practice(s)*	*School Counselor Roles*
Elementary	Disproportionate placement of students in gifted & talented programming by race	Examining disaggregated placement and referral data	Presenting school data in both numeric and graphic formats
		Small-group reflective "think-alouds" focused on explaining the existence of the disproportionality	Leading the think-aloud process by modeling and facilitating small-group reflections
Middle	Student challenges adjusting to middle school structure	Learning about how students experience the transition to middle school and using that knowledge to adjust school processes and structures	Organizing and modeling staff-student learning exchanges focused on the observations, experiences, and perceptions related to student transitions to middle school
High	Shifting toward student-directed learning in which teachers facilitate the development of knowledge rather than solely dispensing it	Teaching staff learn about the theory of adaptive change (Heifetz, Grashow, & Linsky, 2009) and how it can inform their own shifts in pedagogical practice	School counselors lead learning/reflection circles in which 8–10 teaching staff share and process their feelings, attitudes, and thoughts regarding the expectation that they change their teaching to emphasize student agency

the unique form and structure of each school's program. Homeroom advisory programs are fairly common in schools, particularly with the middle grades. They are built and facilitated with the intent of increasing student opportunities to feel connected with the adults in their school (Shulkind & Foote, 2009). When students feel connected to at least one adult in schools, they are more likely to attend and perform well academically (Blum, 2005) and less likely to use drugs and alcohol, participate in violence, and initiate sexual activity at early ages (McNeely, Nonnemaker, & Blum, 2002).

Homeroom advisory programs are designed to create opportunities for school staff members and small groups of students to have ongoing opportunities to interact and build deeper relationships than those that typically develop within classrooms. These homeroom advisory programs are designed to allow students and staff to meet on a scheduled basis with the purpose of creating a more personalized

Table 9.3   Examples of CACREP School Counseling Standards and Descriptions

CACREP School Counseling Standard	Description
C.2.	Knows how to design, implement, manage, and evaluate programs to enhance the academic, career, and social/emotional development of students
C.5.	Understands group dynamics—including counseling, psychoeducational, task, and peer helping groups—and the facilitation of teams to enable students to overcome barriers and impediments to learning
F.2.	Advocates for school policies, programs, and services that enhance a positive school climate and are equitable and responsive to multicultural student populations
I.4.	Knows current methods of using data to inform decision making and accountability (e.g., school improvement plan, school report card)
K.1.	Understands the relationship of the school counseling program to the academic mission of the school
K.2.	Understands the concepts, principles, strategies, programs, and practices designed to close the achievement gap, promote student academic success, and prevent students from dropping out of school
L.1.	Conducts programs designed to enhance student academic development
M.1.	Understands the ways in which student development, well-being, and learning are enhanced by family-school-community collaboration
M.2.	Knows strategies to promote, develop, and enhance effective teamwork within the school and the larger community
M.3	Knows how to build effective working teams of school staff, parents, and community members to promote the academic, career, and social/emotional development of students
M.4.	Understands systems theories, models, and processes of consultation in school system settings
N.3.	Consults with teachers, staff, and community-based organizations to promote student academic, career, and social/emotional development
O.1.	Knows the qualities, principles, skills, and styles of effective leadership
O.2.	Knows strategies of leadership designed to enhance the learning environment of schools
O.4.	Understands the important role of the school counselor as a system change agent
O.5.	Understands the school counselor's role in student assistance programs, school leadership, curriculum, and advisory meetings

and caring environment for academic planning and support, conveying school policies and procedures, recognizing successes and accomplishment, and building school culture (Juvonen, Le, Kaganoff, Augustine, & Constant, 2004). Often, in order to further optimize and honor the relationships and connections built between students and staff, teachers will loop with students across multiple school years. Homeroom advisory programs have become an endemic part of middle schools (Galassi, Gulledge, & Fox, 1997).

Homeroom advisory programs are once again well-matched with school counselor training and practices. Clearly, school counselors are tremendous assets for advisory programs seeking to help students connect with caring adults so that the schools become more personalized for our youth (Klem & Connell, 2004). With their knowledge of the social and emotional development of youth, school counselors can help shape faculty advisor expectations for behavior and relationships with the students in their homerooms. Additionally, who better than school counselors to inform advisors about appropriate and healthy relationship boundaries as well as behaviors or expressions that might require special intervention with counseling either within or outside of the school?

EXTENDING LEARNING AND LEADERSHIP FROM SCHOOL STAFF TO THE COMMUNITY

Finally, school counselors should also consider using their collaborations within the school to bring in the community around the school and its wisdom and gifts. Motivated by the powerful and radical idea that *every community* around every school has all the resources needed to address and solve even the most seemingly intractable issues and problems (McKnight & Block, 2010), school counselors could serve as liaisons and hosts who could bring the strengths and assets, wisdom, and experiences of community members into the school and classroom guidance curriculum.

Just as youth often feel disconnected from their schools, they also too often feel disconnected from their communities (Fernandes-Alcantara & Thomas, 2009). Similarly, schools have often struggled to position themselves as places that honor and respect communities and members enough to welcome their involvement and not simply their presence (Epstein, 2001). However, if the school works concertedly and intentionally to bring in the voices and stories of community members, then the opportunities for a more dynamic curriculum begin to emerge.

This dynamic curriculum can provide a foundation for students to learn not only about their community, as it is rooted in "place and is informed by the local context and condition," but also "about themselves, their history, and their ecology" (Guajardo, Guajardon, & Casaperalta, 2008, p. 5). Another virtue of listening to and learning from the community is that the learners extend beyond students to the school staff. The unfortunate (yet understandable) reality is that in many places, particularly in urban communities, school staff no longer live in the areas where they teach and kids learn. This is a disconnection of a different form and that relational disconnect necessarily contributes to a curricular one. By supporting the development of sustained and collaborative relationships between the school and the community, school counselors position themselves as leaders in not only their schools but also their schools' communities.

School counselors can lead and support the development of collaborative relationships between the school and community in a number of ways. Just one example would be for school counselors to steward student engagement in community asset mapping either as part of their classroom guidance curriculum or through their homeroom advisory programs. Community asset mapping (Kretzmann & McKnight, 1993) is a process that helps the student and adult researchers, as well as community members, view their community for its strengths, gifts, and assets rather than for its limitations and deficiencies. The process itself can be highly relational and take the form of conversations students have with people in their community's neighborhoods in order to learn about the richness of the place in which they live and learn (Guajardo et al., 2008). Notably, community asset mapping processes involve students in the school going out into the community rather than the more traditional approach of inviting members of community into schools.

MARKETING COMPREHENSIVE SCHOOL GUIDANCE PROGRAMS

Regardless of the potential partners with whom school counselors are endeavoring to collaborate, it is important that school counselors effectively market what they do and how they do it. There are many great reasons why school counselors should consider the marketing of their comprehensive school guidance programs as essential aspects of their roles (Thompson, 2013). Within the context of collaborating in order to develop, facilitate, and evaluate classroom guidance, a number of these reasons are even more important.

First and foremost, marketing comprehensive school counseling programs can ultimately assist school counselors in improving their work and increasing their impact within schools and communities. By engaging in marketing, school counselors can address the persisting lack of understanding other educators have about school counselors' roles, their practices, and the comprehensive programs they enact and in which they engage others (Beesley, 2004). Through clarifying understandings of school counseling, school counselors are creating the conditions for improving their work and impact because when others involved with schools are not sufficiently clear about what school counselors do, that work becomes much more challenging (Dotson, 2009). Given the difficulty some school counselors experience when trying to gain entry into classrooms, in-school marketing of the role of school counselors and the potential impact of classroom guidance will likely lead to greater access.

Second, marketing comprehensive school guidance programs provides opportunities to not only communicate about them to the community but (perhaps more importantly) can also serve as an invitation for the community to be more involved (Ritchie, 1989). As described previously, increased collaboration with the community is essential for more culturally informed classroom guidance curricular content and pedagogy. When school counselors successfully market their comprehensive school counseling programs, they will be better able to tap into the rich community wisdom, knowledge, and experience that can help inform their classroom guidance.

Finally, marketing comprehensive school counseling programs help to create greater transparency by actively informing key stakeholders about the important and valuable aims and interventions of the programs and the school counselors who design and implement them. By informing school staff, the community, and students themselves about the work emanating from their comprehensive school counseling programs, school counselors are not only informing their collective stakeholders in their work but they are also increasing the array of voices that can influence and improve the work. For instance, if families and community members know that school counselors will be facilitating classroom guidance lessons about financial literacy, that awareness can lead to increased opportunities for those family and community members with gifts in the area of finance to contribute.

There are innumerable possible marketing practices that school counselors can employ and, as a result of our ever-increasing technological advances, those possibilities are growing exponentially. Some of the possibilities for marketing outside of the school can include ways that extend school counselor expertise beyond the school walls, such as speaking to community groups and providing training to other professionals (Thompson, 2013). School counselors should also familiarize themselves with the potential power and impact of social media. They might begin by providing valuable information through social media such as Twitter, blogs, and the school website.

Within the school, school counselors can market their comprehensive school counseling programs by

- developing yearly calendars that inform students, families, and staff about important school dates and events;
- using flyers, brochures, pamphlets, and posters to communicate about services, programs, and events facilitated by school counselors;
- using social media to communicate important dates and opportunities (in accordance with district policies regarding social media use);
- inviting administrators to sit in on classroom guidance sessions;
- conducting workshops for teachers, staff, and students around areas such as communication, group processes, cultural awareness and appreciation, and so on; and
- providing lists or menus of services that comprehensive school counseling programs offer and posting them in classrooms throughout the school (Thompson, 2013).

KEYSTONES

- Classroom guidance curriculum can be developed from multiple sources: the ASCA Mindsets & Behaviors for Student Success, the broader academic curriculum (including Common Core curriculum), and the unique needs and assets of the school and community.
- School counselors are well-positioned to both consult and engage in leadership with other school staff, students, parents and families, and the community in order to help meet student needs through classroom guidance curriculum.
- School counselor engagement in collective leadership around classroom guidance curriculum provides opportunities to improve educational outcomes for students through powerful programs such as PLCs and homeroom advisory programs.
- School counselors have the potential to serve as invaluable conduits for community wisdom, strengths, and assets to flow into their schools and enhance both learning and teaching.

ONLINE RESOURCES

Common Core State Standards

- Common Core State Standards: http://www.CoreStandards.org
- Common Core Works: http://www.CommonCoreWorks.org
- National Governors Association's Center for Best Practices: http://www.nga.org/cms/center

Community Strengths

- Abundant Communities: http://www.abundantcommunity.com/
- Community Learning Exchange: www.communitylearningexchange.org/
- Search Institute's *40 Developmental Assets*: http://www.search-institute.org/content/40-developmental-assets-adolescents-ages-12-18

Curriculum Design

- Understanding By Design: http://www.ascd.org/research-a-topic/understanding-by-design-resources.aspx
- Dr. John Nash, "Design Thinking": https://www.youtube.com/watch?v=cT1vvewfAno

REFERENCES

Amatea, E., & West-Olatunji, C. (2007). Joining the conversation about educating our poorest children: Emerging leadership roles for school counselors in high poverty schools. *Professional School Counseling, 11*, 81–89.

American School Counselor Association (ASCA). (2005). *The ASCA national model: A framework for school counseling programs* (2nd ed.). Alexandria, VA: Author.

American School Counselor Association (ASCA). (2014a). *ASCA mindsets & behaviors for student success: K–12 college- and career-readiness standards for every student.* Alexandria, VA: Author.

American School Counselor Association (ASCA). (2014b). *The professional school counselor and Multi-Tiered Systems of Support.* Alexandria, VA: Author. Retrieved April 6, 2015, from https://www.schoolcounselor.org/asca/media/asca/PositionStatements/PS_MultitieredSupportSystems.pdf

Beesley, D. (2004). Teachers' perceptions of school counselor effectiveness: Collaborating for student success. *Education, 125*, 259–270.

Bemak, F., & Chung, R. C. (2005). Advocacy as a critical role for urban school counselors: Working toward equity and social justice. *Professional School Counseling, 8*(3), 196–202.

Blum, R. W. (2005). A case for school connectedness. *The Adolescent Learner, 62*(7), 16–20

Borders, L. D., & Shoffner, M. F. (2003). School counselors: Leadership opportunities and challenges in the schools. In J. D. West, C. J. Osborn, & D. L. Bubenzer (Eds.), *Leaders and legacies: Contributions to the profession of counseling* (pp. 51–64). New York, NY: Brunner-Routledge.

Bryan, J. A., & Griffin, D. (2010). A multidimensional study of school-family-community partnership involvement: School, school counselor, and training factors. *Professional School Counseling, 14*, 75–86.

Bryan, J., & Holcomb-McCoy, C. (2007). An examination of school counsellor involvement in school-family-community partnerships. *Professional School Counseling, 10*(5), 441–454.

Clark, M. A., & Breman, J. C. (2009). School counselor inclusion: A collaborative model to provide academic and social-emotional support in the classroom setting. *Journal of Counseling and Development, 87*(1), 6–11.

Darling-Hammond, L., & Friedlaender, D. (2008). Creating excellent and equitable schools. *Educational Leadership, 65*(8), 14–21.

Dollarhide, C. T. (2003). School counselors as program leaders: Applying leadership contexts to school counseling. *Professional School Counseling, 6*, 304–309.

Dotson, T. (2009). Advocacy and impact: A comparison of administrators' perceptions of the high school counselor role. *Professional School Counseling, 12*, 480–487.

Epstein, J. L. (2001). *School, family, and community partnerships: Preparing educators and improving schools*. Boulder, CO: Westview Press.

Fernandes-Alcantara, A. L., & Thomas G. (2009). *Disconnected youth: A look at 16- to 24-year olds who are not working or in school*. Washington, DC: Congressional Research Service.

Galassi, J. P., Gulledge, S. A., & Fox, N. D. (1997). Middle school advisories: Retrospect and prospect. *Review of Educational Research, 67*(3), 301–338.

Garbacz, S. A., Woods, K. E., Swanger-Gagné, M. S., Taylor, A. M., Black, K. A., & Sheridan, S. M. (2008). Conjoint behavioral consultation: The effectiveness of a partnership centered approach. *School Psychology Quarterly, 23*, 313–327.

Guajardo, M., Guajardon, F., & Casaperalta, E. (2008). Transformative education: Chronicling a pedagogy for social change. *Anthropology & Education Quarterly, 39*(1), 3–22.

Gysbers, N. C., & Henderson, R. (2001). Comprehensive guidance and counseling programs: A rich history and bright future. *Professional School Counseling, 4*, 246–254.

Heifetz, R. A., Grashow, A., & Linsky, M. (2009). *The practice of adaptive leadership: Tools and tactics for changing your organization and the world*. Cambridge, MA: Business Review Press.

House, R. M., & Hayes, R. L. (2002). School counselors becoming key players in school reform. *Professional School Counseling, 5*, 249–256.

Janson, C., & Militello, M. (2009). Beyond serendipity: Intentional principal and school counselor collaboration and inquiry. In F. Connolly & N. Protheroe (Eds.), *Principals and counselors partnering for student success* (pp. 75–106). Washington, DC: Educational Research Service and Naviance.

Janson, C., Militello, M., & Kosine, N. (2008). Four views of the professional school counsellor and principal relationship: A Q methodology study. *Professional School Counseling 11*(6), 353–361.

Janson, C., Stone, C., & Clark, M. A. (2009). Stretching leadership: A distributed perspective to understanding and preparing school counselor leaders. *Professional School Counseling, 13*(2), 98–106.

Juvonen, J., Le, V. N., Kaganoff, T., Augustine, C., & Constant, L. (2004). *Focus on the wonder years: Challenges facing the American middle school*. Santa Monica, CA: RAND Corporation.

Klem, A., & Connell, J. (2004). *Relationships matter: Linking teacher support to student engagement and achievement*. Philadelphia, PA: Institute for Research and Reform in Education.

Kretzmann, J. P., & McKnight, J. L. (1993). *Building communities from the inside out: A path toward finding and mobilizing a community's assets*. Chicago, IL: ACTA.

Lapan, R. T., Gysbers, N. C., & Sun, Y. (1997). The impact of more fully implemented guidance programs on the school experiences of high school students: A statewide evaluation study. *Journal of Counseling and Development, 75*, 292–302.

Marzano, R. J., Pickering, D. J., & Pollock, J. E. (2001). *Classroom instruction that works: Research-based strategies for increasing student achievement*. Alexandria, VA: Association for Supervision and Curriculum Development.

McDonnell, L. (2004). *Politics, persuasion, and educational testing*. Cambridge, MA: Harvard University Press.

McKnight, J., & Block, P. (2010). *The abundant community: Awakening the power of families and neighborhoods*. Chicago, IL: American Planning Association.

McLaughlin, M. W., & Talbert, J. E. (2006). *Building school based teacher learning communities. Professional strategies to improve student achievement*. New York, NY: Teachers College Press.

McMahon, H. G., Mason, E. C. M., & Paisley, P. O. (2009). School counselor educators as educational leaders promoting systemic change. *Professional School Counseling, 13*(2), 116–124.

McNeely, C. A., Nonnemaker, J. M., & Blum, R. W. (2002). Promoting school connectedness: Evidence from the National Longitudinal Study of Adolescent Health. *Journal of School Health, 72*(4), 138–146.

Militello, M., Gajda, R., & Bowers, A. (2009). The role of accountability policies and alternative certification on principals' perceptions of leadership preparation. *Journal of Research on Leadership Education, 4*(2), 30–66.

Militello, M., & Janson, C. (2007). Socially focused, situationally driven practice: A study of distributed leadership among school principals and counselors. *Journal of School Leadership, 17*(4), 409–442.

Myrick, R. D. (2003). *Developmental guidance and counseling: A practical approach* (3rd ed.). Minneapolis, MN: Educational Media Corporation.

National Governors Association Center for Best Practices & Council of Chief State School Officers. (2010). *Common core state standards*. Washington, DC: Authors.

Paisley, P. O., & McMahon, H. G. (2001). School counseling for the 21st century: Challenges and opportunities. *Professional School Counseling, 5*, 106–115.

Porter, A., McMaken, J., Hwang, J., & Yang, R. (2011). Common core standards: The new U.S. intended curriculum. *Educational Researcher, 40*(3), 103–116.

Rafoth, M. A., & Foriska, T. (2006). Administrator participation in promoting effective problem solving teams. *Remedial and Special Education, 27*, 130–135.

Ravitch, D. (2010). *The death and life of the great American school system: How testing and choice are undermining education*. New York, NY: Basic Books.

Ritchie, M. H. (1989). Enhancing the public image of school counseling: A marketing approach. *The School Counselor, 37*, 54–61.

Sanders, W. L., & Rivers, J. C. (1996). *Cumulative and residual effects of teachers on future student academic achievement (research progress report)*. Knoxville: University of Tennessee Value-Added Research and Assessment Center.

Sheridan, S. M., Eagle, J. W., & Doll, B. (2006). An examination of the efficacy of conjoint behavioral consultation with diverse clients. *School Psychology Quarterly, 21*, 396–417.

Sheridan, S. M., & Kratochwill, T. R. (2007). *Conjoint behavior consultation: Promoting family school connections and interventions* (2nd ed.). New York, NY: Springer.

Sheridan, S. M., Kratochwill, T. R., & Bergan, J. R. (1996). *Conjoint behavioral consultation: A procedural manual*. New York, NY: Plenum Press.

Shulkind, S. B, & Foote, J. (2009, September). Creating a culture of connectedness through middle school advisory programs. *Middle School Journal, 41*(1), 20–27.

Thompson, R. A. (2013). *School counseling: Best practices for working in schools*. New York, NY: Routledge.

Whiston, S. C., & Quinby, R. F. (2009). Review of counseling outcome research. *Psychology in the Schools, 46*(3), 267–272.

Chapter 10

OUTCOME RESEARCH AND FUTURE DIRECTIONS OF CLASSROOM GUIDANCE

E. C. M. MASON
DePaul University

STEPHANIE EBERTS
Louisiana State University

LAUREN STERN WYNNE
Longwood University

"As a result of the meeting, the teachers and I devised a classroom guidance lesson that would emphasize the concepts of conversion between decimals and percentages by teaching students how different grades could change a course average and how to calculate their grade point averages. This lesson set out to reinforce mathematics competencies assessed on the state high-stakes test, a subject area that was critical to the school's adequate yearly progress. Furthermore, the lesson would also reinforce the importance of grade point averages—a school counseling goal. One teacher volunteered his classes first, and after a day of five back-to-back math periods, we discussed the strengths and weaknesses of the lesson and made some small adjustments. Before long, the word spread to the other math teachers, and I was scheduled to be in their classes in the following weeks."

Mason, 2010, p. 28

Mason's story of aligning mathematics standards with the school counseling program and its goals demonstrates the kind of cross-curricular collaboration that is essential to creating outcomes as well as the kind of creative approach that is vital to the future of classroom guidance programming.

This chapter considers the significance of classroom guidance a central component of a comprehensive school counseling program. Further, it invites the reader to consider what classroom guidance programming will look like in years to come. While some aspects of classroom guidance programming may remain over time, changes to education as a whole will undoubtedly shift how school counselors reach students in the classroom setting. This chapter should leave the reader hopeful and curious about the future of classroom guidance programming.

After reading this chapter about outcome research and future directions of classroom guidance programming, you will be able to

- understand the research and outcomes regarding successful classroom guidance programming,
- describe the importance of the prevention and intervention aspects of classroom guidance programming,
- explain various formats and frameworks for the delivery of classroom guidance programming,
- describe the relationship between the school counselor and the teacher in classroom guidance programming,
- apply a college- and career-readiness focus in classroom guidance programming, and
- consider the use of technology in classroom guidance programming, now and in the future.

RESULTS OF EFFECTIVE CLASSROOM GUIDANCE PROGRAMMING

Effective classroom guidance lessons are historically preventive or remedial in nature (Erford, 2014). School counselors are urged to use data to show the effectiveness of their programmatic curricula, starting with a needs assessment to figure out the best intervention for the issue and then using an evaluation to measure whether or not the curriculum has been effective (American School Counselor Association [ASCA], 2012; Council for Accreditation of Counseling & Related Educational Programs [CACREP], 2009). Strong, well-delivered curricula have the potential to change the climate of a school. Through intentional planning, evaluation, and promotion of the results, a school counselor can advocate for his or her students through curriculum-based instruction.

Core Curriculum

School counselors are in a unique position to deliver a curriculum that focuses on the development of social and emotional skills, career development, college readiness, and academic skills. No other individual in the school building is able to focus exclusively on these areas. One example of how a classroom guidance curriculum can benefit a school is that of one of the authors, Stephanie E. Eberts, who was a school counselor in New Orleans when Hurricane Katrina devastated the Louisiana and Mississippi gulf region:

CASE STUDY

Stephanie

In 2005, I had been the school counselor at a small private elementary and middle school in New Orleans for five years. On August 28, 2005, Hurricane Katrina landed in New Orleans with devastating impact, and our school did not reopen until the following year. The city and the school were barely functioning when we returned in January of 2006. Though we had only been in school for a few days prior to our evacuation, the delivery of my guidance program was already in place for the school year, and the full developmentally based curriculum had been in place since before I had become the counselor at the school. Though the curriculum was adjusted each year to meet the needs of each grade level, the foundation of the program was preventive in nature and focused on skill building in the areas of social/emotional development and academic and career skills. This foundation did not change. When I returned after our long evacuation period, I feared I would not have the tools I needed to meet the needs of my students and community. I could not have been more wrong. The comprehensive guidance program provided me the time in the classroom that I needed, and it allowed my students to discuss how to cope with the changes they were facing. For example, the fourth-grade curriculum focused on coping with challenging situations. Prior to the storm, many of the identified situations were about friendships or test taking whereas after the storm, the students identified challenges related to loss (of friends, family members, homes) and difficulty managing academics after a half a year in a different school. I was able to see the power of an effective guidance curriculum. The curriculum itself did not need to change, and the relationships with students and the teachers were already in place. So while the curriculum base did not change, the content of the discussions did. To this day, it was the most validating experience in my career as a school counselor. I knew that year that school counselors really impact the lives of students and help communities to become resilient, and this is achievable through classroom guidance programming.

Hopefully, very few school counselors' comprehensive school counseling programs will be tested by something as difficult as a natural disaster, but through this example, it is easy to see how impactful a strong classroom guidance curriculum can be in the life of a school. Though classroom guidance is only one part of the comprehensive school counseling program, it is essential to reaching and serving the needs of all students.

Delivery

Not all classroom guidance programming can be delivered in the traditional setting. The case example above refers to a program in which the school counselor delivered a 10-week curriculum at every grade level in all classes over the course of one school year. However, due to large student caseloads and difficulty scheduling, this sort of delivery of classroom guidance is not always possible. There are a number of different ways that counselors have been successful in implementing their curricula, such as delivery via

- larger groups of two or more classes combined,
- schoolwide or grade-level assemblies,
- trained peer mediators or peer leaders to provide content in classes,
- trained teachers in advisory periods,
- cross-curricular interventions that involve multiple staff or subject areas, and
- technology with information that can be accessed by students online, such as webinars.

Advisory periods are sometimes used at the middle school and high school level, and they are implemented in a variety of ways. These periods are usually shortened class periods or homerooms in which students meet with an appointed advisor who is a faculty member. These programs are designed to help students and teachers build relationships that will support the students' academic goals. The school counselor can train the advisory teachers assigned to deliver a curriculum that meets the needs of the students. Variations in delivery of the program can be a deterrent to this sort of implementation, but often, it is an effective way to reach a large number of students. Cross-curricular interventions are collaborative interventions that go beyond a single subject and involve several staff. In cross-curricular interventions, several teachers will link curricular objectives to deepen the students' understanding of certain topics (see Mason's sample at the beginning of the chapter or the teacher and counselor accountability section of this chapter). Schmidt (2014) suggests that impactful guidance curriculum is an integral part of the school's curriculum. He believes that in order to be effective, the school counselor must infuse his or her teachings throughout the school community through a variety of delivery methods.

Best Practices and Research-Based Interventions

How do school counselors know that their classroom guidance programming is effective? Besides meeting the needs of the students, the school counselor should be using evidence-based interventions (those based on research). Seeking out these programs can be a challenge for new and seasoned school counselors alike. Many districts and states respond to this challenge by offering resources and standards of practice for their school counselors through state-approved curricula, programs, or lessons. There are also other national resources available to support school counselors in finding evidence-based interventions. For example, the Ronald H. Fredrickson Center for School Counseling Outcome Research and Evaluation (CSCORE; http://www.umass.edu/schoolcounseling/) offers a host of researched programs as well as evaluation tools for school counselors to use in their own data collection. Examples of some evidence-based programs detailed on the CSCORE website (http://www.umass.edu/schoolcounseling/resources-for-counselors.php) are Second Step (social and academic success), Student Success Skills (academic development), Project Achieve (social skills), and Roads to Success (college preparation). In order for school counselors to continue to advocate for their positions in schools, it is necessary to not only evaluate how their programs impact their students but also to use evidence-based programs. The future of classroom guidance programming should also include scholars and practitioners conducting or participating in the rigorous research of programs so as to create a stronger curriculum base that is shown to be effective with various student populations.

PREVENTION RATHER THAN INTERVENTION

Classroom guidance programming serves *all* students in a school and addresses anticipated developmental needs across the elementary, middle, and high school grade levels (Myrick, 1987). Classroom guidance programming teaches students about the mindsets and behaviors that support their academic, social/emotional, college readiness, and career development in a manner that is holistic, developmental, and sequential (ASCA, 2012). The school counseling profession continues its decades-long focus on prevention through classroom guidance programming to help students know how to plan for the future and cope with the current personal, academic, and sometimes systemic challenges that detract from their academic, career, and social/emotional goals (Gysbers, 2004).

Types of Prevention Addressed
by Classroom Guidance Programming

Borrowing terms from public health and depending on the assessed need, classroom guidance programming can be defined as primary, secondary, or tertiary prevention. However, classroom guidance typically falls under the realm of primary prevention. Primary prevention efforts focus on stopping problems before they occur (McMahon, Mason, Daluga-Guenther, & Ruiz, 2014; Walker & Shinn, 2002). Given the developmental lens through which school counselors view their students, they plan classroom guidance with the goal of teaching students the mindsets and behaviors they need to stay on track academically as well as to cope with the social and emotional changes that are universal to most children in school settings. For example, working with kindergarten students using the Ready to Learn program (Brigman & Webb, 2003) is a tool for primary prevention because the lessons teach students how to listen, pay attention, ask questions, and not give up when they are learning something new or challenging. These are examples of the ASCA behavior standards, learning strategies, self-management skills, and social skills. Helping students learn *how* to learn promotes academic coping and resilience and contributes to a positive learning environment. The vast majority of classroom guidance programming focuses on primary prevention and the ASCA Mindsets & Behaviors for Student Success (2014) through instruction about healthy choices, positive learning behaviors, social and refusal skills, coping and resilience strategies, and follow-through skills to support home-to-school, school-to-school, and school-to-work transitions.

Classroom guidance programming also serves as a secondary prevention tool as needed. Secondary prevention focuses on intervening in a classroom after exposure to a risk or event to reverse the potential negative impact on students (McMahon et al., 2014; Walker & Shinn, 2002). For example, if a classroom teacher is shifted to another school due to changing enrollments or needs to take an unexpected medical leave, a classroom of students may feel lost, confused, or upset. Often, a counselor can facilitate a classroom guidance lesson about change and how to cope with and adapt effectively to what is happening in the classroom in a manner that calms students' nerves and helps them feel hopeful and open to the teacher who will take over the position. It can be very powerful if the new teacher is able to participate in the intervention to learn about and from his or her students, and in return, they can learn about their new teacher. This type of event happens more often than one would think and for various reasons, and classroom guidance can reverse the negative impact of the unexpected transition and help the class get back to normal levels of functioning.

At times, classroom guidance represents a form of tertiary prevention. Tertiary prevention activities seek to reduce the negative impact of an event or a set of risk factors (McMahon et al., 2014; Walker & Shinn, 2002). Classroom guidance is sometimes facilitated in response to an event that has a potentially severe impact on a class or the entire school. In the case of a student's death, counselors may develop classroom guidance programming about healthy grieving that addresses the unique situation and aids students in seeking assistance as needed to cope in constructive rather than destructive ways. The goals of the lesson are to limit the potential negative impact on personal and academic functioning and to identify and engage the protective factors and resources available to students.

Creating a Climate for Learning through Classroom Guidance

Classroom guidance programming promotes positive learning environments. When school counselors use classroom guidance programming to facilitate team building, collaborative problem-solving, and activities that enhance belonging, classrooms are more peaceful and safe. Using needs assessments and collaborating with teachers to identify students' needs and strengths helps school counselors identify what each class needs and the best timing for delivery of classroom lessons. Meeting with classes early in the year to help build relationships through classroom guidance can help set a tone for each individual class that is positive and includes the unique perspectives of all the individuals in the room. For example, if a school counselor knows that his or her school population is highly transient, he or she may recognize that it will be important for the class to have a procedure for welcoming (and saying good-bye to) students that is positive and encouraging, because the class group may change throughout the year. Facilitating a conversation with students about what they think this procedure should look like offers each class the opportunity to define how they want to respond to each other in positive ways. This same approach can be applied to designing procedures for dealing with classroom conflicts or behavior issues.

Classroom Meeting Training

Classroom meeting training as a form of classroom guidance offers each class a skill set for managing the ups and downs of learning in a group that can serve the class all year and potentially reduce unnecessary referrals to school counselors or administrators. Based on cooperation, shared power, and encouragement (Edwards & Mullis, 2003), classroom meeting training can be facilitated as classroom guidance in regular and special education classrooms with students of all ages (Bucholz & Sheffler, 2009). Teacher attendance and participation in classroom meeting training is vital because the teacher is an important member of the class who participates in the meetings as well. While this is an intervention with older roots, its role in the prevention of classroom-based problems remains vital.

Multi-Tiered Systems of Support

Response to Intervention (RTI), a multi-tiered model of student intervention recommended by the Individuals with Disabilities Act, is a data-driven process with the goal of helping all students receive the support or intervention needed to decrease behavior disruptions, increase instructional time, or enhance learning and achievement (Gruman & Hoelzen, 2011). The tiers provide for increasingly targeted and intensive interventions depending upon the individual student's documented needs. At RTI's most basic level, schoolwide or classroom-level interventions are in place to serve *all* students and create an environment that supports learning and instruction. Schoolwide positive behavior support or positive behavioral interventions & supports (PBIS), are behavioral applications of RTI and are well-supported in the literature as a means of creating a positive climate for learning (Martens & Andreen, 2013). (For additional information, visit http://www.pbis.org.) Classroom guidance programming is an efficient vehicle for delivering several of the preventative and educational universal interventions in a schoolwide positive behavior support plan, including defining the schoolwide behavior expectations and teaching and reteaching those expectations (Ockerman, Mason, & Feiker-Hollenbeck, 2012). School counselor participation on the school PBIS committee offers opportunities to collaborate and advocate for systemic change and may lead to more opportunities to directly impact students through preventative classroom guidance.

Prevention Topics Covered in Classroom Guidance

Assessment of school and contextual data as well as the ASCA Mindsets & Behaviors for Student Success (2014) offer helpful insight into which prevention topics to incorporate into classroom guidance programming. Student, educator, and parent/caregiver assessments provide additional information about the areas of greatest need in a school population. The recently published ASCA Mindsets & Behaviors for Student Success offers 35 standards that can be utilized in classroom guidance curriculum development across the three broad domains of academic, career, and social/emotional development (ASCA, 2014). It is vital to approach all three domains in a balanced manner when developing an implementation plan for a comprehensive classroom guidance curriculum that supports the current academic achievement of students to prepare them for each academic transition (i.e., grade to grade, level to level) as well as the ultimate goal of helping all students be college and career ready.

School counselors must also consider their role in promoting the mental health of students as they plan and implement their classroom guidance programs. Growing empirical support for the positive impact of universal social and emotional learning (SEL) programs that are well-developed and well-conducted in school settings underscores their importance in helping students be more successful in school and life (Durlak, Weissberg, Dymnicki, Taylor, & Schellinger, 2011; Zins & Elias, 2006). Waters and Sroufe (1983) believe competent people are able "to generate and coordinate flexible, adaptive responses to demands and to generate and capitalize on opportunities in the environment" (p. 80). This definition resonates with the role of school counselors in the holistic development of students in K–12 settings. Classroom guidance can be used to assess for mental health concerns affecting students as well as to teach students developmentally appropriate strategies for coping with anxiety, stress, discouragement, and interpersonal conflict as a means of promoting perseverance, resilience, and self-care in learning, employment, and community settings. Further information about SEL is available from the Collaborative for Academic, Social, and Emotional Learning at http://www.casel.org. Prevention topic categories to consider may include but are not limited to the following:

- Academic success skills (Brigman & Webb, 2003, 2004)
- Anxiety prevention and coping skills training (Barrett, Webster, Turner, & May, 2003)
- Hope/resilience/dropout prevention (Pedrotti, Edwards, & Lopez, 2008)
- Violence prevention/social skills (Committee for Children, 1997a, 1997b)
- Suicide prevention (Erikson & Abel, 2013)
- Health and wellness (Walsh, Kenny, Weineke, & Harrington, 2008)

The categories above contain numerous subtopics and may serve best as unit titles under which a number of related classroom guidance programming can be developed, implemented, and evaluated. Earlier chapters describe this process more fully for further reference.

Classroom guidance programming stands out as an effective, efficient, and dynamic agent of prevention at all grade levels. The saying that "an ounce of prevention is worth a pound of cure" emphasizes its potential in making a difference in the lives of children as they develop into capable workers, caring citizens, and compassionate partners and caregivers.

TEACHER AND COUNSELOR ACCOUNTABILITY

In recent years, school counselors have been held to similar stringent accountability requirements as teachers. The ASCA has included accountability in its national model as a critical component to building an understanding of the effectiveness of comprehensive school counseling programs. As each state certification/license agency moves away from the requirement that school counselors have classroom teaching experience in order to become certified/licensed, the future of school counseling is reliant on future practitioners learning how to be effective both in and out of the classroom. Part of this effectiveness is measured through formal performance evaluations, but school counselors must also use teaching skills, plan developmentally appropriate curricula that align with school and national standards, collaborate with teachers, and manage a classroom.

The future of school counseling and school counselor accountability lies in the hands of the practitioners and those who prepare and educate them. School counseling preparation programs should not only educate future school counselors on to how to implement their classroom guidance and comprehensive programs but they must also prepare new professionals to work in the classroom setting. Courses that focus on developmentally appropriate lesson plan and curricular development, demonstrate how to assess commercial programs and curricula, provide strategies for classroom management, and prepare future school counselors without teaching experience for the unique systems, procedures, and initiatives in modern-day education reform are essential. Courses that emphasize the use of group skills to manage a classroom and run effective groups will also help future school counselors to implement classroom guidance curricula with greater success. It is also important to note that there are still many teachers who are becoming school counselors, and it is a difficult paradigm shift to make from being a classroom teacher to being a school counselor. School counselor preparation courses should acknowledge this shift, especially as school counseling students with teaching experience enter practicum and internship.

Program Evaluation

The ASCA National Model (2012) is very specific in its emphasis on programmatic evaluation for school counselors. Incorporating different types of evaluation into the school counseling program will yield the clearest and most helpful results. Action research models provide a helpful framework for school counselors trying to determine the effectiveness of interventions such as classroom guidance programming. Action research models assist the school counselor who is also simultaneously the researcher and the intervener by emphasizing the significance of the intervention in the local context rather than making it necessary for results to be generalized to other settings. As such, action research supports measuring against oneself and one's own practices as a school counselor and encourages a cycle of continuous improvement within any given unique school counseling intervention (Mason & McMahon, 2009; Mason & Uwah, 2007; Plummer et al., 2014; Rowell, 2005, 2006).

Schmidt (2014) refers to five different types of evaluation to help strengthen a program: informal and formal, formative and summative, process, needs assessment, and outcome. With regard to classroom guidance programming, informal evaluations refer to those that happen in an unstructured manner, such as polling students with a show of hands, while formal evaluations are more systemic and structured in nature, such as a scheduled classroom observation by an administrator. Both of these types of evaluation can offer feedback for improvement and send the message to the stakeholders in the school community that everyone plays a role in the strengthening of the school counseling program. Formative evaluations are ongoing efforts to collect data and information, such as pre- and posttests during classroom guidance lessons; summative evaluations aid in the decisions about how to improve upon a program, such as end-of-the-year surveys for staff about the classroom guidance curriculum. Process evaluations reveal how the logistics of implementation will occur, such as how much time will be spent delivering classroom guidance, when during the school day, and in which classes. Needs assessment evaluations are used to assess the needs of the school community and help identify topics for potential classroom guidance programming. Outcome evaluations relate to the overarching goals that the school counseling program was trying to accomplish. For example, a program's goal may be to decrease behavioral referrals by 5% in the fifth grade. Outcome evaluations, in the way of a review of discipline records, ascertain whether or not the program helped meet this goal; the classroom guidance curriculum may have been one intervention that contributed toward this goal.

Consultation and Collaboration

Consultation and collaboration with teachers, administrators, and other stakeholders are also key elements to the accountability efforts of school counselors. Participating in team-, grade-, or department-level meetings to find out about the issues the teachers are facing can assist the counselor in developing appropriate classroom guidance programming. It also enables the counselors to build the collegial relationships that are vital to the success of a school counseling program. Similarly, working with teachers to plan curricula that is collaborative where standards are concerned allows students to integrate academic, career, and social/emotional skills within their classes (Mason, 2010). For example, if the students are learning about the civil rights movement in history or social studies, they can gain a deeper understanding of the material if they are also reading a book that takes place during that time in their English class. The school counselor can teach about how discrimination impacts students today (in their social, academic, and working lives) in their classroom guidance lessons. This sort of cross-curricular collaboration not only benefits the students, it also helps school counselors to become an integral part of the school's curriculum and to gain credibility with teachers. These collaboration and consultation efforts also help with counselor accountability, especially when data and evaluation tools are used, by showing teachers, administrators, and other stakeholders the value of the work that counselors are doing in the classroom.

COLLEGE- AND CAREER-READINESS FOCUS

The school counseling profession grew out of the vocational guidance movement in the early 1900s and has not wavered in its goal to support students' career development (Gysbers, 2001). College- and career-focused classrooms or large-group guidance sessions are powerful, parsimonious school counseling interventions that help students learn how their interests, skills, and values relate to career clusters and how to utilize effective skills for learning, working, and making educational transitions. Because classroom guidance is an intervention offered to all students in a comprehensive guidance program, it provides the opportunity for every student to explore postsecondary options and to develop an understanding of how current academic decisions affect future college and career planning and implementation in a supported, preventative, and constructive manner.

Defining College and Career Readiness

Though the exact definition of *college and career readiness* is still under debate (Conley, 2012b), the concept of college and career readiness and how it can be applied in the student development process continues to be rigorously studied and discussed from different perspectives. Organizations such as the United States Department of Education, ACT, College Board, and American Institutes for Research as well as university-based scholars regularly report data that underscore the dire need for a continued focus on college and career readiness:

- While 93% of middle school students report a goal of attending college, only 44% graduate, and only 26% graduate within six years of enrollment (Conley, 2012a, 2012b).
- Only 25% of high school graduates who took the ACT test were ready for college-level work (ACT, 2012).
- Less than 25% of two-year college students who require remedial classes earned a degree or certificate within eight years of enrollment. Only 40% of community college students who did not require remediation completed their degree or certificate program in eight years (Bailey, 2009).

- In the next decade, 63% of all jobs in the United States will require some post-secondary training and 90% of jobs in growing industries with higher wages will require some postsecondary education (Carnevale, Smith, & Strohl, 2010).

The data collected about underserved populations also continue to illuminate a gap in equity and access:

- Thirty-two percent of White high school graduates who took the ACT in 2012 met all four of the College Readiness Benchmarks. Only 5% of African American students and 13% of Hispanic students met all four benchmarks (ACT, 2012).
- Students considered English language learners are twice as likely to drop out of high school as their English-proficient peers (Rumberger, 2006).
- Only 15% of high school students with disabilities attended a four-year college compared to 37% of young adults in the general population (Sanford, Newman, Wagner, Cameto, Knokey, & Shaver, 2011).
- Underserved groups, such as minorities, students with a lower socioeconomic status, and first-generation college students, require additional support accessing the federal financial aid system (College Board National Office for School Counselor Accountability, 2010).
- A lack of career readiness is the single best predictor of indecisiveness in undergraduate students than any other combination of variables (Gaffner & Hazler, 2002).

The renewed focus on college and career readiness as a primary outcome measure of student achievement and indicator of potential success in postsecondary studies drives the work of professional educators. School counselors advocate for the inclusion of college- and career-based development by creating and delivering a classroom guidance curriculum that incorporates national and state-level mandates. Student access to postsecondary options increases when school counselors lead classroom guidance activities that enhance postsecondary awareness and develop skills for exploration, planning, and attainment (Chen-Hayes, Ockerman, & Mason, 2013; Hines & Lemon, 2011). National and state-level mandates and policies such as No Child Left Behind, the reauthorization of the Elementary and Secondary Education Act, adoption of the Common Core Standards for College and Career Readiness, the College Board's National Office of School Counselor Advocacy (NOSCA), the National Association of College Admissions Counseling, and the recent Reach Higher campaign led by First Lady Michelle Obama and backed by Secretary of Education Arne Duncan offer direct and indirect support of the school counselor's role in the college- and career-readiness process.

College and Career Lessons

When school counselors at every level develop and implement comprehensive, developmental school counseling programs, they encourage students' academic, career, and social/emotional development (ASCA, 2012). All three domains support college and career readiness, and a discussion of how each classroom or large-group guidance lesson topic is related to students' current and future academic and career success helps them begin to build a bridge to reach their postsecondary goals. School counselors are in a unique role to develop and implement a college- and career-focused guidance curriculum in collaboration with other professional educators, caregivers, community resources, and representatives of postsecondary institutions (Chen-Hayes et al., 2013; Hines & Lemons, 2011). For example, school counselors can enlist the support of local employers (who represent different career clusters) to participate in classroom guidance programming to share what being career ready looks like from their perspective. Parents and caregivers often look for ways to participate in their children's education. School counselors can ask them to participate in classroom guidance programming or accept their offer to connect with local resources parents know who can serve as potential speakers. Colleges and technical school representatives will leap at the opportunity to meet with students in classrooms to describe the programs they offer. For example, inviting a university admissions representative to talk about their STEM (science, technology, engineering, and mathematics) major programs during science and math classes is a way to collaborate with teachers of these subjects who are trying to teach content as well as inspire students to pursue jobs in these fields. University and technical school admissions representatives can also present on financial aid resources that help students understand how postsecondary training can be more affordable and increase their long-term earning potential for an array of employment opportunities.

Engaging at the Elementary School and Middle School Levels

From the moment students enter school in kindergarten, the developmental, sequential nature of a strong comprehensive school counseling program sets the stage for developing the mindsets elementary school, middle school, and high school students need to successfully transition to postsecondary educational settings and the world of work (ASCA, 2014). For example, an elementary school counselor can begin to introduce students to a myriad of jobs from different career clusters to help students name careers beyond what their caregivers do for a living. A classroom guidance activity focused on creating an ABC-type alphabet book of different jobs that highlights what they do and what school subjects relate to the career cluster under which the job falls is pretty simple but very powerful. This type of classroom guidance activity helps students connect the ways in which school and work are related. When students work on the activity collaboratively, a school counselor can verbally highlight how being able to work with others toward a common goal is an academic and career-readiness skill regardless of field. Middle school counselors can present information in classroom guidance lessons about how elective courses (e.g., connections, exploratory, or specials classes) relate to career clusters and how they can try out areas of interest in their course selections. Middle school is also an appropriate level for presenting class-room guidance lessons that involve creating basic resumes, doing mock job inter-views, or hosting large-scale career or college fairs.

COMPONENTS OF COLLEGE AND CAREER READINESS

The National Office for School Counselor Advocacy (2010) outlines eight compo-nents of a college- and career-readiness-focused school counseling program. Infusion of all eight components into classroom guidance planning offers a solid framework for developing classroom guidance lessons that promote equity and access to postsec-ondary and work settings. Developmental modifications allow the components of college knowledge to be addressed in an age-appropriate manner in elementary, middle, and high school classrooms. They include the following:

1. College aspirations
2. Academic planning for college and career readiness
3. Enrichment and extracurricular engagement
4. College and career exploration and selection processes
5. College and career assessments
6. College affordability planning
7. College and career admission processes
8. Transition from high school graduation to college enrollment

The challenge of helping all students graduate on time and be college and career ready is daunting, given the unique needs of individual students and schools; therefore, NOSCA encourages school counselors to examine school data and cultural/systemic aspects to determine the style of intervention that makes the most sense, based on the school setting.

Even though this is a textbook about working with students in groups, school counselors can prepare students on an individual level to be more engaged in classroom guidance by helping them know about upcoming classroom guidance sessions. In this way, the fabric of college and career readiness is woven into each student interaction (Hines & Lemons, 2011) and students begin to prepare mentally for the next classroom guidance lesson, which can help them participate more actively. The following case study illuminates how this type of interaction might sound:

CASE STUDY

Anish

Anish, a rising tenth grader, is meeting with his counselor to enroll at the local high school in his family's new neighborhood. After reviewing Anish's prior school achievement and progress toward meeting graduation requirements, the counselor inquires about his college and career aspirations by saying, "What do you hope to be doing after you graduate?" While it might seem like putting the cart before the horse, it makes sense to ask this question before a course schedule is officially created. Not only does the counselor build rapport with the student and family, she also begins to help students understand her role in the school as a college and career specialist who can help students learn about their interests, preferences, abilities, and values in the college and career decision-making process.

When Anish expresses a desire to become an engineer or a scientist, his counselor can begin helping him explore what core and elective courses may help him explore these interests while in high school and the level of course rigor required for a more successful postsecondary transition. For example, in addition to presenting all of the elective options, his counselor highlights the sequence of engineering courses and array of science classes that are available at this new school. They discuss college admissions requirements for many STEM programs, which include taking calculus prior to high school graduation. She also lets him know whom to contact about joining the Engineering Club, where he can participate in fun and competitive activities that relate to his interests. These conversations also occur in classroom guidance lessons with large groups of students.

Prior to the end of the meeting, Anish's counselor asks if his prior school counselors ever visited his classrooms to provide information and facilitate activities related to strategies for school success, life skills, or career development. His counselor is attempting to gather data about how his prior school counselors implemented their college and career guidance focus in the classroom. Anish confirms that he knew his counselors from visiting his classes and that he liked what they had to share. His new counselor lets him know that the counselors at his new school will be visiting his sophomore social studies class to help the students learn how to use an online college and career development tool that they can access at school or home to help begin making decisions about where they are headed after high school and what high school classes will be helpful in their career exploration. He says that sounds like a great idea because he is not sure what type of engineer or scientist he might like to be. The counselor shares about additional classroom and large-group guidance sessions that will take place during junior and senior year that will help Anish learn more about the college- and career-planning process and gives dates for upcoming caregiver guidance sessions about financial aid options and how to help with the college application process. His parents are thrilled to learn that his school takes such a proactive approach to college and career planning and feel relieved because they did not complete their education in this country and are unsure of all the ways to help Anish plan for college. His counselor could be this informative because of the developmental, sequential nature of a comprehensive guidance program and because of her awareness of the role of elementary and middle school counselors in the college- and career-guidance process as a result of vertical planning and teaming across the school levels.

College- and career-focused classroom guidance programming offers many opportunities to advocate for equity and access to postsecondary study and work options. School counselors can utilize the power of legislation and national initiatives to increase their time working with students in classrooms and large groups. When all of the students receive general information and training about college and career readiness in large-group guidance, school counselors often have more time to tailor individual and small-group college- and career-focused interventions to meet the unique needs of the student population.

DIVERSITY AND SOCIAL JUSTICE

Diversity and social justice are elemental to the nature of the school counselor's work. As an advocate and change agent, school counselors must be able to work with diverse populations and should seek to address issues of social justice (ASCA, 2012; Education Trust, 2003; Holcomb-McCoy, 2007; Holcomb-McCoy & Chen-Hayes, 2011; House & Sears, 2002; Ockerman & Mason, 2012).

Diversity

Schools are full of diversity, so cultural competence and proficiency are essential skills of the school counselor. It is not unusual for school counselors to be the only ones in the building trained to acknowledge and support cultural variables that impact student achievement. Cultural variables are inclusive of many aspects of a student's or family's identity and can include such factors as race, ethnicity, economic status, religious or faith-based practices, sexual orientation, gender identity, or ability. While school counselors will likely not leave their graduate programs prepared to address the needs of all populations, a framework that values cultural diversity in general can help in approaching most any population. Below is a non-exhaustive list of populations with whom school counselors should anticipate working:

- Students with disabilities (cognitive, physical, and emotional/behavioral)
- English language learners
- Lesbian, gay, bisexual, transgender, or questioning populations
- Students living in poverty or temporary living situations
- Military students and families

School counselors should be aware that the ASCA Mindsets & Behaviors for Student Success (ASCA, 2014) may align differently with the cultural values of various student groups or may not align at all in some cases. When choosing standards for lessons, selecting activities, and choosing the delivery method, school counselors should carefully consider the cultural impact on students. School counselors should also value the need for ongoing self-reflection and professional development so as to be aware of their own biases and to seek to learn the skills needed to work with populations with whom they are less familiar (Holcomb-McCoy, 2007; Holcomb-McCoy & Chen-Hayes, 2011; Ockerman & Mason, 2012). Such practices will help school counselors in the classroom by aiding them in planning culturally proficient and respectful lessons, differentiating activities for a variety of learners, and anticipating and managing diversity-related interactions during the delivery of lessons.

Social Justice

Social justice refers to advocacy efforts around issues of inequity. Inequities can come in a variety of forms where student achievement is concerned, including lack of or gaps in access or opportunity or discrimination against certain groups of students (Holcomb-McCoy, 2007; Holcomb-McCoy & Chen-Hayes, 2011; Ockerman & Mason, 2012). The following are samples of common inequities that may require social justice action:

- Lower enrollment rates of minority students in more rigorous courses (Honors, AP) compared to non-minority students

- More disciplinary actions taken against students with Individual Education Plans compared to other students
- Lower homework completion rates for low-income students with limited access to technology
- Lack of knowledge about all available postsecondary options for students of families without college graduates

Being able to act as an advocate and change agent and to address issues of social justice means that school counselors must know how to draw from a variety of schoolwide data sources such as test scores, grades, graduation rates, attendance records, and disciplinary records (Dimmitt, Carey, & Hatch, 2007; Hatch, 2013). Using these sources, the school counselor must make important decisions about what content should go into lesson plans so that classroom guidance programming becomes a primary intervention for closing achievement and equity gaps between groups of students. Classroom guidance itself is a social justice action by design because it ensures that *all* students interact with and receive support from the school counselor as part of a comprehensive school counseling program.

College and career readiness is a social justice issue. Globally, the U.S. has fallen behind dramatically with respect to the number of college graduates produced as compared to other countries (Organization for Economic Cooperation and Development, 2014). Therefore, in particular, school counselors must work at *all levels* to increase the number of college and postsecondary graduates, which means a focus on classroom guidance programming that emphasize college- and career-readiness skills.

Consider the following case study in which Karlyn, a school counselor in Chicago, used classroom guidance programming to increase the percentage of eighth-grade students who applied to non-neighborhood high schools.

CASE STUDY

Karlyn

In Chicago, eighth-grade students have the option of going to their neighborhood high school for Grades 9 through 12 or they can apply to other high schools in the city that offer more rigorous college preparatory programs, International Baccalaureate programs, premilitary, arts, math and science, or other specialty programs. Application

(Continued)

(Continued)

to these high schools involves obtaining a minimum score on an entrance test, submission of grades, and other components. Depending upon the school, admission is often highly competitive.

As a new school counselor, Karlyn discovered that about 75% of her students went to the neighborhood school, while only 25% went on to non-neighborhood schools. While the neighborhood school was adequate, it was evident from previous data that eighth-grade students simply were not exposed to all their high school options and neither were their families. Karlyn used classroom guidance programming to make sure all eighth graders knew about their high school options and followed up with additional supports, including group and individual meetings to help students complete applications, and presentations on high school options for families. At the end of the year, Karlyn was able to report a complete flip in the data: 75% of the eighth graders had been accepted to non-neighborhood schools, and 25% went on to the neighborhood high school.

By attending to the social justice issue at hand, Karlyn was able to put more of her eighth graders on the path to being college and career ready because they were provided additional information, which in turn gave them greater access and opportunity.

VIRTUAL EDUCATION/SCHOOLS AND THE ONLINE ENVIRONMENT

Classrooms are no longer adequate learning environments without at least some use of technology. Students now and in the future will be digital natives, and as such, technology is a daily part of their lives and learning (Prensky, 2010). Therefore, it is imperative for school counselors to utilize technology in the classrooms as well as within the rest of their jobs (Sabella & Booker, 2003). It is important, however, that school counselors use technology in thoughtful, intentional, and pedagogically appropriate ways rather than just for the sake of using technology alone. School counselors must model and teach students digital citizenship as part of productive educational, career-long, and lifestyle practices. It is very appropriate for school counselors to teach classroom lessons on online safety, online image management, cyberbullying, or Internet addiction.

As a practicing school counselor, it is important to keep up with technology in general as well as with the tools that can assist the school counselor in his or her work. Technologies that can be used in classrooms are constantly changing, and those that are mentioned here may become outdated and obsolete as newer, more sophisticated tools come on the scene. Keeping up with technology is one way to ensure that classroom guidance lessons are fresh, engaging, and innovative even as the content remains applicable over time.

Presentation Tools

One way to incorporate technology in the school counseling program is through the presentation of classroom or large-group guidance. While standard tools such as Microsoft PowerPoint are still widely used, other presentation tools such as Prezi, Haiku Deck, Voicethread, LiveBinder, and Smore provide engaging features such as movement during the presentation, nonlinear formats, eye-catching graphics, themes and fonts, and offline interactivity through audio, video, and text. Additional tools can be integrated with presentations to gather data from students during presentations in the form of pre- and posttests, polls, or surveys. Tools such as PollEverywhere or Poll Code require the use of mobile applications or access to the Internet for data entry. Given the rise of "bring your own device" (BYOD) or "bring your own technology" (BYOT) and "one-to-one" tablet programs (one tablet or laptop for each student) in schools, devices are becoming a tool for engaging students in classroom guidance programming. Not only can school counselors use such tools to present directly to students but they can also model these tools for students to use for their own presentations and projects. Additionally, these tools can be used synchronously while the school counselor is in front of a class or asynchronously so that students can view them outside of class.

Mobile Applications

Classroom guidance is no longer strictly relegated to the walls of the classroom itself. Technology allows for classroom guidance programming to be delivered on devices that can be accessed nearly anywhere and consumed *asynchronously* (not at the same time that a class physically meets). Most of the presentation tools offered above have mobile apps, which means that classroom guidance content, as part of the school counseling program's core counseling curriculum, can be edited, presented, and viewed on tablets and smartphones. Given the varying accessibility to technology in schools, it is known that while some students (particularly those from low-income areas) may not have desktops, laptops, or tablets, the 2013 Pew report (Teens and Technology) indicates that 93% of teens have access to a computer (Madden, Lenhart, Duggan, Cortesi, & Gasser, 2013). In addition, the report indicates that nearly 73% of all students have smartphones, and many teens report accessing the Internet mostly from their smartphones. As school counselors plan classroom and large-group lessons that utilize technology, it is important to keep these findings in mind. Technology tools should be used in and for lessons that are as easily accessible as possible to all student populations.

Social Media

Social media has a growing presence in education and is certainly used widely by school-age students. Social media allows for interaction online, which, if used with intentionality and care, can be additive to a school counseling program, including classroom guidance programming. Current social media include such tools as Facebook, Twitter, Tumblr, Pinterest, and Instagram. In addition, there are education-specific tools such as Edmodo, which mimic popular social networking tools but are only open to school-based groups or classes.

In addition to using social media for a variety of reasons (including to promote the school counseling program or to reach families, staff, and students), school counselors can consider using social media for classroom guidance programming. For example, a lesson on positive self-talk and coping may involve a class using Pinterest to find inspiring messages and quotes. A lesson on careers may involve students using Instagram to take pictures of various people at their jobs or setting up a career-related poll on a unique Facebook page for a longer career unit. Or a lesson on scholarships and financial planning for college may involve a class reviewing tweets for a related hashtag on Twitter.

Flipped Classroom Guidance

Flipped teaching originated from high school science teachers Bergmann and Sams (2012) and has significant implications for the way school counselors deliver classroom and large-group guidance. The essence of flipped teaching is that students review content online prior to meeting. Once the class is physically together, time is spent in activities and discussion that engage students in application of the content. From the standpoint of Bloom's model (Bloom, 1956), flipped teaching allows for more complex levels of learning such as analysis, synthesis, evaluation, and creation to happen in the classroom under the guidance of the teacher while more basic levels such as comprehension and application are relegated to self-paced, online methods (Brame, 2013). In flipped teaching, the lecture portion is delivered in an online format and viewed at the students' convenience. Online or video lectures can be delivered by the actual teacher of the course or can be recorded videos from other sources or experts. Either way, they are intended to teach basic concepts of the lesson. Bergmann and Sams used YouTube, but there are other online tools that can be used to deliver content. Khan Academy (http://www.khanacademy.org), a nonprofit founded by Salman Kahn in 2006, is a vast collection of free instructional videos on many school-based subjects that teachers of those subjects can use as part of their lessons. There is also an entire website devoted to flipped teaching (http://www.flippedlearning.org), and the literature base on flipped teaching and learning continues to grow.

Consider the following case study for delivering a classroom guidance lesson for third graders on the topic of bullying with a flipped approach.

CASE STUDY

Malik

Malik, the school counselor, prepares a PowerPoint with the main points of the lesson and creates and edits a short video with advice from third graders on the topic. He uploads these to Voicethread and then narrates each slide. Some of the slides contain discussion questions that the viewers should consider about the topic. The completed Voicethread runs about eight to 10 minutes in length. Next, Malik, prepares an e-mail and a flyer to go out to all third-grade students and families with instructions to view the Voicethread in preparation for his visits to third-grade classrooms the next week as part of the school's anti-bullying campaign. Included in the e-mail and the flyer is a link to the Voicethread. Students are required to view the Voicethread, but parents and families are encouraged to watch it as well. In addition, a link is provided to a brief pre/post survey using Google forms, which students are instructed to complete before and after the lesson.

In collaboration with all third-grade teachers, Malik schedules classroom visits of approximately 30 minutes in length. Face-to-face time in the classroom includes a brief review of the Voicethread to make sure key concepts are understood (approximately five minutes). More time, however, is spent on the discussion questions (up to 10 minutes) and on a hands-on activity (15 minutes) in which the students design and share an anti-bullying poster. Students who may not have access to a computer at home can view the Voicethread at the public library or with the app on most mobile devices, or accommodations may be made so that they can view it at school. If the pre/post survey cannot be accessed online or students have specific needs, Malik provides paper copies.

Global Learning

One way that technology can increase global knowledge is through the use of tools that allow for connecting nationally and internationally. Some schools and classrooms engage in conversations and learning with classrooms in other parts of the country or the world. Through the use of tools such as Skype or FaceTime, counselors can engage in dialogue between classrooms and groups of students. Increasing students' global knowledge will help to make them more engaged students and more competitive in the world's marketplace.

Consider the following case study for an eighth-grade lesson on conflict resolution using technology to connect with students in another country.

CASE STUDY

Natalya

Natalya, the school counselor, coordinates with the social studies teacher to plan the lesson and the interaction. The two decide that the lesson will cover several class meetings over a three-week period, two of which will involve the school counselor. Using Skype in the Classroom, a free service by Skype that connects classrooms around the world, the counselor finds an eighth-grade classroom teacher in Argentina who wishes to partner for the interaction. The two teachers and Natalya discuss via Skype the details of the students' upcoming interaction, including the lesson and objectives, preparation activities, language fluency, and follow-up activities. Using e-mail, the three educators continue to communicate through the completion of the three-week unit.

The first lesson involving the school counselor utilizes a prerecorded lecture that students view prior to class that reviews basic concepts of conflict resolution. In this lesson, Natalya relates some of the concepts to the students' recent study of the Civil War. Included in this lecture is a brief online pretest about conflict resolution. During class time, Natalya leads the students in several activities related to the conflict resolution concepts and in developing questions for the classroom in Argentina. These questions are generally about how the students solve their own conflicts and how they witness conflicts being solved publicly in their own towns or country. The classroom in Argentina engages in a similar lesson during the same week. After the lesson, the teacher and Natalya work together to refine the questions and send them to the teacher in Argentina via e-mail; they receive questions from her in a similar manner.

The second lesson takes place the following week; the primary objective is for the two classrooms to speak to each other. Before the lesson, the three educators do an after-school test run of their equipment to check visual clarity and audio quality. Using Skype, the teacher and Natalya are able to project the video feed of the Argentinian classroom onto the screen in the classroom. Natalya takes the lead in facilitating discussions about conflict resolution between the two groups of students. Both teachers assist in facilitating the discussion by noting other related class concepts and generally keeping the discussion on track.

The third lesson is primarily the responsibility of the teacher and involves the students writing reflection papers from the Skype conversation that are then shared with the classroom in Argentina. Natalya assists by helping the teacher in preparing some of the questions for the paper. She also seeks permission from the teacher to send the students, via e-mail, a posttest on conflict resolution concepts that she has developed for data collection purposes.

The case study above demonstrates several points covered in this chapter, such as collaborating with teachers to align standards, use of accountability tools, incorporation of technology, and global learning.

KEYSTONES

- Classroom guidance programming can be delivered in a variety of formats.
- Effective classroom guidance programming is data driven and takes advantage of available evidence-based programs.
- Classroom guidance programming is ideally preventative in nature, can cover a wide range of topics, and is designed to serve all students.
- Teacher and school counselor collaboration is essential to the development and delivery of classroom guidance programming.
- School counselor preparation programs must train new professionals to be ready for school and classroom environments.
- School counselors are accountable for the effectiveness of their classroom guidance programming and should use a variety of measures for evaluation.
- College and career readiness is an essential focus for classroom guidance programming at all levels.
- School counselors must recognize their roles as advocates for all students and the role of classroom guidance programming in helping to close achievement gaps and addressing issues of social justice.
- Incorporating technology is a significant aspect of the future of classroom guidance programming, both in design and implementation.

ADDITIONAL RESOURCES

Center for Excellence in School Counseling and Leadership (CESCAL): http://www.cescal.org

Collaborative for Academic, Social, and Emotional Learning (CASEL): http://www.casel.org

College Board National Office of School Counselor Advocacy (NOSCA): http://nosca.college board.org/

Edudemic: http://www.edudemic.com

Edutopia: http://www.edutopia.org

Flipped Learning: http://www.flippedlearning.org

Khan Academy: http://www.khanacademy.org

Matthew Sowers, "Flipped Counselor" YouTube Channel: https://www.youtube.com/channel/ UCP-rvn89zwDVtbGy4_E7QzA

National Association of College Admissions Counseling (NACAC): http://www.nacacnet.org

Positive Behavioral Interventions & Supports (PBIS): http://www.pbis.org

School Counselors' Online Professional Exchange (SCOPE): http://www.scope4scs.org

REFERENCES

ACT. (2012). *The condition of college & career readiness 2012: National report.* Retrieved April 9, 2015, from http://www.act.org/research/policymakers/cccr12/

American School Counselor Association (ASCA). (2012). *ASCA national model.* Alexandria, VA: Author.

American School Counselor Association (ASCA). (2014). *ASCA mindsets & behaviors for student success: K–12 college- and career-readiness standards for every student.* Alexandria, VA: Author.

Bailey, T. (2009). Challenge and opportunity: Rethinking the role and function of developmental education in community college. *New Directions for Community Colleges, 145,* 11–30.

Barrett, P. M., Webster, H., Turner, C. M., & May, C. (2003). *Introduction to FRIENDS—A program for enhancing life skills promoting psychological resilience.* Retrieved from http://www .friendsinfo.net/downloads/friendsintro.pdf

Bergmann, J., & Sams, A. (2012). *Flip your classroom: Reach every student in every class every day.* Eugene, OR: International Society for Technology in Education.

Bloom, B. S. (1956). *Taxonomy of educational objectives: The classification of educational goals.* New York, NY: Longmans, Green.

Brame, C. (2013). *Flipping the classroom.* Nashville, TN: Vanderbilt University Center for Teaching. Retrieved April 9, 2015, from http://cft.vanderbilt.edu/guides-sub-pages/flipping-the-classroom/

Brigman, G., & Webb, L. (2003). Ready to learn: Teaching kindergarten students school success skills. *Journal of Educational Research, 96,* 286–292.

Brigman, G., & Webb, L. (2004). *Student success skills: Classroom manual.* Boca Raton, FL: Atlantic Education Consultants.

Bucholz, J. L., & Sheffler, J. L. (2009). Creating a warm and inclusive classroom environment: Planning for all children to feel welcome. *Electronic Journal for Inclusive Education, 2*(4).

Carnevale, A. P., Smith, N., & Strohl, J. (2010). *Help wanted: Projections of job and education requirements through 2018.* Retrieved April 9, 2015, from http://files.eric.ed.gov/fulltext/ ED524310.pdf

Chen-Hayes, S. F., Ockerman, M. S., & Mason, E. C. M. (2013). *101 solutions for school counselors and leaders in challenging times.* Thousand Oaks, CA: Corwin.

College Board National Office for School Counselor Accountability. (2010). *Eight components of college and career readiness counseling.* New York, NY: College Board Advocacy and Policy Center. Retrieved April 9, 2015, from http://media.collegeboard.com/digitalServices/pdf/nosca/11b_4416_8_Components_WEB_111107.pdf

Committee for Children. (1997a). *Second step: A violence prevention curriculum, grades 1–3* (2nd ed.). Seattle, WA: Author.

Committee for Children. (1997b). *Second step: A violence prevention curriculum, grades 4–5* (2nd ed.). Seattle, WA: Author.

Conley, D. T. (2012a). The complexity of college and career readiness. Educational Policy Improvement Center at the University of Oregon, Power Point Presentation at the New School. Retrieved April 9, 2015, from http://www.acrpro-training.org/TheComplexityofCollegeandCareerReadiness.pdf

Conley, D. T (2012b). *Defining and measuring college and career readiness.* Washington, DC: National High School Center, American Institutes for Research. Retrieved April 9, 2015, from http://programs.ccsso.org/projects/Membership_Meetings/APF/documents/Defining_College_Career_Readiness.pdf

Council for Accreditation of Counseling & Related Educational Programs (CACREP). (2009). *2009 standards for accreditation.* Alexandria, VA: Author.

Dimmitt, C., Carey, J. C., & Hatch, T. (2007). *Evidence-based school counseling: Making a difference with data-driven practices.* Thousand Oaks, CA: Corwin.

Durlak, J. A., Weissberg, R. P., Dymnicki, A. B., Taylor, R. D., & Schellinger, K. B. (2011). The impact of enhancing students' social and emotional learning: A meta-analysis of school based universal interventions. *Child Development, 82*(1), 405–432.

Education Trust. (2003). *A new core curriculum for all: Aiming high for other people's children.* Retrieved April 9, 2015, from http://edtrust.org/resource/a-new-core-curriculum-for-all-aiming-high-for-other-peoples-children/

Edwards, D., & Mullis, F. (2003). Classroom meetings: Encouraging a climate of cooperation. *Professional School Counseling, 7*(1), 20–29.

Erford, B. T. (Ed.). (2014). *Transforming the school counseling profession* (4th ed.). Columbus, OH: Pearson Merrill.

Erikson, A., & Abel, N. R. (2013). A high school counselor's leadership in providing school-wide screenings for depression and enhancing suicide awareness. *Professional School Counseling, 16*(5), 283–289.

Gaffner, D. C., & Hazler, R. J. (2002). Factors related to indecisiveness and career indecision in undecided college students. *Journal of College Student Development, 43*(3), 317–326.

Gruman, D. H., & Hoelzen, B. (2011). Determining responsiveness to school counselling interventions using behavioral observations. *Professional School Counseling, 14,* 183–190.

Gysbers, N. C. (2001). School guidance and counseling in the 21st century: Remember the past into the future. *Professional School Counseling, 5,* 96–105.

Gysbers, N. C. (2004). Comprehensive guidance and counseling programs: The evolution of accountability. *Professional School Counseling, 8,* 1–14.

Hatch, T. (2013). *The use of data in school counseling.* Thousand Oaks, CA: Corwin.

Hines, P. L., & Lemons, R. W. (2011). *Poised to lead: How school counselors can drive college and career readiness.* Washington, DC: Education Trust. Retrieved April 9, 2015, from http://files.eric.ed.gov/fulltext/ED527908.pdf

Holcomb-McCoy, C. (2007). *School counseling to close the achievement gap: A social justice framework for success.* Thousand Oaks, CA: Corwin.

Holcomb-McCoy, C., & Chen-Hayes, S. F. (2011). Culturally competent school counselors: Affirming diversity by challenging oppression. In B. T. Erford (Ed.), *Transforming the school counseling profession (3rd ed., pp. 90–109).* Boston, MA: Pearson.

House, R. M., & Sears, S. J. (2002). Preparing school counselors to be leaders and advocates: A critical need in the new millennium. *Theory into Practice, 41*, 154–162.

Madden, M., Lenhart, A., Duggan, M., Cortesi, S., & Gasser, U. (2013, March 13). *Teens and technology 2013.* Retrieved April 9, 2015, from http://www.pewinternet.org/2013/03/13/main-findings-5/

Martens, K., & Andreen, K. (2013). School counselors' involvement with a school-wide positive behavior support system: Addressing student behavior issues in a proactive and positive manner. *Professional School Counseling, 16*(5), 313–322.

Mason, E. C. M. (2010). Leveraging classroom time. *ASCA School Counselor*, July/August, 27–29.

Mason, E. C. M., & McMahon, H. G. (2009). Supporting academic improvement among 8th graders at risk of retention: A study using action research. *Research in Middle Level Education, 33*(1).

Mason, E. C. M., & Uwah, C. J. (2007, Fall). An eight-step research model for school counselors. *The Georgia School Counselors Association Journal*, 1–5.

McMahon, H. G., Mason, E. C. M., Daluga-Guenther, N., & Ruiz, A. (2014). Towards an ecological model of school counseling. *Journal of Counseling and Development, 92*(4), 459–471.

Myrick, R. D. (1987). *Developmental guidance and counseling: A practical approach.* Minneapolis, MN: Educational Media Corporation.

National Office for School Counselor Advocacy. (2010). *Eight components of college and career readiness counseling.* New York, NY: The College Board.

Ockerman, M. S., & Mason, E. C. M. (2012). Developing school counseling students' social justice orientation through service learning. *Journal of School Counseling, 10*(5).

Ockerman, M. S., Mason, E. C. M., & Feiker-Hollenbeck, A. (2012). Integrating RtI with school counseling programs: Being a proactive professional school counselor. *Journal of School Counseling, 10*(15).

Organization for Economic Cooperation and Development. (2014). *Education at a glance: OECD indicators 2013.* Retrieved April 16, 2015, from http://www.oecd.org/edu/eag2013%20%28eng%29--FINAL%2020%20June%202013.pdf

Pedrotti, J. T., Edwards, L. M., & Lopez, S. J. (2008). Promoting hope: Suggestions for school counselors. *Professional School Counseling, 12*(2), 100–107.

Plummer, B. D., Galla, B. M., Finn, A., Patrick, S. D., Meketon, D., Leonard, J., . . . Duckworth, A. L. (2014). A behind-the-scenes guide to school-based research. *Mind, Brain, and Education, 8*(1), 15–20.

Prensky, M. (2010). *Teaching digital natives: Partnering for real learning.* Thousand Oaks, CA: Corwin.

Rowell, L. L. (2005). Collaborative action research and school counselors. *Professional School Counseling, 9*, 28–36.

Rowell, L. L. (2006). Action research and school counseling: Closing the gap between research and practice. *Professional School Counseling, 9*, 376–384.

Rumberger, R. W. (2006). *Tenth grade dropout rates by native language, race/ethnicity, and socioeconomic status.* Berkeley: University of California Linguistic Minority Research Institute. Retrieved April 9, 2015, from http://escholarship.org/uc/item/2903c3p3

Sabella, R., & Booker, B. L. (2003). Using technology to promote your guidance and counselling program among stakeholders. *Professional School Counseling, 6,* 206–213.

Sanford, C., Newman, L., Wagner, M., Cameto, R., Knokey, A. M., & Shaver, D. (2011). The post-high school outcomes of young adults with disabilities up to 6 years after high school: Key findings from the National Longitudinal Transition Study-2 (NLTS2). *National Center for Special Education Research.* Retrieved April 9, 2015, from http://files.eric.ed.gov/fulltext/ED523539.pdf

Schmidt, J. J. (2014). *Counseling in schools: Comprehensive programs of responsive services for all students.* Boston, MA: Pearson.

Walker, H. M., & Shinn, M. R. (2002). Structuring school-based interventions to achieve integrated primary, secondary, and tertiary prevention goals for safe and effective schools. *Interventions for Academic and Behavior Problems II: Preventive and Remedial Approaches,* 1–26.

Walsh, M. E., Kenny, M. E., Weineke, M. A., & Harrington, K. R. (2008). The Boston Connects program: Promoting learning and health development. *Professional School Counseling, 12*(2), 166–169.

Waters, E., & Sroufe, L. A. (1983). Social competence as a developmental construct. *Developmental Review, 3,* 79–97.

Zins, J. E., & Elias, M. J. (2006). Social and emotional learning. In G. G. Bear & K. M. Minke (Eds.), *Children's needs III: Development, prevention, and intervention* (pp. 1–13). Bethesda, MD: National Association of School Psychologists.

APPENDIX A

ASCA Mindsets & Behaviors for Student Success:

K-12 College- and Career-Readiness Standards for Every Student

The ASCA Mindsets & Behaviors for Student Success: K-12 College- and Career Readiness for Every Student describe the knowledge, skills and attitudes students need to achieve academic success, college and career readiness and social/emotional development. The standards are based on a survey of research and best practices in student achievement from a wide array of educational standards and efforts. These standards are the next generation of the ASCA National Standards for Students, which were first published in 1997.

The 35 mindset and behavior standards identify and prioritize the specific attitudes, knowledge and skills students should be able to demonstrate as a result of a school counseling program. School counselors use the standards to assess student growth and development, guide the development of strategies and activities and create a program that helps students achieve their highest potential. The ASCA Mindsets & Behaviors can be aligned with initiatives at the district, state and national level to reflect the district's local priorities.

To operationalize the standards, school counselors select competencies that align with the specific standards and become the foundation for classroom lessons, small groups and activities addressing student developmental needs. The competencies directly reflect the vision, mission and goals of the comprehensive school counseling program and align with the school's academic mission.

Research-Based Standards

The ASCA Mindsets & Behaviors are based on a review of research and college- and career-readiness documents created by a variety of organizations that have identified strategies making an impact on student achievement and academic performance. The ASCA Mindsets & Behaviors are organized based on the framework of noncognitive factors presented in the critical literature review "Teaching Adolescents to Become Learners" conducted by the University of Chicago Consortium on Chicago School Research (2012).

This literature review recognizes that content knowledge and academic skills are only part of the equation for student success. "School performance is a complex phenomenon, shaped by a wide variety of factors intrinsic to students and the external environment" (University of Chicago, 2012, p. 2). The ASCA Mindsets & Behaviors are based on the evidence of the importance of these factors.

Organization of the ASCA Mindsets & Behaviors

The ASCA Mindsets & Behaviors are organized by domains, standards arranged within categories and subcategories and grade-level competencies. Each is described below.

Domains

The ASCA Mindsets & Behaviors are organized in three broad domains: academic, career and social/emotional development. These domains promote mindsets and behaviors that enhance the learning process and create a culture of college and career readiness for all students. The definitions of each domain are as follows:

Academic Development – Standards guiding school counseling programs to implement strategies and activities to support and maximize each student's ability to learn.

Career Development – Standards guiding school counseling programs to help students 1) understand the connection between school and the world of work and 2) plan for and make a successful transition from school to postsecondary education and/or the world of work and from job to job across the life span.

Social/Emotional Development – Standards guiding school counseling programs to help students manage emotions and learn and apply interpersonal skills.

Standards

All 35 standards can be applied to any of the three domains, and the school counselor selects a domain and standard based on the needs of the school, classroom, small group or individual. The standards are arranged within categories and subcategories based on five general categories of noncognitive factors related to academic performance as identified in the 2012 literature review published by the University of Chicago Consortium on Chicago School Research. These categories synthesize the "vast array of research literature" (p. 8) on noncognitive factors including persistence, resilience, grit, goal-setting, help-seeking, cooperation, conscientiousness, self-efficacy, self-regulation, self-control, self-discipline, motivation, mindsets, effort, work habits, organization, homework completion, learning strategies and study skills, among others.

> **Category 1: Mindset Standards** – Includes standards related to the psychosocial attitudes or beliefs students have about themselves in relation to academic work. These make up the students' belief system as exhibited in behaviors.

> **Category 2: Behavior Standards** – These standards include behaviors commonly associated with being a successful student. These behaviors are visible, outward signs that a student is engaged and putting forth effort to learn. The behaviors are grouped into three subcategories.

> a. **Learning Strategies:** Processes and tactics students employ to aid in the cognitive work of thinking, remembering or learning.

> b. **Self-management Skills:** Continued focus on a goal despite obstacles (grit or persistence) and avoidance of distractions or temptations to prioritize higher pursuits over lower pleasures (delayed gratification, self-discipline, self-control).

> c. **Social Skills:** Acceptable behaviors that improve social interactions, such as those between peers or between students and adults.

The ASCA Mindsets & Behaviors for Student Success: K-12 College- and Career-Readiness Standards for Every Student

Each of the following standards can be applied to the academic, career and social/emotional domains.

Category 1: Mindset Standards
School counselors encourage the following mindsets for all students.

1. Belief in development of whole self, including a healthy balance of mental, social/emotional and physical well-being
2. Self-confidence in ability to succeed

3. Sense of belonging in the school environment

4. Understanding that postsecondary education and life-long learning are necessary for long-term career success

5. Belief in using abilities to their fullest to achieve high-quality results and outcomes

6. Positive attitude toward work and learning

Category 2: Behavior Standards
Students will demonstrate the following standards through classroom lessons, activities and/or individual/small-group counseling.

Learning Strategies	*Self-Management Skills*	*Social Skills*
1. Demonstrate critical-thinking skills to make informed decisions	1. Demonstrate ability to assume responsibility	1. Use effective oral and written communication skills and listening skills
2. Demonstrate creativity	2. Demonstrate self-discipline and self-control	2. Create positive and supportive relationships with other students
3. Use time-management, organizational and study skills	3. Demonstrate ability to work independently	3. Create relationships with adults that support success
4. Apply self-motivation and self-direction to learning	4. Demonstrate ability to delay immediate gratification for long-term rewards	4. Demonstrate empathy
5. Apply media and technology skills	5. Demonstrate perseverance to achieve long- and short-term goals	5. Demonstrate ethical decision-making and social responsibility
6. Set high standards of quality	6. Demonstrate ability to overcome barriers to learning	6. Use effective collaboration and cooperation skills
7. Identify long- and short-term academic, career and social/emotional goals	7. Demonstrate effective coping skills when faced with a problem	7. Use leadership and teamwork skills to work effectively in diverse teams
8. Actively engage in challenging coursework	8. Demonstrate the ability to balance school, home and community activities	8. Demonstrate advocacy skills and ability to assert self, when necessary
9. Gather evidence and consider multiple perspectives to make informed decisions	9. Demonstrate personal safety skills	9. Demonstrate social maturity and behaviors appropriate to the situation and environment
10. Participate in enrichment and extracurricular activities	10. Demonstrate ability to manage transitions and ability to adapt to changing situations and responsibilities	

Grade-Level Competencies

Grade-level competencies are specific, measurable expectations that students attain as they make progress toward the standards. As the school counseling program's vision, mission and program goals are aligned with the school's academic mission, school counseling standards and competencies are also aligned with academic content standards at the state and district level.

ASCA Mindsets & Behaviors align with specific standards from the Common Core State Standards through connections at the competency level. This alignment allows school counselors the opportunity to help students meet these college- and career-readiness standards in collaboration with academic content taught in core areas in the classroom. It also helps school counselors directly align with academic instruction when providing individual and small-group counseling by focusing on standards and competencies addressing a student's developmental needs. School counselors working in states that have not adopted the Common Core State Standards are encouraged to align competencies with their state's academic standards and can use the competencies from the ASCA Mindsets & Behaviors as examples of alignment.

ASCA Mindsets & Behaviors Database

The grade-level competencies are housed in the ASCA Mindsets & Behaviors database at *www.schoolcounselor.org/studentcompetencies*. School counselors can search the database by keyword to quickly and easily identify competencies that will meet student developmental needs and align with academic content as appropriate. The database also allows school counselors to contribute to the competencies by sharing other ways to meet or align with a specific standard.

Citation Guide

When citing from this publication, use the following reference:

American School Counselor Association (2014). *Mindsets and Behaviors for Student Success: K-12 College- and Career-Readiness Standards for Every Student.* Alexandria, VA: Author.

Resources Used in Development of ASCA Mindsets & Behaviors

The following documents were the primary resources that informed ASCA Mindsets & Behaviors.

Document	Organization	Description
ACT National Career Readiness Certificate	ACT	Offers a portable credential that demonstrates achievement and a certain level of workplace employability skills in applied mathematics, locating information and reading for information.
ASCA National Standards for Students	American School Counselor Association	Describes the knowledge, attitudes and skills students should be able to demonstrate as a result of the school counseling program.
AVID Essentials at a Glance	AVID	Promotes a college readiness system for elementary through higher education that is designed to increase schoolwide learning and performance.
Building Blocks For Change: What it Means to be Career Ready	Career Readiness Partner Council	Defines what it means to be career-ready, and highlights the outcome of collaborative efforts of the Career Readiness Partner Council to help inform policy and practice in states and communities.
Career and Technical Education Standards	National Board of Professional Teaching Standards	Defines the standards that lay the foundation for the Career and Technical Education Certificate.
Collaborative Counselor Training Initiative	SREB	Offers online training modules for middle grades and high school counselors that can improve their effectiveness in preparing all students for college, especially those from low-income families who would be first-generation college students.
Cross Disciplinary Proficiencies in the American Diploma Project	Achieve	Describes four cross disciplinary proficiencies that will enable high school graduates to meet new and unfamiliar tasks and challenges in college, the workplace and life.
Eight Components of College and Career Readiness Counseling	College Board	Presents a comprehensive, systemic approach for school counselors to use to inspire and prepare all students for college success and opportunity, especially students from underrepresented populations.
English Language Arts Standards	National Board of Professional Teaching Standards	Defines the standards that lay the foundation for the English Language Arts Certificate.

(Continued)

(Continued)

Document	Organization	Description
Framework for 21st Century Learning	Partnership for 21st Century Skills	Describes the skills, knowledge and expertise students must master to succeed in work and life; it is a blend of content knowledge, specific skills, expertise and literacies.
NETS for Students 2007	International Society for Technology in Education	Describes the standards for evaluating the skills and knowledge students need to learn effectively and live productively in an increasingly global and digital world.
Ramp-Up to Readiness	University of Minnesota	Provides a schoolwide guidance program designed to increase the number and diversity of students who graduate from high school with the knowledge, skills and habits necessary for success in a high-quality college program.
Social and Emotional Learning Core Competencies	CASEL	Identifies five interrelated sets of cognitive, affective and behavioral competencies through which children and adults acquire and effectively apply the knowledge, attitudes and skills necessary to understand and manage emotions, set and achieve positive goals, feel and show empathy for others, establish and maintain positive relationships and make responsible decisions.
Teaching Adolescents to Become Learners: The Role of Non-Cognitive Factors in Shaping School Performance	The University of Chicago Consortium on Chicago School Research	Presents a critical literature review of the role of noncognitive factors in shaping school performance.
What is "Career Ready"?	ACTE	Defines what it means to be career-ready, involving three major skill areas: core academic skills, employability skills, and technical and job-specific skills.

Appendix B

**Ethical Standards
for School Counselors**

PREAMBLE

The American School Counselor Association (ASCA) is a professional organization whose members are school counselors certified/licensed in school counseling with unique qualifications and skills to address all students' academic, personal/social and career development needs. Members are also school counseling program directors/ supervisors and counselor educators. These ethical standards are the ethical responsibility of school counselors. School counseling program directors/supervisors should know them and provide support for practitioners to uphold them. School counselor educators should know them, teach them to their students and provide support for school counseling candidates to uphold them.

Professional school counselors are advocates, leaders, collaborators and consultants who create opportunities for equity in access and success in educational opportunities by connecting their programs to the mission of schools and subscribing to the following tenets of professional responsibility:

- Each person has the right to be respected, be treated with dignity and have access to a comprehensive school counseling program that advocates for and affirms all students from diverse populations including: ethnic/racial identity, age, economic status, abilities/disabilities, language, immigration status, sexual orientation, gender, gender identity/expression, family type, religious/spiritual identity and appearance.

(Adopted 1984; revised 1992, 1998, 2004 and 2010)

- Each person has the right to receive the information and support needed to move toward self-direction and self-development and affirmation within one's group identities, with special care being given to students who have historically not received adequate educational services, e.g., students of color, students living at a low socio-economic status, students with disabilities and students from non-dominant language backgrounds.
- Each person has the right to understand the full magnitude and meaning of his/her educational choices and how those choices will affect future opportunities.
- Each person has the right to privacy and thereby the right to expect the school-counselor/student relationship to comply with all laws, policies and ethical standards pertaining to confidentiality in the school setting.
- Each person has the right to feel safe in school environments that school counselors help create, free from abuse, bullying, neglect, harassment or other forms of violence.

In this document, ASCA specifies the principles of ethical behavior necessary to maintain the high standards of integrity, leadership and professionalism among its members. The Ethical Standards for School Counselors were developed to clarify the nature of ethical responsibilities held in common by school counselors, supervisors/directors of school counseling programs and school counselor educators. The purposes of this document are to:

- Serve as a guide for the ethical practices of all professional school counselors, supervisors/directors of school counseling programs and school counselor educators regardless of level, area, population served or membership in this professional association;
- Provide self-appraisal and peer evaluations regarding school counselors' responsibilities to students, parents/guardians, colleagues and professional associates, schools, communities and the counseling profession; and
- Inform all stakeholders, including students, parents and guardians, teachers, administrators, community members and courts of justice, of best ethical practices, values and expected behaviors of the school counseling professional.

A.1. Responsibilities to Students

Professional school counselors:

a. Have a primary obligation to the students, who are to be treated with dignity and respect as unique individuals.

b. Are concerned with the educational, academic, career, personal and social needs and encourage the maximum development of every student.

c. Respect students' values, beliefs and cultural background and do not impose the school counselor's personal values on students or their families.

d. Are knowledgeable of laws, regulations and policies relating to students and strive to protect and inform students regarding their rights.

e. Promote the welfare of individual students and collaborate with them to develop an action plan for success.

f. Consider the involvement of support networks valued by the individual students.

g. Understand that professional distance with students is appropriate, and any sexual or romantic relationship with students whether illegal in the state of practice is considered a grievous breach of ethics and is prohibited regardless of a student's age.

h. Consider the potential for harm before entering into a relationship with former students or one of their family members.

A.2. Confidentiality

Professional school counselors:

a. Inform individual students of the purposes, goals, techniques and rules of procedure under which they may receive counseling. Disclosure includes the limits of confidentiality in a developmentally appropriate manner. Informed consent requires competence on the part of students to understand the limits of confidentiality and therefore, can be difficult to obtain from students of a certain developmental level. Professionals are aware that even though every attempt is made to obtain informed consent it is not always possible and when needed will make counseling decisions on students' behalf.

b. Explain the limits of confidentiality in appropriate ways such as classroom guidance lessons, the student handbook, school counseling brochures, school Web site, verbal notice or other methods of student, school and community communication in addition to oral notification to individual students.

c. Recognize the complicated nature of confidentiality in schools and consider each case in context. Keep information confidential unless legal requirements demand that confidential information be revealed or a breach is required to prevent serious and foreseeable harm to the student. Serious and foreseeable harm is different for each minor in schools and is defined by students' developmental and chronological age, the setting, parental rights and the nature of the harm. School counselors consult with appropriate professionals when in doubt as to the validity of an exception.

d. Recognize their primary obligation for confidentiality is to the students but balance that obligation with an understanding of parents'/guardians' legal and inherent rights to be the guiding voice in their children's lives, especially in value-laden issues. Understand the need to balance students' ethical rights to make choices, their capacity to give consent or assent and parental or familial legal rights and responsibilities to protect these students and make decisions on their behalf.

e. Promote the autonomy and independence of students to the extent possible and use the most appropriate and least intrusive method of breach. The developmental age and the circumstances requiring the breach are considered and as appropriate students are engaged in a discussion about the method and timing of the breach.

f. In absence of state legislation expressly forbidding disclosure, consider the ethical responsibility to provide information to an identified third party who, by his/her relationship with the student, is at a high risk of contracting a disease that is commonly known to be communicable and fatal. Disclosure requires satisfaction of all of the following conditions:

- Student identifies partner or the partner is highly identifiable
- School counselor recommends the student notify partner and refrain from further high-risk behavior
- Student refuses
- School counselor informs the student of the intent to notify the partner
- School counselor seeks legal consultation from the school district's legal representative in writing as to the legalities of informing the partner

g. Request of the court that disclosure not be required when the release of confidential information may potentially harm a student or the counseling relationship.

h. Protect the confidentiality of students' records and release personal data in accordance with prescribed federal and state laws and school policies including the laws within the Family Education Rights and Privacy Act (FERPA). Student information stored and transmitted electronically is treated with the same care as traditional student records. Recognize the vulnerability of confidentiality in electronic communications and only transmit sensitive information electronically in a way that is untraceable to students' identity. Critical information such as a student who has a history of suicidal ideation must be conveyed to the receiving school in a personal contact such as a phone call.

A.3. Academic, Career/College/Post-Secondary Access and Personal/Social Counseling Plans

Professional school counselors:

a. Provide students with a comprehensive school counseling program that parallels the ASCA National Model with emphasis on working jointly with all students to develop personal/social, academic and career goals.

b. Ensure equitable academic, career, post-secondary access and personal/social opportunities for all students through the use of data to help close achievement gaps and opportunity gaps.

c. Provide and advocate for individual students' career awareness, exploration and post-secondary plans supporting the students' right to choose from the wide array of options when they leave secondary education.

A.4. Dual Relationships

Professional school counselors:

a. Avoid dual relationships that might impair their objectivity and increase the risk of harm to students (*e.g.*, counseling one's family members or the children of close friends or associates). If a dual relationship is unavoidable, the school counselor is responsible for taking action to eliminate or reduce the potential for harm to the student through use of safeguards, which might include informed consent, consultation, supervision and documentation.

b. Maintain appropriate professional distance with students at all times.

c. Avoid dual relationships with students through communication mediums such as social networking sites.

d. Avoid dual relationships with school personnel that might infringe on the integrity of the school counselor/student relationship.

A.5. Appropriate Referrals

Professional school counselors:

a. Make referrals when necessary or appropriate to outside resources for student and/or family support. Appropriate referrals may necessitate informing both parents/guardians and students of applicable resources and making proper plans for transitions with minimal interruption of services. Students retain the right to discontinue the counseling relationship at any time.

b. Help educate about and prevent personal and social concerns for all students within the school counselor's scope of education and competence and make necessary referrals when the counseling needs are beyond the individual school counselor's education and training. Every attempt is made to find appropriate specialized resources for clinical therapeutic topics that are difficult or inappropriate to address in a school setting such as eating disorders, sexual trauma, chemical dependency and other addictions needing sustained clinical duration or assistance.

c. Request a release of information signed by the student and/or parents/guardians when attempting to develop a collaborative relationship with other service providers assigned to the student.

d. Develop a reasonable method of termination of counseling when it becomes apparent that counseling assistance is no longer needed or a referral is necessary to better meet the student's needs.

A.6. Group Work

Professional school counselors:

a. Screen prospective group members and maintain an awareness of participants' needs, appropriate fit and personal goals in relation to the group's intention and focus. The school counselor takes reasonable precautions to protect members from physical and psychological harm resulting from interaction within the group.

b. Recognize that best practice is to notify the parents/guardians of children participating in small groups.

c. Establish clear expectations in the group setting, and clearly state that confidentiality in group counseling cannot be guaranteed. Given the developmental and chronological ages of minors in schools, recognize the tenuous nature of confidentiality for minors renders some topics inappropriate for group work in a school setting.

d. Provide necessary follow up with group members, and document proceedings as appropriate.

e. Develop professional competencies, and maintain appropriate education, training and supervision in group facilitation and any topics specific to the group.

f. Facilitate group work that is brief and solution-focused, working with a variety of academic, career, college and personal/social issues.

A.7. Danger to Self or Others

Professional school counselors:

a. Inform parents/guardians and/or appropriate authorities when a student poses a danger to self or others. This is to be done after careful deliberation and consultation with other counseling professionals.

b. Report risk assessments to parents when they underscore the need to act on behalf of a child at risk; never negate a risk of harm as students sometimes deceive in order to avoid further scrutiny and/or parental notification.

c. Understand the legal and ethical liability for releasing a student who is in danger to self or others without proper and necessary support for that student.

A.8. Student Records

Professional school counselors:

a. Maintain and secure records necessary for rendering professional services to the student as required by laws, regulations, institutional procedures and confidentiality guidelines.

b. Keep sole-possession records or individual student case notes separate from students' educational records in keeping with state laws.

c. Recognize the limits of sole-possession records and understand these records are a memory aid for the creator and in absence of privileged communication may be subpoenaed and may become educational records when they are shared or are accessible to others in either verbal or written form or when they include information other than professional opinion or personal observations.

d. Establish a reasonable timeline for purging sole-possession records or case notes. Suggested guidelines include shredding sole possession records when the student transitions to the next level, transfers to another school or graduates. Apply careful discretion and deliberation before destroying sole-possession records that may be needed by a court of law such as notes on child abuse, suicide, sexual harassment or violence.

e. Understand and abide by the Family Education Rights and Privacy Act (FERPA, 1974), which safeguards student's records and allows parents to have a voice in what and how information is shared with others regarding their child's educational records.

A.9. Evaluation, Assessment and Interpretation

Professional school counselors:

a. Adhere to all professional standards regarding selecting, administering and interpreting assessment measures and only utilize assessment measures that are within the scope of practice for school counselors and for which they are trained and competent.

b. Consider confidentiality issues when utilizing evaluative or assessment instruments and electronically based programs.

c. Consider the developmental age, language skills and level of competence of the student taking the assessments before assessments are given.

d. Provide interpretation of the nature, purposes, results and potential impact of assessment/evaluation measures in language the students can understand.

e. Monitor the use of assessment results and interpretations, and take reasonable steps to prevent others from misusing the information.

f. Use caution when utilizing assessment techniques, making evaluations and interpreting the performance of populations not represented in the norm group on which an instrument is standardized.

g. Assess the effectiveness of their program in having an impact on students' academic, career and personal/social development through accountability measures especially examining efforts to close achievement, opportunity and attainment gaps.

A.10. Technology

Professional school counselors:

a. Promote the benefits of and clarify the limitations of various appropriate technological applications. Professional school counselors promote technological applications (1) that are appropriate for students' individual needs, (2) that students understand how to use and (3) for which follow-up counseling assistance is provided.

b. Advocate for equal access to technology for all students, especially those historically underserved.

c. Take appropriate and reasonable measures for maintaining confidentiality of student information and educational records stored or transmitted through the use of computers, facsimile machines, telephones, voicemail, answering machines and other electronic or computer technology.

d. Understand the intent of FERPA and its impact on sharing electronic student records.

e. Consider the extent to which cyberbullying is interfering with students' educational process and base guidance curriculum and intervention programming for this pervasive and potentially dangerous problem on research-based and best practices.

A.11. Student Peer Support Program

Professional school counselors:

a. Have unique responsibilities when working with peer-helper or student-assistance programs and safeguard the welfare of students participating in peer-to-peer programs under their direction.

b. Are ultimately responsible for appropriate training and supervision for students serving as peer-support individuals in their school counseling programs.

B. RESPONSIBILITIES TO PARENTS/GUARDIANS

B.1. Parent Rights and Responsibilities

Professional school counselors:

a. Respect the rights and responsibilities of parents/guardians for their children and endeavor to establish, as appropriate, a collaborative relationship with parents/guardians to facilitate students' maximum development.

b. Adhere to laws, local guidelines and ethical standards of practice when assisting parents/guardians experiencing family difficulties interfering with the student's effectiveness and welfare.

c. Are sensitive to diversity among families and recognize that all parents/guardians, custodial and noncustodial, are vested with certain rights and responsibilities for their children's welfare by virtue of their role and according to law.

d. Inform parents of the nature of counseling services provided in the school setting.

e. Adhere to the FERPA act regarding disclosure of student information.

f. Work to establish, as appropriate, collaborative relationships with parents/guardians to best serve student.

B.2. Parents/Guardians and Confidentiality

Professional school counselors:

a. Inform parents/guardians of the school counselor's role to include the confidential nature of the counseling relationship between the counselor and student.

b. Recognize that working with minors in a school setting requires school counselors to collaborate with students' parents/guardians to the extent possible.

c. Respect the confidentiality of parents/guardians to the extent that is reasonable to protect the best interest of the student being counseled.

d. Provide parents/guardians with accurate, comprehensive and relevant information in an objective and caring manner, as is appropriate and consistent with ethical responsibilities to the student.

e. Make reasonable efforts to honor the wishes of parents/guardians concerning information regarding the student unless a court order expressly forbids the involvement of a parent(s). In cases of divorce or separation, school counselors exercise a good-faith effort to keep both parents informed, maintaining focus on the student and avoiding supporting one parent over another in divorce proceedings.

C. RESPONSIBILITIES TO COLLEAGUES AND PROFESSIONAL ASSOCIATES

C.1. Professional Relationships

Professional school counselors, the school counseling program director/site supervisor and the school counselor educator:

a. Establish and maintain professional relationships with faculty, staff and administration to facilitate an optimum counseling program.

b. Treat colleagues with professional respect, courtesy and fairness.

c. Recognize that teachers, staff and administrators who are high-functioning in the personal and social development skills can be powerful allies in supporting student success. School counselors work to develop relationships with all faculty and staff in order to advantage students.

d. Are aware of and utilize related professionals, organizations and other resources to whom the student may be referred.

C.2. Sharing Information with Other Professionals

Professional school counselors:

a. Promote awareness and adherence to appropriate guidelines regarding confidentiality, the distinction between public and private information and staff consultation.

b. Provide professional personnel with accurate, objective, concise and meaningful data necessary to adequately evaluate, counsel and assist the student.

c. Secure parental consent and develop clear agreements with other mental health professionals when a student is receiving services from another counselor or other mental health professional in order to avoid confusion and conflict for the student and parents/guardians.

d. Understand about the "release of information" process and parental rights in sharing information and attempt to establish a cooperative and collaborative relationship with other professionals to benefit students.

e. Recognize the powerful role of ally that faculty and administration who function high in personal/social development skills can play in supporting students in stress, and carefully filter confidential information to give these allies what they "need to know" in order to advantage the student. Consultation with other members of the school counseling profession is helpful in determining need-to-know information. The primary focus and obligation is always on the student when it comes to sharing confidential information.

f. Keep appropriate records regarding individual students, and develop a plan for transferring those records to another professional school counselor should the need occur. This documentation transfer will protect the confidentiality and benefit the needs of the student for whom the records are written.

C.3. Collaborating and Educating Around the Role of the School Counselor

The school counselor, school counseling program supervisor/director and school counselor educator:

a. Share the role of the school counseling program in ensuring data-driven academic, career/college and personal/social success competencies for every student, resulting in specific outcomes/indicators with all stakeholders.

b. Broker services internal and external to the schools to help ensure every student receives the benefits of a school counseling program and specific academic, career/college and personal/social competencies.

D. RESPONSIBILITIES TO SCHOOL, COMMUNITIES AND FAMILIES

D.1. Responsibilities to the School

Professional school counselors:

a. Support and protect students' best interest against any infringement of their educational program.

b. Inform appropriate officials, in accordance with school policy, of conditions that may be potentially disruptive or damaging to the school's mission, personnel and property while honoring the confidentiality between the student and the school counselor.

c. Are knowledgeable and supportive of their school's mission, and connect their program to the school's mission.

d. Delineate and promote the school counselor's role, and function as a student advocate in meeting the needs of those served. School counselors will notify appropriate officials of systemic conditions that may limit or curtail their effectiveness in providing programs and services.

e. Accept employment only for positions for which they are qualified by education, training, supervised experience, state and national professional credentials and appropriate professional experience.

f. Advocate that administrators hire only qualified, appropriately trained and competent individuals for professional school counseling positions.

g. Assist in developing: (1) curricular and environmental conditions appropriate for the school and community; (2) educational procedures and programs to meet students' developmental needs; (3) a systematic evaluation process for comprehensive, developmental, standards-based school counseling programs, services and personnel; and (4) a data-driven evaluation process guiding the comprehensive, developmental school counseling program and service delivery.

D.2. Responsibility to the Community

Professional school counselors:

a. Collaborate with community agencies, organizations and individuals in students' best interest and without regard to personal reward or remuneration.

b. Extend their influence and opportunity to deliver a comprehensive school counseling program to all students by collaborating with community resources for student success.

c. Promote equity for all students through community resources.

d. Are careful not to use their professional role as a school counselor to benefit any type of private therapeutic or consultative practice in which they might be involved outside of the school setting.

E. RESPONSIBILITIES TO SELF

E.1. Professional Competence

Professional school counselors:

a. Function within the boundaries of individual professional competence and accept responsibility for the consequences of their actions.

b. Monitor emotional and physical health and practice wellness to ensure optimal effectiveness. Seek physical or mental health referrals when needed to ensure competence at all times.

c. Monitor personal responsibility and recognize the high standard of care a professional in this critical position of trust must maintain on and off the job and are cognizant of and refrain from activity that may lead to inadequate professional services or diminish their effectiveness with school community members. Professional and personal growth are ongoing throughout the counselor's career.

d. Strive through personal initiative to stay abreast of current research and to maintain professional competence in advocacy, teaming and collaboration, culturally competent counseling and school counseling program coordination, knowledge and use of technology, leadership, and equity assessment using data.

e. Ensure a variety of regular opportunities for participating in and facilitating professional development for self and other educators and school counselors through continuing education opportunities annually including: attendance at professional school counseling conferences; reading *Professional School Counseling* journal articles; facilitating workshops for education staff on issues school counselors are uniquely positioned to provide.

f. Enhance personal self-awareness, professional effectiveness and ethical practice by regularly attending presentations on ethical decision-making. Effective school counselors will seek supervision when ethical or professional questions arise in their practice.

g. Maintain current membership in professional associations to ensure ethical and best practices.

E.2. Multicultural and Social Justice Advocacy and Leadership

Professional school counselors:

a. Monitor and expand personal multicultural and social justice advocacy awareness, knowledge and skills. School counselors strive for exemplary cultural competence by ensuring personal beliefs or values are not imposed on students or other stakeholders.

b. Develop competencies in how prejudice, power and various forms of oppression, such as ableism, ageism, classism, familyism, genderism, heterosexism, immigrationism, linguicism, racism, religionism and sexism, affect self, students and all stakeholders.

c. Acquire educational, consultation and training experiences to improve awareness, knowledge, skills and effectiveness in working with diverse populations: ethnic/racial status, age, economic status, special needs, ESL or ELL, immigration status, sexual orientation, gender, gender identity/expression, family type, religious/spiritual identity and appearance.

d. Affirm the multiple cultural and linguistic identities of every student and all stakeholders. Advocate for equitable school and school counseling program policies and practices for every student and all stakeholders including use of translators and bilingual/multilingual school counseling program materials that represent all languages used by families in the school community, and advocate for appropriate accommodations and accessibility for students with disabilities.

e. Use inclusive and culturally responsible language in all forms of communication.

f. Provide regular workshops and written/digital information to families to increase understanding, collaborative two-way communication and a welcoming school climate between families and the school to promote increased student achievement.

g. Work as advocates and leaders in the school to create equity-based school counseling programs that help close any achievement, opportunity and attainment gaps that deny all students the chance to pursue their educational goals.

F. RESPONSIBILITIES TO THE PROFESSION

F.1. Professionalism

Professional school counselors:

a. Accept the policies and procedures for handling ethical violations as a result of maintaining membership in the American School Counselor Association.

b. Conduct themselves in such a manner as to advance individual ethical practice and the profession.

c. Conduct appropriate research, and report findings in a manner consistent with acceptable educational and psychological research practices. School counselors advocate for the protection of individual students' identities when using data for research or program planning.

d. Seek institutional and parent/guardian consent before administering any research, and maintain security of research records.

e. Adhere to ethical standards of the profession, other official policy statements, such as ASCA's position statements, role statement and the ASCA National Model and relevant statutes established by federal, state and local governments, and when these are in conflict work responsibly for change.

f. Clearly distinguish between statements and actions made as a private individual and those made as a representative of the school counseling profession.

g. Do not use their professional position to recruit or gain clients, consultees for their private practice or to seek and receive unjustified personal gains, unfair advantage, inappropriate relationships or unearned goods or services.

F.2. Contribution to the Profession

Professional school counselors:

a. Actively participate in professional associations and share results and best practices in assessing, implementing and annually evaluating the outcomes of data-driven school counseling programs with measurable academic, career/college and personal/social competencies for every student.

b. Provide support, consultation and mentoring to novice professionals.

c. Have a responsibility to read and abide by the ASCA Ethical Standards and adhere to the applicable laws and regulations.

F.3 Supervision of School Counselor Candidates Pursuing Practicum and Internship Experiences:

Professional school counselors:

a. Provide support for appropriate experiences in academic, career, college access and personal/social counseling for school counseling interns.

b. Ensure school counselor candidates have experience in developing, implementing and evaluating a data-driven school counseling program model, such as the ASCA National Model.

c. Ensure the school counseling practicum and internship have specific, measurable service delivery, foundation, management and accountability systems.

d. Ensure school counselor candidates maintain appropriate liability insurance for the duration of the school counseling practicum and internship experiences.

e. Ensure a site visit is completed by a school counselor education faculty member for each practicum or internship student, preferably when both the school counselor trainee and site supervisor are present.

F.4 Collaboration and Education about School Counselors and School Counseling Programs with other Professionals

School counselors and school counseling program directors/supervisors collaborate with special educators, school nurses, school social workers, school psychologists, college counselors/admissions officers, physical therapists, occupational therapists and speech pathologists to advocate for optimal services for students and all other stakeholders.

G. MAINTENANCE OF STANDARDS

Professional school counselors are expected to maintain ethical behavior at all times.

G.1. When there exists serious doubt as to the ethical behavior of a colleague(s) the following procedure may serve as a guide:

1. The school counselor should consult confidentially with a professional colleague to discuss the nature of a complaint to see if the professional colleague views the situation as an ethical violation.

2. When feasible, the school counselor should directly approach the colleague whose behavior is in question to discuss the complaint and seek resolution.

3. The school counselor should keep documentation of all the steps taken.

4. If resolution is not forthcoming at the personal level, the school counselor shall utilize the channels established within the school, school district, the state school counseling association and ASCA's Ethics Committee.

5. If the matter still remains unresolved, referral for review and appropriate action should be made to the Ethics Committees in the following sequence:

- State school counselor association
- American School Counselor Association

6. The ASCA Ethics Committee is responsible for:

- Educating and consulting with the membership regarding ethical standards
- Periodically reviewing and recommending changes in code
- Receiving and processing questions to clarify the application of such standards. Questions must be submitted in writing to the ASCA Ethics Committee chair.
- Handling complaints of alleged violations of the ASCA Ethical Standards for School Counselors. At the national level, complaints should be submitted in writing to the ASCA Ethics Committee, c/o the Executive Director, American School Counselor Association, 1101 King St., Suite 625, Alexandria, VA 22314.

G.2. When school counselors are forced to work in situations or abide by policies that do not reflect the ethics of the profession, the school counselor works responsibly through the correct channels to try and remedy the condition.

G.3. When faced with any ethical dilemma school counselors, school counseling program directors/supervisors and school counselor educators use an ethical decision-making model such as Solutions to Ethical Problems in Schools (STEPS) (Stone, 2001):

1. *Define the problem emotionally and intellectually*

2. *Apply the ASCA Ethical Standards and the law*

3. *Consider the students' chronological and developmental levels*

4. *Consider the setting, parental rights and minors' rights*

5. *Apply the moral principles*

6. *Determine your potential courses of action and their consequences*

7. *Evaluate the selected action*

8. *Consult*

9. *Implement the course of action*

INDEX